HIGMAN

A Collection

HIGMAN
A Collection

Foreword by Roger Ebert

Edited by
Tom Adams with Betty Brandenburg

Thomas • Berryhill Press
Lafayette, California

Higman
A Collection

Copyright ©1998 by Thomas Berryhill Press

ISBN: 0-9648638-4-7 (Hardcover)
ISBN: 0-9648638-5-5 (Paperback)

Address for information
Thomas•Berryhill Press
Box 178
Lafayette, California 94549
(925) 284-7176

Printed in the United States
10 9 8 7 6 5 4 3 2 1

Cover: Photograph by Karl Brandenburg

This book is printed on recycled paper

To Marion Higman

and

Anne, Alice and Elizabeth

To Betty & Eric

Tom Adams

10 . 8 . 02

CONTENTS

ACKNOWLEDGMENTS

Scores of persons gave assistance and support as we compiled and edited this first book that incorporates some aspects of Howard Higman's social thought and humor.

From the beginning, the Higman family encouraged us to proceed with this important and, at times, difficult journey. Anne R. Higman provided photographs and advice. Many of his friends assisted us. Space does not allow for all to be mentioned. A few are: Juli and Peter Steinhauer, Bob and Ellie Hunter, John and Isabelle Murphy, Richard and Linda Loose, Sonny Dunford, Ann Lanier, June and Rick Adams, Betty Weems, Jane and Charles Butcher, Joan Higman Davies, Lura Middleton, Frank Dell'apa and Kathryn Armstrong. Generous financial assistance was provided by Phillip Adams.

Roger Ebert eagerly accepted our invitation to write the Foreword and Karl Brandenburg provided the cover's photograph. The back cover photograph of Howard Higman and Tom Adams standing among the flags during the opening procession to Macky Auditorium during Higman's last conference, the Forty-Seventh, 1994 was taken by Edith Dell'apa.

Julia Perez directed the manuscript production team that included Tania Odessa, Roberta Smith, John Mack, Kathleen Smith and Scott Silber. Edith Dell'apa and Richard Loose provided technical and editorial services and Richard Schwartz offered invaluable design assistance.

Art and book design was was done by Richard Carron of Adworx, and General Printing of Berkeley, California, was our printer.

Finally, we thank Pam Penfold of the University of Colorado Alumni Association as well as Howard's and our beloved University of Colorado. This book was especially prepared for presentation at the Fiftieth Anniversary of the World Affairs Conference, April 1998.

CITATION

HOWARD HIGMAN

University of Colorado Medal

HOWARD HIGMAN, a provocative teacher and a man of incisive opinion and judgment, has been committed to the betterment of the University of Colorado for the past thirty-five years. During that time, he has supported and earned the respect of eight presidents.

He is the "father" of the Conference on World Affairs, a forum for artistry, controversy, and social and political commentary which has drawn thousands to Boulder each of the last thirty-four years. Luminaries who have participated in the Conference include Ralph Nader, Henry Kissinger, and Buckminster Fuller to name a few.

A devoted public servant, Professor Higman has been immersed in a multitude of noble projects, including founding the Rocky Mountain American Association for the United Nations, and the Colorado Council on Migrant and Seasonal Agricultural Workers and Families. He has also served as director of the regional training centers of VISTA and ACTION.

During World War II, Professor Higman served in several capacities with the powerful War Production Board, the agency charged with channeling raw materials into war weapons, and using most productively the available supply of workers. In 1945-46, he was deputy director of the shipbuilding division of the United States Department of Labor.

Most importantly, he is an educator with revolutionary ideas who has inspired good students to improve, and gifted ones to excel. His classroom methods consist of challenging students and eliciting a response from them. In all Professor Higman has taught more than 10,000 students and 2,000 VISTA volunteers and other trainees.

A Boulder native, Professor Higman earned bachelor's and master's degrees from the University of Colorado. He is listed in "American Men of Science" and has written numerous scholarly and professional publications.

In recognition of his superior teaching and outstanding public service record, the Board of Regents is pleased and proud to award the University of Colorado Medal to Howard Higman.

This citation was read at the Commencement of the University of Colorado on May 22, 1981.

Arnold R. Weber
President

H. H. Arnold
Secretary of the University
and of the Board of Regents

INTRODUCTION

Howard Higman, the late professor, taught sociology for thirty- nine years at the University of Colorado at Boulder. At 79, he continued to direct the Conference on World Affairs, an annual gathering of some of the world's best minds, and now in its fiftieth year. Higman died at age 80 in 1995.

Higman earned his bachelor's and master's degrees at CU and then taught in the sociology department from 1946 until 1985. He administered the VISTA (Volunteers in Service to America) training program in Colorado during Presidents Lyndon Johnson's and Richard Nixon's terms. He trained thousands for various poverty programs, including persons in the VISTA, WIN (Work Incentive), YOC (Youth Opportunity Center), the Colorado Migrant Council, the national staff of ACTION, and many more.

During the 1950's, *Esquire* magazine named him one of the ten most popular professors on America's college campuses. In 1966, he was selected by the American Friends Service Committee as one of ten Americans to travel to Moscow to take part in a two-week seminar, with ten Soviets, on world peace, national life and individual responsibility.

From 1951 into the late 1980's, Howard Higman was the subject of numerous FBI investigations. One informant said, "He has loyal friends and bitter enemies...no one can buy Higman because he has far too big an ego." As professor and social activist, Higman was at ease on Indian Reservations, in Barrios and inner cities where he prepared legions of volunteers and staff who sought to help heal the nation's ills. Thousands of undergraduate and graduate students took his courses at the CU campuses, almost ten thousand poverty workers studied with him, hundreds of thousands attended his forty- seven

i

World Affairs Conferences and thousands of doctors, lawyers, social workers, criminal justice personal, nurses and other professionals attended his lectures.

This collection of lectures, writings, observations and personal accounts provides the reader with an autobiographical look at a man who touched many during his lifetime. In the first chapter, we learn about his childhood and college days that prepared him to become the ultimate teacher. In Chapter Two, he takes us through the prolonged and, at times, comical antics of J. Edgar Hoover's FBI investigations. Taken from the actual documents obtained through the Freedom of Information Act, we learn how his beloved university community responded to this Byzantine witch hunt.

Higman was famous for his lectures. Two stand out as examples of putting sociology into action. *Rings and Things* and *Genetic Society* were heard by thousands; many returning over and over to grasp the lessons presented in Chapter Three.

In Chapter Four, his views on violence and order are told by Ernest Manley, Higman's alter ego. For more than three decades, Higman taught a popular course, Sociology of War. He became an authority on violence, war and order. This soliloquy remains relevant today, years after its creation.

The Conference on World Affairs is Higman's enduring legacy. As a driving force behind its creation, the annual conference celebrates its fiftieth anniversary in 1998. In Chapter Five, Higman describes it's origin and uniqueness.

In 1964, quite by accident, Higman became a soldier in the War on Poverty. Some of his contributions to action sociology are presented in Chapter Six.

In Chapter Seven, *The Information Society* provides a clear example of Higman's capacity to render understandable this complicated and ever-changing aspect of modern society. Historical and future trends are merged.

While Higman usually eschewed predictions and forecasting, he did indulge in hindsight and foresight in two essays, the one about the passing of the 1970's and the other about what to concern ourselves with in the approaching 1980's. Chapter Eight allows his wit and genius to unfold.

The final chapter, entitled *Snippets,* enables the reader to sample some of Higman's outrageous, dramatic, hilarious and profound comments. Never at a loss for words, for he was a consummate linguist, Higman thrusts us into his world of people, ideas and sentiments.

Thus, we have a compilation of Higman's views on many topics, prepared especially for the Fiftieth Anniversary of the Conference on World Affairs, Boulder, Colorado, April 1998.

—Tom Adams and Betty Brandenburg

Roger Ebert received an Honorary Doctorate of Humanities
from the University of Colorado, 1993.
L to R. Chaz Ebert, President Judith Albino, Ebert, Howard Higman

FOREWORD

HOWARD HIGMAN: A Considerable Man

by Roger Ebert

There died in Boulder on Nov. 22, 1995 a man named Howard Higman, who liked to be part of a good conversation. Nearly 50 years earlier, he had founded the Conference on World Affairs, an event in his image and likeness, which brought each year approximately 110 good talkers to the campus of the University of Colorado and set them to talking. It was not an academic conference. There were no professional rewards for attending. No papers were read. Half of the speakers on every panel knew little or nothing about the subject. The sessions were free and open to everybody. All of these rules reflected Howard's personality in one way or another; he was a man who lived in the moment, who prized spontaneity and inspiration, who structured the Conference to dislodge its participants from the safety of their specialties, and confront them with new ideas.

Howard, who presided over some of these sessions in person and all of them in spirit, was authoritarian, dictatorial, infuriating, presumptuous, brilliant and lovable. He was large. He contained multitudes. He would have filled Falstaff with envy. He had many careers—he was a professor, and directed a Vista training program, and wrote and lectured and "interfered in politics." But the Conference was his life. He ran it almost in spite of the University, which gave him some money but exerted little control. He did not endear himself by banning anyone from Colorado from speaking on his panels ("We can hear them the rest of the year"). He deliberately made the Conference the opposite of those precious academic events at which jargon is traded for tenure. There were always a few ambassadors and foreign correspondents and ministers to justify the "World" in the title, but it was really a Conference on Everything Conceivable. A democrat to his marrow, he invited all sorts of people—poets, diplomats, witches, physicists, communitarians, bricklayers, utopians and Indian chiefs—and he didn't announce the subjects of their panels until they had arrived in Boulder, so they wouldn't have time to prepare, and would have to depend on what they really knew and communicate it in plain English.

Howard Higman was born in Boulder in 1915, and lived all of his life in the same rambling brown shingle house on 11th street. There he brought his bride Marion, there they raised their daughters Elizabeth, Anne and Alice, there numerous graduate students occupied the garden apartment and became part of an extended family and an endless conversation. And there on Tuesday nights of Conference weeks he and Marion would feed roast beef to the Conferees, after which everyone would gather around an upright piano to sing "It's a Sin to Tell a Lie."

Among the framed portraits, letters and drawings on the wall of a downstairs bathroom was his grammar school report card. One had the sense from him of a man unusually anchored in time and place, Boulder-born, Boulder-made, one of those magnets around which the history of a city forms. In his recollections in this volume, he remembers in minute detail his childhood and young manhood, those who helped him, those who hindered him, the turning points of a lifetime; at times he seems almost to be standing outside his life and watching it sail past like a proud warship.

On two or three occasions when I found myself in Boulder at non-Conference times of the year, and had dinner with Howard, the conversation often touched on his early life, on his childhood, on his sense of walking at seventy down the same streets he walked when he was seven.

He suggests in the passages of autobiography in this book that he was a precocious child, adrift in a sea of somewhat distant and elder adults, able to impress with his knowledge and his firm conviction that his opinions were worth knowing. That mask or role suited him for a lifetime. Even as an old man, there was something of the impetuous, bright boy about Howard, who would shout for attention, issue decrees, supply marching orders and wade into arguments with the joy of a born debater.

Watching him over many years, I formed a feeling that his memoirs seem to confirm: He was shaped during years when he was often lonely, when his opinions were slighted by his elders, when he could get attention only in opposition, when there was nobody to talk to. The Conference in a sense was the kind of family he wanted as a child—and the childhood he never had. We were all his playmates. There was no such thing as rudeness in his behavior, just as there never is on a playground, because everyone proceeds from the same basis of vulnerability, insecurity, competition and familiarity. Perhaps that is why he was so adamant in refusing to let participants read papers or prepare their remarks, and why he cheerfully put them on panels about which they presumably knew nothing. He wanted to strip them of an adult's defenses of position, credentials and reputation and set them at work again as curious adolescents, dazzled by the universe of knowledge, and delighted by unexpected connections.

Reading this book, I was impressed with the fact that Howard was always in love with the University of Colorado. Its president, whoever he or she was, was always his commander in chief, and Howard always the loyal foot soldier, or so he asserts, although some of his generals might remember it differently. He took jobs in other places, worked in Washington and Europe, but it was his destiny to return to Boulder and to teach there.

I was also born in a university town (Urbana), grew up there and attended the university, and I can appreciate some of his feelings. The university buildings would have attracted his curiosity and shadowed his imagination from an early age. As a boy he would have had heroes among the athletes, and as a young man be intrigued by the ideas floating up the hill. The first heroes of his adulthood would have been his teachers, and to teach at the University of Colorado would have always seemed to him a different and more significant thing than to teach anywhere else. Those who had him in class remembered a spellbinding lecturer who drew facts and theories from many different disciplines to weave his views. In full sail in pursuit of a passionate principle, Howard was not so much a teacher as a preacher, casting out ignorance, praising truth.

He wrote, he published, he administered, he served on committees, he held offices, but if you seek his legacy, attend the Conference, and look about you. Insofar as an institution can embody a life, the Conference was Howard, and Howard was the Conference. Howard began the Conference as United Nations Week, right after the war. Eleanor Roosevelt and R. Buckminster Fuller were there in the early years. The Conference grew. It became an honor to be invited to attend. Higman and his committee drew a dark veil of secrecy around the selection process. "Who invited you?" he asked me in an early year. If you were invited, you got a letter which informed you that you were requested to travel to Boulder at your own expense, perform for a week on panels not of your choosing, be paid nothing for your labors, and sleep in somebody's guest bedroom. You were not allowed to arrive late in the week or leave early. And if you didn't gratefully embrace these conditions you would not be invited back.

At a time when famous speakers can pull down $10,000 to $25,000 for an hour's work, this would seem like an offer they could refuse. Yet over the years the people who attended the Conference included not only Fuller (whose encyclopedic interests set the tone), but Russell Baker, Steve Allen, Odetta, poet laureate Howard Nemerov, pundit Jeff Greenfield, Ted Turner, astronaut Rusty Schweikart, novelist Malcolm Bradbury, historian Henry Steele Commager, publisher Peter Mayer, musicians Les McCann, Ben Sidron, Dave Grusin and Johnny Mandel, Ralph Nader, legal advisor Sonya Hamlin, Barry Commoner, columnist Joseph Kraft, *London Sunday Times* editor Andrew Neil, Eddie Albert, novelist Peter Tauber, sexual liberationist Betty Dotson, architect Paolo Soleri, artist Robert Irwin, playwright Arthur Kopit, essayist Henry Fairlie, Henry Kissinger, and countless other academics, artists, statesmen and eccentrics.

If you were to write a letter to most of these people asking them to appear anywhere for an evening, you would most likely be referred to their agents. Yet year after year the Conferees voluntarily returned, forming a sort of family that kept in touch in other places during the rest of the year, sharing their private knowledge of Boulder in the spring. It was something they did for themselves. Many felt, as I always did, that the Conference was the time when you found out about what was new: Over the years I was exposed there for the first time in any organized and thoughtful way to Black power, feminism, gay rights, computers, the Internet, New Age ideas, new directions in cosmology and Darwinism, and the deconstruction of deconstructionism. Once I was on a panel titled "Everyone Can Draw," with the artist and therapist Annette Goodheart. She persuaded me that the title of the panel was the simple truth, and I started to draw, and a year later published a book illustrated by 45 of my own drawings. I presented a copy of the book to Howard Higman as a tribute. He looked at my drawings and observed that the panel should have been titled "Not Everyone Can Draw Well."

No Conference was held in 1995. Howard had finally offended too many people in the University hierarchy, and there were those who objected to the cost of the event (although any other university would have wept with joy at obtaining such speakers for a week at such a pittance). Howard had retired and lost his campus clout, and a segment of his board felt it was time for a new generation to take over. Howard was having none of that.

The Conference was suspended amid the turmoil of his lifetime of drinking, his shaky health in his late 70s, and his conviction that the conference could be run by no one but himself. Whether this last point was true was completely beside the point, because it went without saying that as long as Howard was alive no one else would run it.

The Conference began again in April 1996. To say it was held in his memory is an understatement. It was held in his indignant shadow. There were those who said the Conference could not possibly survive Howard, that it was part and parcel of his presence, but it has indeed survived and prospered, in part because Howard's original conception was so sound, in part because the new director, Sven Steinmo, has made reasonable improvements while protecting the Conference's essential spirit.

It was the critic Leonard Feather who found the perfect description for the Conference: "The Leisure of the Theory Class." Texas columnist Molly Ivins, when she was writing for *The New York Times*, recorded a typical Conference scene: A gray-haired critic sitting comfortably in a chair by the fire after one of the dinner parties, looking down at the cute young thing curled up at his ankles and asking "And what do you do?" To which she replied, "I'm an admiral."

I was asked once by the *Boulder Daily Camera* why I attended the Conference, and I simply said, "I come back to see Howard." That this large, loud and frequently rude man could inspire love seems unlikely, but it is so. Howard Higman was the nearest I will come, I imagine, to the experience of meeting Dr. Samuel Johnson. Like Johnson, he was learned on many matters and opinionated on more. He had not just an appetite but a hunger for food, drink, ideas and conversation. Johnson had his Boswell, and it is one of the purposes of this volume to function in the way of a Boswell, to record that we met an extraordinary man and remember him and want to share our memories.

Traditions, it is said, are a way of holding time at bay. Certainly the annual conference unfolded in a series of traditional patterns. The opening night party, in recent decades held at Betty Weems' house, had newcomers circulating warily while veterans greeted each other with cries of glee. Howard positioned himself at the entry stairs to bark out his recognition of returning participants. He was a man whose manner embraced you and held you at a certain distance, both at once; he was happy to see you again, and hoped you would not disappoint him. I would sit across the room and watch him, and see him look with satisfaction over the throng he had gathered. This unlikely, even impossible, event was going to happen for one more year. He stood back and watched what he had wrought, like a child delighted with the functioning of a complex and ingenious toy.

Tuesdays, I have said, were always for roast beef at Howard and Marion's. Guests circulated through a warren of rooms (I never counted the rooms in the house, but it seemed to unfold endlessly, like Gormenghast). Shelves were crammed with a lifetime of reading. It was a house built, like the man who was raised in it, for hospitality on a large scale. Wednesdays we were set free to spend with our hosts and friends, Thursdays were hosted by Jane Butcher in her vast and jolly home, and Friday, up in the big mansion on the hill, we ate primavera, prepared for many years by Betty Brandenburg, Howard's colleague. At many of these events Howard would wear a coat of many colors—a boldly extroverted sports coat of no known style or fashion, which served him more as a vestment. (After he died and the annual Higman Memorial Lecture was established, I suggested that this coat be worn every year by the speaker. At first it was feared it had been given to charity, but after two years it emerged, something like the indestructable Shroud of Turin, and will play a role in the annual ritual).

Howard during these evenings was not always sober, for of his drinking he made no secret, but he was solid as a rock and missed nothing, and as one's years of attendance piled up his warmth only grew; faithful conferees were rewarded by a vast hug and generous compliments. In his last years I would sometimes wonder if I were bidding Howard farewell, for his health seemed precarious even though his energy always held. As events worked out there was no year that could be called "Howard's last conference," because in 1994 he was looking forward to the next year and in 1995 the Conference was suspended because of the wars between Howard and his partisans, and those who had become convinced (not without reason) that there were changes to be made. It went without saying that no compromise was possible, and in a sense the non-Conference of 1995 was a moment of silence in the long, noisy discourse of the years, followed later in the year by Howard's own death.

Howard died on the anniversary of the Kennedy assassination. On the day of his death, his daughter Alice brought a harpist into his hospital room to play for him. "Oh, I know Professor Higman," the harpist said. "He was my professor in 1957. He was the best teacher I ever had."

Higman, the young professor

1

THE EARLY YEARS

My father left his home in Liskeard, England, in about 1870 when he was 12 or 13. He crossed the Atlantic as a stowaway on a boat, then walked across the United States. People used to think the pioneers came across the country in wagons, but actually, many walked. Took my father four years. He got to Central City, Colorado, when he was about 17, to mine gold. Central City was full of Welshmen and Cousin Jacks, which means Cornwall and Eastern England, the tip of England. If you go up to Central City now and examine the graveyards, you'll see all the names there. It was there that my father smoked and drank and mined.

America is characterized by class mobility. The town was divided into the roughs and the respectable. There was a straight dichotomy as severe as black and white in Atlanta in the old days. The roughs swore, drank, danced, whored and built an opera house. They put a hat in the street, and the miners tossed in bundles of gold, and by nightfall they had ten times as much money as they needed to build the opera house and hire famous women to come and sing to them.

Across the street from the opera house was the Methodist Church. The Methodists were the respectables, and they were also British and skinny and narrow. They didn't dance, smoke, play cards or drink. My mother's family were respectables. They had come from Racine, Wisconsin, to Central City. The respectables were goldsmiths and blacksmiths. My mother was born in Central City. When the glory days in Central City played out, her parents, Henry and Priscilla, moved down to Boulder and built a house which is at 440 Arapahoe.

It's there now, a little old brick house with a keyhole window, just at the mouth of Boulder Canyon.

After the mining world ended, my father gave up his wicked ways. He married my mother and walked across the street and became a Methodist. Gave up smoking, drinking, everything. He told my brother once that he went to pay his saloon bill, and it was more than he made all week, so he gave it up. He didn't touch alcohol or tobacco or play cards or dance henceforth, nor accept credit of any kind. My mother was never allowed to borrow 5 cents in any way, shape, or form from anybody for any purpose. Everything they had they had already paid for.

My father came out east, north of Boulder, and built a farm. He was temperamentally incapable of farming, got in rows with his bull, ruined his farm equipment, and managed to burn down his haystack—so he turned the farm over to my mother and my older brother, Sid, and came into town, slowly moving his way into construction, and ending up a building contractor.

From 1915 to 1930, he built houses in Boulder, bought and built houses and sold them. Built the house I live in now. And then he retired. He was 69 or something, and he just went fishing. He had two cars: one for daily and one for Sunday. The daily car was a dirty Essex— he went fishing in it all the time. The day before he died he was chopping wood. Physically he was very powerful, very strong, but he had no lungs left from the hard rock mining. He had emphysema and died at 72. He was never an invalid, he just suffocated. My mother lived another 20 years.

My father had some reverence for Queen Victoria, and the name for Europe was *the old country*. As far as I knew, when I was 6 years old, everybody was white, Christian and Protestant. Protestants came in a hierarchy. The top Protestants were Presbyterians and Episcopalians. The difference between them was that the Presbyterians were a little more Calvinistic in terms of hard work, thrift and parsimony. So the big Presbyterians sort of owned the town, and my parents were Presbyterians, even if they had been Methodists in Central City.

Episcopalians were inclined to be a bit social, maybe professional as opposed to being shrewd merchants. Then the strata went down to Baptists. Catholics were just out of it.

My mother was Joseph Henry Higman's wife, Mrs. Joseph Henry Higman. She never called my father Joe. She never referred to him as anything other than Mr. Higman. To me, she referred to him as *your father*. To him, she didn't call him anything. She wouldn't speak to him unless he was looking at her. It was heavy Calvinism. My father was very meticulous about order in every way. Meals were served exactly on time. Dinner was at six sharp, and it was called supper. The noon meal was called dinner.

My father came home late one evening, about ten minutes after six. He looked sheepish. I had never seen him look sheepish before. My mother was nervous, as if some terrible thing must have happened. Dinner was ready. He looked at her, and he must have seen curiosity in her body language, but she didn't dare ask him. So he generously gave her an explanation. He said, "Oh, I forgot I hadn't driven and I had to walk home." My mother said, "Well, why didn't you come on the street car?" And he looked at her and said, "I didn't have a nickel." He would not turn to a friend and ask for a nickel. That's how severe the Calvinism was.

The basic virtue was to *do it yourself*— self-reliance. You don't cooperate, you don't share, you don't engage in those immoral Catholic things like charity—going around sponsoring indolence, alcohol, stupidity, laziness and welfare. Franklin Roosevelt was the height of evil; if you fed all those relief-ers they will all beget relief-ers; soon half the nation will be on relief and you'd be taking care of them. Survival of the fittest, that's what Calvinism was all about. The Presbyterians believed in the sociological views of Herbert Spencer without knowing it. They also believed in predestination. Everything has its meaning and its place and is appropriate. "God moves in mysterious ways, His wonders to perform." What happens when everything is already determined in advance is that you don't manipulate the world. You don't fix things. You don't have social problems. You have poverty. It's just a fact.

Unemployment isn't unemployment. My father would not have a word in his vocabulary for unemployment because there wasn't such a thing. The first person to use the word *unemployment* was William Killing Ogburn in 1920. My father never had an employer. If you'd told him he was unemployed when he was 13, he'd have said that he was not, he was going to America. While he was on the boat and walking across America, he wasn't unemployed, he was going to Central City. When he got there he wasn't unemployed, he dug. When he couldn't dig anymore, he came down and staked out a piece of land under the Homestead Act. He wasn't unemployed. He worked. He planted seeds. He got hold of a pig and a chicken. He milked a cow, made butter, got some horses. What you used to do in the world was work, and if you didn't work, it was a moral defect, not an economic problem. Those who did not work were called *indigents;* they had a moral defect. All you had to do was move on and work. The idea of unemployment only comes in 1920 when the economy changes and you have to have someone else's permission to work. You have to have an employer.

My father had two years of school—first and second grade. He taught himself to read and write, and long after that he taught himself arithmetic, so he could keep his own books. And he probably wrote a letter to his mother in England, but I don't think he ever got one back. I don't know how much schooling my mother had. I would bet she had an eighth grade education. In those days to be a graduate meant to be a graduate of the eighth grade. Boulder High School was invented as a college preparatory school. People who went to college at the turn of the century were rare. Even bankers and lawyers and doctors didn't go to college. Over half the lawyers in Congress in 1930 had never been to college. The idea of a university or a college as a vocational training center is entirely new. The training system for vocations was an apprentice system. The way my father learned to be a contractor was by going and being a carpenter's helper. It's all in Dickens. Dickens isn't full of college students.

You had patriotism also. You had statues down on the court-house lawn, cannonballs piled into pyramids, and you had the Fourth of July and Armistice Day, and speakers in the theater and you'd fly

American flags. My mother was president of the Daughters of the Veterans of the Union; her father, my grandfather, the one who is buried in Blackhawk, was one of the *boys in blue*, a soldier in the Civil War.

The Daughters met at least once a week and celebrated their fathers' soldiering in the 1865 war. You were constantly carrying flowers and flags, and putting them on graves. You did the same in the American Legion, from the First World War. But these activities slowly disappeared and ended with the disinterest in the Vietnam War. My father belonged to a fraternal organization, the Odd Fellows, and he belonged to the Republican Party—almost a civic duty.

I Was Born A Coward

I came along very late in my parents' life, born in 1915 when my father was 54 and my mother was about 47. I had a sister, Josephine, who was eight years older, and another sister, Wynn, who was 12 years older than I. My brother Sid was 26 when I was born. He had a daughter the same age as I; I was born an uncle. Another sister, Norine, was 30 when I was born. Sociologically speaking, my mother and father were actually my grandparents, since I was the same age as their grandchildren.

I had been born premature (weighed less than 3 pounds); been expected to die within two weeks. They couldn't find me in the nursery until someone discovered I had been buried with three hot-water bottles in a grape basket. I heard it was the chief of police who promised my father not to worry, I wouldn't live two weeks. This was before the days of abortions. Nobody wanted me. The rumor was out that my father suffered terrible embarrassment as his wife swelled up. In those Calvinist days, you weren't supposed to engage in sex except for the deliberate purpose of producing a child, which everybody knew they didn't want. Each of his children was eight years apart, which is kind of strange. I was born on the Colorado University campus in a building which is still there.

I went to church on Sunday, the 11 o'clock service, and sat beside my mother and father. Then I went back in the afternoon and also to the Sunday evening service. I went to prayer meetings on Wednesday nights and tagged along with my mother once a week to meetings of the Golden Circle and Ladies Aides. We ate leftover sandwiches. Then I got into student activities, which the church called Christian Endeavor. I competed all the time in reciting the Bible and winning prizes and read a lot about salvation.

When I was three or four years, five maybe, we were living in a house in the 700 block of Mapleton in Boulder. I remember getting into trouble by finding a trap-door under the sink and when you opened it there was a valve that turned off all the water in the house, which I was able to do. The only other thing I recall is my eight-year-old sister baby-sitting me. She had pigtails braided down the back, owned roller skates and seemed to be the enemy. An older sister had run away with a high school boy, married him and became what was called a camp follower.

The bias in my family was strongly for vocational education in the schools and spiritual education in the church. My mother had the McGuffey Readers and she read to me. They were no longer used when I went to school, but they were used at home because they were her textbooks. They are very difficult. The words are difficult and they are spelled out phonetically in pronunciation and spelling. The stories are all very sad. They are all extremely Puritan, with moral values.

There is a long poem I remember she often read called, *Somebody's Darling is Dying Today*. It's all about a soldier who was killed in the Civil War; a young boy, blond, blue eyes, with curls hanging down his face. He was in the hospital dying. And then there was one about a man who killed people for greed. He buried them, and every time he came back to their graves, they were uncovered. The corpses lying there were exposed. You can't get over it. And in *The Wreck of the Hesperus*, there was a shipwreck, the drunkard. All this literature kept telling you about the wicked, evil world and the ways of sin.

I remember feeling a shock when I went to first grade and the textbooks were all so pretty. They had colored pictures and stories like, Dick has a dog, the dog's name is Chip. Somebody's dog is dying today.

During that time I had an accident which I did not understand, but no one else did either. I apparently knelt on a sewing needle that had dropped on the rug and stuck straight up into my leg. The doctor who was called said it was rheumatism. He painted my knee with iodine. It swole up, and he put a light bulb over it, a purple light, with a green shade, but it didn't do any good.

That doctor died and we got another one. He did more things. So I took the second grade at home in bed, and the teacher came at three o'clock every day. She stayed about fifteen minutes, picked up yesterday's work and left me with lessons. We finally ascended to a proper doctor, Dr. Carr, in the Physicians Building, and he had this fancy machine that looked like a tray. You could put it on your knee and look to see the bones; it was called a fluoroscope. He said there were two halves of a needle in the knee. It had broken in the joint. The doctor and my father talked over whether they should take it out.

I overheard them talking and my father said, "What will we do?"

And he said, "Well, we turned it sideways so we could mark it with an indelible pencil." When they did, it scattered and went somewhere else and the doctor said to my father, "Well, we could chop that knee up and then we could find it." I wondered in my little head why they just didn't use a magnet. But in any case, my father said "What will we do?"

He said "Well, with luck it will calcify—calcium will grow around it and attach it to the bones."

My father said, "What else?"

Dr. Carr said, "Well if it doesn't, it will get in his blood stream and go into his heart and kill him."

My father said, "If we chop it up what will happen?"

"Well, you'll probably have a boy with a stiff straight leg".

And I remember shuddering in my brain when my father said, "Well I don't think I want a son with a stiff straight leg. Let's let it go."

Obviously I didn't have gymnasium, and I couldn't roller-skate, ice-skate, play basketball, football or any of the sports except wrestling. And so I had no balance or equilibrium. When the knee was all right, I could walk, though it hurt sometimes.

When I was six to ten, and my mother and father who were getting too old for anything as obstreperous as I was, shipped me out to my oldest sister, Norine. She had a son, Clarence, two years older than I, a daughter, Charlotte, one year older, who lived in Greeley and was married to the publisher of the newspaper over there; a daughter, Priscilla, my age, a daughter, Frances, one year younger and a husband. They lived on a poverty-stricken dirt farm, halfway between Frederick and Fort Lupton. They had moved there from Platteville in the 1920's, and were dirt farmers, with cows, a creamery and sugar beets. The only people lower than they were the Mexicans who came and lived in the beet house and topped beets. I used to call them the beet toppers.

In the agricultural summer, I was sent out there. We picked tomatoes and cucumbers, shocked wheat, herded cows, stacked hay, gathered up hay, milked cows and separated milk into cream. All summer, people came and picked up big containers of milk. Little Frances was tiny enough to crawl under the granary and gather eggs. A little older and you could slop pigs. A little older, you could herd cows. A little older, you could milk the cows. But I never got to that. I could run the cream separator. I ran the stacker horse and Clarence ran the buck rake. A spring wagon was used on Sunday to go to church, and we had a flivver Ford, a tractor, a windmill and a pump. When the windmill wouldn't work, gasoline pumps were used to get water to fill the trough for the cattle and horses.

I hated it because my nieces teased me all the time. I was the fragile city boy, and they were the tough country kids. I hated

Sunday most, because on Sunday you had peer group society. Sunday you got terminally scrubbed in the morning. You were washed in a tub like a piece of machinery, picked up naked and stuck in the tub. Women scrubbed your back with brushes and water and all your clothes were taken off. We didn't do that in Boulder. I was scrubbed, stood up, bounced around, dried and dressed then marched off to church in Frederick. We came back to this enormous dinner on Sunday that ran for three hours, with three kinds of pies, chicken and all kinds of vegetables. They had food, but they didn't have much of anything else. They had this long meal that went on till three in the afternoon, and then the women spent about an hour washing dishes and gossiping in the kitchen. It always startled me, because they would all march out at the end of dish washing, about four in a row, to an outhouse which had a row of holes for defecation, and they'd sit and talk collectively as they defecated in this long house.

The men would sit around on this one day of the week wearing suits, sitting around the parlor, which was only open on Sundays and they gossiped, using soft voices, about politics and affairs and all the children, of which I was one. There was always company, about twenty people for dinner in a different house each Sunday. Collectively, you met on Sundays.

The kids would all go play in the hayloft. They were full of daring, and the hayloft was slightly dangerous with pitchforks and such. There was sexual exploration and defeat; it was kind of like an organized football game. I could only compete with city knowledge that they didn't have — knowledge of electricity and batteries and wire. I could set up bell systems and press buttons and make bells ring.

It was work. You weren't spoiled. It seems to me I didn't like it. I'm not sure I was aware I didn't like it at the time. It's because I think I thought that everybody did it. I didn't know that everybody didn't do it. I was afraid of my nieces and nephews, and they were slightly afraid of me. There was a sense that if they did anything bad to me, their mother would whop them because she was my sister.

Our family moved from Arapahoe over to 1135 Eleventh Street, where my father allowed his wife to rent rooms to college girls; there were no dormitories then. The house was full of freshmen and sophomore college girls, with light housekeeping privileges; meaning they could cook downstairs in the basement, with iceboxes (not refrigerators), a gas stove and oil cloth tablecloths. Well, I was picked up as the *house mascot*, I guess, because I was six and wandering loose through the building. I got engaged to one of them, Gladys Crawford. We were engaged to be married, and I remember she brought me a diamond ring, which I later heard she bought at Woolworth's for fifteen cents. I wandered around being Gladys Crawford's prospective husband. I didn't understand exactly why everyone treated me like you'd treat a fragile pet at a sports event, but I found it quite comfortable, until I learned by overhearing people that I probably wouldn't marry Gladys Crawford. Later I picked up with the daughter of a lumber man in Boulder and escorted her to school. Then, finally, she confessed to me her father said she couldn't marry me because he was a lumber man and I was going to be a Presbyterian minister. You see, I'd fallen in love with Doctor Carr, the Presbyterian minister in Boulder, and kept winning prizes by reciting things and being awarded Bibles. I went through all the regimen of childhood in the Presbyterian church, for which I will be eternally grateful.

I never could engage in sports: I didn't engage in conflict, so I didn't win. That led me, of course, into a life in which I never took a chance that I was aware of taking. In retrospect I see that I must have taken hundreds of them, but I didn't know it; I didn't do it voluntarily. I've never bought a lotto ticket or bet on a game or outcome or score. I had trouble staying in the poker club, although I often won. But I didn't really like competing for winning and losing.

Anyway, through grammar school I seemed to be protected and too sensitive. I paid attention to my first grade teacher, Miss Fortnum, who came to my house to tutor me when I had the bad knee. Then Miss Barnhill came through third grade, and then Daisy Johnson, through fifth grade. And Julia Blair, who was a fresh young Pi-Phi. Of course she got married and quit, pretty quickly.

My father built a house in 1926, three blocks up on Eleventh Street, down the hill from three professors' houses. They came to Colorado because of the aridity of the air to arrest TB. Playing in professors' basements indoctrinated me into the cult of secure professors, meaning persons with academic tenure, who gossiped about and weren't afraid of administrators. The reason they weren't, I now understand, is that they were arrested tuberculars. They didn't care if they got increased salaries because they had taken huge decreases in salaries to come here from the east in the first place.

The University was fortunate. Russell George taught Geology. Professor Willard was the first American to be a vice president of the Royal Historical Society. Professor Eckert was the world authority on the Vatican. And Professor Eckley was involved in the fixation of nitrogen from the air. He became very rich. It's fun to drive around the hill and see these gorgeous houses. The University of Colorado became world famous because of these world famous professors. T. D. A. Cockerell, whom Russell George said, "T. D. A. Cockerell means Theodore Does Advertise Cockerell," was a world authority on zoology. And his wife, a botanist, grew hybrid hollyhocks. George Fulmer Reynolds, who was the first Wreath lecturer from Boulder, wrote on Elizabethan staging.

An Apartment of My Own

As I nosed around as a little boy, my older sister was in high school. When my father built the house, he put a room in the basement with a door and a fireplace. He took me down there and said, "Bill, (my parents called me Bill) this is your room. You can have your Uni-Hill friends over, but don't bring them upstairs; your mother and I are through with Uni-hill kids. If you want to have dinner with your mother and me, you can come up the back stairs or, if you don't, you've got a little hot-plate. You can do as you please."

I was perceived by my parents to be something that would happen in its own way. It limited my father's influence with me. He would shake his head sideways and say, "What are you doing?" I would not play. We did not quarrel. He gave up. It got to be useless. It's not that he did not like me. He did not know what I was up to. He forbade me to use alcohol or tobacco. He did not approve of attorneys whom he thought were immoral, so if I wanted to become an attorney, he would not pay for it.

The worst thing I ever did to him was come home with a package of cigarettes squeezed up out of my sweater pocket, exposed about an inch. I sat down across the table from him. He looked over at me and said, "Are those cigarettes?" I looked back at him and said, "No." I could just see him saying, "What am I going to do with this boy?" That was the end of it.

In his last years, I liked him. I'd go in late and go upstairs to him. He liked a big hunk of mouse-cheese with butter on it and hot milk. I'd fix it and he would drink the milk and sometimes talk. I mean we didn't have actual conversations that described my life or what I was up to or what I was doing. It was just, "How are ya?"

I was the only fifth grader with an apartment. I didn't understand its import or its future. That meant the ninth grade boys thought I was just dandy. So a bunch ganged over in my house and sent me on frequent errands all the time. By the time I was in ninth grade, I began to figure out how to run the place myself. I went to State Preparatory School. I did not get to participate in any athletics, or wear athletic letters, so I invented the name for the athletes, the Panthers. We'd furl the flag over the balcony in Longmont at basketball games.

Vicariously, I managed to stay in the main circle of decision-makers. I quickly discovered that there were various subgroups of decision-makers that didn't respect each other. I was curious and managed to belong to lots of groups. I wasn't loyal to any of them, but I didn't, of course, ever get kicked out of any. They never caught me hurting them because I never tried to; I wasn't competing. So I belonged to the hippie group, the dancing group and the drinking group. We drank rot-gut whiskey in little glass bottles, even though it was against the law. I ran around with Jim McKenna and Robert George. The Dean of Women, Elizabeth Stein, thought I was a dandy kid, and when she said she was making me head of the National Honor Society, someone said, "You can't do that, he was drunk at the basketball game." She said, "My Howard Higman would never allow liquor to touch his lips." So I became President of the National Honor Society.

When I entered college I was rushed all summer because people thought I was a leader who would drag other precious Boulder High School kids into the right fraternities. I spent the summer running around with Dick Jones and Mary Dart, a girl he later didn't marry I guess. I was this little boy running around with grown-ups. I spent my whole life being a little boy running around with grown-ups. I rarely ran around with my peer group. A sign of sheer cowardice. My father didn't permit me to join a fraternity, so my sister Wynn paid my college fraternity bills. Wynn said, "Please don't tell him, Howard." So we didn't mention that I belonged to a fraternity. We just deceived him.

When I was in junior high and high school, we were living on the Hill in the shadow of the university. My father went to check on life insurance after going to the university to see how much it cost to get a BA degree. He took a life insurance policy and the man came to the house every Thursday to pick up a small payment. My father took it out because he was old and knew he might not be here long. He was right about that. I was a sophomore in high school, taking gym, when I got a phone call saying that he was dead. He was 72 years old.

In my junior year in college I got interested in politics. In 1936, we were interested in the conflict between big business and the Roosevelt administration. When big business rejected the New Deal, Frances Perkins suggested that Roosevelt work with the Unions. My Christian values from childhood were being enacted on a political front.

I took a course from Joe Cohen, which was a dangerous thing to do. He was the absolute arbiter of the honors program, Phi Beta Kappa, everything terrific. I took a course in the summer and got along fine. All the books were Marxist things, and we subscribed to the *Moscow Daily News.* It was during the terrible Stalinist purges in Russia. If there'd been a Party, and they'd asked me to join, I probably would have.

In high school and college I had this sort of Jekyll and Hyde personality. In college, in the fraternity, in order to protect myself, I played captain, social chairman and finally, president. Then I would sneak out to go join the intellectuals who had no fraternity. In my sophomore year I was forced to take a required course on the history of English literature. I fell madly in love with the teacher, Ned West, and became deeply interested in the seduction poets such as Sucking and Lovelace as well the anonymous ballads and Charles Lamb. I was drafted by my English teacher to take a role as a page in a play. A lot of the people there were anti-frat. Probably a lot of them were gay, but in those days they did not have that idea. They talked about Oscar Wilde. They had blue eyes and drank tea and got Masters Degrees in English Literature.

A rumor circulated in the fraternity that I was a homosexual because I knew the people in English Literature. I was president of the fraternity, I held court on Sunday nights for any infractions of the rules. I hailed these two guys from Montana before the court and accused them of slander and lying; they did not have anything they could produce.

As a student activist, I wrote articles for campus publications. The following created a stir.

POLITICS AND THE A.S.U.C.
by
Howard H. Higman

It is, I believe, dangerous from some points of view, to write an essay on politics in student government in anything but a facetious tenor. Politics in student government is a joke. I shall, however, discuss this laughing matter from the rather more serious position of the student considering his own welfare.

In the first place, it may be stated that there should be no objection to politics. Some social group on this campus recently pointed a scornful finger at other groups, charging politics. Now the implication of this action was, of course, that there is something objectionable about politics. This is like saying, Jack is a sissy; the implication is that there is something objectionable about being a sissy. A similar charge without the ugly implication is fairly pointless: "Jack is a boy."

It may be suggested that politics has an undesirable meaning only when we refer to those situations where the selection of men is best made on the basis of their efficiency. In the fields of Public Administration, for example, we would ideally choose administrators to administer the law of the land in as efficient a way as possible. Postmasters should be chosen in accordance with their proven ability in mastering the post.

In the college community we have such positions as these in the office of Head Cheerleader, Junior Prom Chairman, Purchasing Agent, Professor of Divorce; they should be chosen because they lead the best cheers, direct the best proms, make the best purchases, and teach the best course on divorce. When these offices are filled with friends, stooges or relatives, liberals rightly object. It is unfortunate that in making their justifiable objections, persons have used the word politics because that now questionable word has a very respectable meaning in its proper place.

Editors Note:

*This essay demonstrates Higman's wit and incisive thoughts as a graduate student. It appeared in the Spring 1939 issue of **Campus Window, A Quarterly Review,** published by the Associated Students of the University of Colorado.*

Politics as the science and art of government might well enter the A.S.U.C. Representative-democratic communities are controlled by legislation made by some democratically chosen body. The A.S.U.C. Commission may be only an administrative board, in which case the positions should be filled by someone more capable than the rank and file to determine the possibility of an efficient execution of the routine. If it is only administrative then we are forced into the dilemma of being without any student legislators to make our law, in which case we must conclude either that our law slips in surreptitiously from some faculty source, or that our law does not exist. If our law comes down from on high we are studying under a dictatorship, benevolent or tyrannical, but nevertheless a dictatorship; and sometimes dictatorships are not administered for the welfare of the population. If our law does not exist, then the existence of a commission to execute it is at least of dubious value.

Now, of course, if the A.S.U.C. Commission were to act as a government of the students, by the students, and for the students-a democratically chosen quasi-executive, quasi-judicial body entrusted with the obligation of representing the majority of student opinion and empowered with the authority to act in the student's behalf—then the students should choose, by election, the office holders on the basis of their ability to convince the voters that they represent the voters' interests and point of view.

A virile student government is a political institution with issues, difference of opinion—liberal, or conservative that conducts campaigns, elections and action; politics, in other words.

What do we find? We find a commission made up of *elected* representatives of the various student *inter-*

ests. The Class President, which is traditionally an honorary position, a sort of popularity contest, represents the interests of his class. The Junior class has few interests other than the Junior Prom; the Senior class, Senior week. The various schools and colleges have interests, so they send *representatives.* During the last year, what interest of the College of Engineering has been protected by the work of their representatives in the Commission? Maybe engineers do have interests, but they are probably protected by their own college officers and not in the A.S.U.C. Commission. Proportionally the College of Music has much more weight than the College of Arts and Sciences on the Commission.

I question that the membership of the Commission represents either the student body or the significant interest groups of the student body.

The interests of the student are his own welfare. It is likely that these interests are, first, Educational; requirements, attendance at lectures, instructional method and personnel, systems of examination, grading systems, the honors system, majors and degrees offered.

Second, Economic; tuition and fees, especially the A.S.U.C. fees, (at many schools the students vote to change fees) housing, working conditions, hours and wages.

Third, Social; minority problems, Greek and Barb interests, health, recreation, intramurals, dances, public and private recreation, cultural activities, artist series and convocations.

Fourth, Extra-curricular; athletics, publications, forensics, dramatics, band and traditions.

Fifth, Regulative; individual conduct, expulsions, probations, free speech.

While I will hesitate to say arbitrarily, "These are the student's interests," this outline is not far off. Now imagine that I, as an enrolled student, believe that my four years and four thousand dollars are best spent to my advantage when I, as a major in political science, get a political science degree rather than one in economics; that it is to my advantage to be given comprehensives instead of ten minute tests; that instructors whose lectures are minus content should be reprimanded; that more money should be spent on the *Window*; that the *Dodo* is not worth its office space; that I shall be paid WPA wages when I work in the library; that my Negro friend can *coke* with me; that the Barbs shall not have the edge; that I shall be given a Wasserman test for syphilis at low cost; that intramurals shall be played for my physical development and not over the telephone, a coin deciding where the points will go; that I want a co-operative student-owned lunch room; that I want beer served in the M.S.U.B.; that I want more dancers and fewer travelogues in Macky; that I want a big band for the prom.

Suppose that I want the *Silver and Gold* to come out every day and that I want a fascist editorial policy; that I want to read therein, uncensored, what Stringham has to say; that I object to the publication of a glorified student directory which costs me ten dollars for the mild satisfaction of seeing my picture seven times.

Suppose that I object to the student seats at the Thanksgiving game, or the lack of them at commencement. Whom shall I vote for, Mouse or Hart? I am conservative. I oppose student-owned campus utilities. I want a student government which will protect the status quo. Whom shall I vote for?

Now a candidate for student office must at all costs avoid having opinions on student affairs. If he has any he must not let them be known. The A.S.U.C. constitution expressly forbids the use of advertisements of platforms. The elections are held in such a manner that one would think; first, that students must have as little time as possible between the announcement of the not-democratically-chosen candidates and the election, thus preventing anyone's discovering the opinions of the candidates, and, second, that the candidates must be prevented from expressing platforms in the *Silver and Gold* or at a general convocation, because the student body might find out for whom they were voting.

It is sufficient condemnation to say that the candidates for the "play" elections are chosen by faculty members and the old commission, which in theory allows the election to be; (1) railroaded by a clever choice of candidates, (2) a rubber-stamp approval of the choice of a commission picking its own successor, (3) controlled by the elimination of persons objectionable to the nominating group.

We have no representative government. The commission does not represent the students because it is not in the last analysis the real choice of the students. We cannot vote, if we vote, for our man, but only for one out of four.

We have no student government. The commission does not govern. Nobody cares.

Either we have no interest in University affairs because we have no student government, or we have no student government because we have no interest in student affairs.

It is difficult to believe that individuals who have passed the age of puberty, and many of whom vote in national elections, spend their energy in child-like combines to get the freshman prom chairman or to win best dressed, that little boys in fraternity houses feud over who shall be president, that little girls quarrel over who shall be pledged to Spur, because they are so coy.

It is difficult to believe that students of this campus are inherently different from students of other campuses who do concern themselves with the things that really affect their lives as students.

Now it is possible that the University officials who control the student's lives have planned it out so well that there are no complaints. Colorado University is a student's utopia. If this is true it is unfortunate; because the outside world is not planned out so well. Those of us who leave college will be forced to live in a world where we have to concern ourselves with the government that affects our daily lives. There, we cannot play and be so certain that some older generation will regulate our lives to our advantage.

It is conceivable that the University might well consider that students train to live in a play world, with play politics, and play interests, that students accustomed to allow some faculty person to regulate their affairs to the point where there is no responsibility on the student, that such students make easy meat for dictators, that such students at best have to learn the ways of democracy by trial-and-error not before but after they graduate from the educational system.

The students of this campus are not facing the problem of frustration by the faculty. In fact, only several weeks ago, President Norlin indicated his wish for more student control in the administration of student affairs.

Granting the weakness of the constitution, either the student government is facing the problem of a student body that is not concerned with its own welfare, or the student body is facing the problem of a student government that is not interested in the welfare of the student body.

World War II

Then the war came. I married a Pi Phi named Marion Hackstaff on the 25th of April and on December 7th the Japanese bombed Pearl Harbor. President Bob Stearns told the graduate students to get commissions in the Navy. I marched over, they turned me down. I had no feet, no metatarsal arches. I stood in line to be drafted as doughboy. At my physical exam I was with Paddox Charles Monroe, who was the nephew of the big shot editor of the Boulder Camera. I was turned down for the Army. My advisor, a brilliant man named Morris Garnsey, said to me, "Well, you've almost finished your Ph. D, but you've got another six months on it; so if you turn it in now, we'll hand you an M. A. with no exam or anything, because an M. A. in the hand will be better to keep you from peeling potatoes than a Ph. D. in progress."

I wanted to serve my country in some way—any way possible. I went to Washington, leaving my pregnant wife in Boulder, to join the Board of Economic Warfare. Somehow that didn't work out; they didn't like my ethnicity, I think. In any case I fell accidentally into the arms of the Shipbuilding Stabilization Committee of the War Production Board, which turned out to be just dandy. Shipbuilding was the biggest monetary activity in the arms industry during World War II.

I came into the office under a set plan A-B, in which the B guy was a labor leader who had never been to college and whose staff had never been to college. They came out of the AFL labor movement. The boss, on the other hand, was Paul R. Porter, a very sophisticated man who had been editor of the student newspaper at Kansas University. He headed a labor magazine in Kenosha, Wisconsin, and was picked to direct the Shipbuilding Stabilization Committee. I was installed in that office. The people in the outer office didn't trust me one bit, because I'd been to college. They banished me to a file room filled with tons of tissue paper, paper, letters and contracts and minutes of meetings, piled in cardboard boxes.

They thought they'd gotten rid of me for a couple of years while I was organizing these files. At Colorado University I had worked in the Norlin library, learning about the dewey decimal classification of books. I was fascinated with the files and, of course, turned it into an enormous job of classifying all letters and knowledge. The result was that when I did come in for a coffee break to the proper office where the others were yacking about the problems they were having, I was able to say, "Oh, but I know, you guys had a meeting down in Tallahassee and I can...." And they'd say, "What?!" I'd say, "Sure." I went to the file room and came back with the file many times. Well, I didn't realize it then but now in retrospect, that's when I realized knowledge is power. I wasn't power hungry at all, I just had to come in there for coffee and a lunch break. When they found out that I wasn't damaging any of them by my college education, and the boss began to notice that I knew more than all of his staff, not because of my brains but because I'd been stuck in the file room for two years, he kept turning to me. And as they noticed that, they decided to treat me the same way Gladys Crawford did when I was six years old; I was the little pet in the office. I was about twenty-six.

I slowly began running around with the boss, Paul Porter, who took me to meetings at the Navy Department and even occasionally to the White House. I was once in the White House, holding papers for Paul, while he was in talking to the President, who had sent orders for him to come to his bedroom. I stood in the hall, with the door ajar, and heard Paul say, "Mr. President, you spend your time in bed." "Yes I do. I just read the papers." Paul asked, "Why do you do that?" "To find out what I did yesterday," the President replied.

That's when I first learned that the person who is to blame or gets the credit probably has very little to do with what he gets the blame for or the credit. When I did my first lecture at the Salzburg seminar, I titled it, *The President is Many Men.*

I stayed in Washington during the war and bought a house. At the War Production Board we had problems like the shortage of manufacturing plants. The solution to the problem was to run the shipyards seven days a week instead of five, eight, or twenty-four hours a day; three shifts of eight hours for seven days. My favorite words in the shipyards were "the account of premium days." The workers got double time on Sunday and time-and-a-half on Saturday. But with the account of premium days they drew lots to see whose Sunday came on Tuesday, Wednesday or Friday. The workers, by agreement with the Union, got double time on their seventh day. The agreements had to be made with the Unions.

The Stabilization Committee was created in the War Production Board, and it functioned to keep the shipyards going by preventing work stoppages due to conflicts between the unions and management. The Stabilization Committee analyzed how a strike would come out if they had one and how to come up with an agreement. The result was the only American tripartite labor agreement I know of; an agreement in which the government is a member along with labor and management. Tripartite agreements are the pattern in Germany.

As the war went on, the Board became more involved with security and preventing terrorism. It controlled inflation by setting wage rates and reviewing them from time to time. I got involved in all of that from 1941 to 1946.

Back to Colorado

Later I was unexpectedly invited to return to Boulder to become a sociology instructor at $6,700 a year. I was making six thousand, and I had a permanent civil service job with the Navy. I was also offered $12,000 to work for United States Steel in New York. I didn't know why at the time, but later found out they were afraid that I might end up on labor's side of the table if they didn't hire me. I came back to Boulder and never left the University.

The letter offering me an instructorship in sociology at CU in Boulder proposed about one-half the salary I would have gotten in New York. Like Hamlet, I wondered whether to go to New York or not to go to New York. I was terrified to be offered a job teaching in Boulder. This was a pre-World War II world. Families were rather stable, the university was small, with the same president for twenty years. The only people hired in our department while I had been a student were Ph. D's, two from Harvard and one from Yale. So I was shocked to be offered a job as an instructor. Today it would be called assistant professor. My wife realized that the longer I stayed away from academia, the harder it would be to take the low salary. I decided, what the hell, one year; I can always keep my contacts in Washington. So we packed our things and moved to Colorado in 1946.

I went to the first faculty meeting as a member instead of as a student. The Dean, Jacob Van Ek, whom I came to worship later, stood before us. We were scared to death of him at the time. He was a Calvinist tyrant who ran the meeting and always said *"We* think this,*"* or "We think that," and I thought that was a kind of royal *we* . Queen Victoria said, *"We* are not amused." But it's taken me all this time to realize he was being truthful. Because a person in charge is not a person but a group, whether or not you can identify it. So it is in fact, a *we.*

I began to notice I was getting much more fame for things I didn't do, good or bad. But being a coward I never defended it or said anything. It turned out that my glorious reputation for supplying Russians with all kinds of information turned out to be false, as revealed in the chapter about the FBI's long investigation of me.

If Howard Higman did not exist, he would have to be invented. But if he were invented, he would be scarcely believable. And of course he would be the first to question the proposition that there really was a Howard Higman.

But he seems to me cast more truly in the mold of Plato's teacher. It is easy to imagine him, walking through the streets of Athens, asking the most troublesome questions of his fellow-citizens. He is claimed by the sociologists, but sociology is only a recent offshoot of philosophy. Whatever his discipline, we laymen would recognize him as a philosopher—and as a natural-born gadfly and corrupter of youth.

When I am asked "Why do people delight continually in conversing with [him]?". I can reply, with the Athenians, that "[We] like to hear the cross examination of the pretenders to wisdom." And if I am ever asked whether the world has made progress in the last 2400 years, I can at least point out that this Socrates has outlasted every Meletus and Anytus who has sought to still his tongue.

—Adam Yarmolinsky
University of Maryland

DN 140-1980
-1-

b7C

b7C
b7D

SECRET

On May 23, 1967,

advised that many of the
employee's statements and opinions are a matter of public
record over the years in the local newspapers and although he
cannot pinpoint any specific statements he has made or stands
he has taken on various issues, his general impressions of
him drawn over the many years he has known him have led him
to the conclusion that he is a highly controversial figure
in the academic community as he always seems to support the
minority opinion in any issue. He continued that it is a
well-known fact in Boulder that the employee uses intoxicants
to excess but that to his knowledge this has never seemed to
interfere with his duties as an instructor at the University
of Colorado nor has it apparently caused him any concern
with officials of the University.

would, with some rather strong
reservations, recommend the employee for a position of trust
and confidence with the United States Government. He stated
his reservations were mainly concerned with the employee's
reputation as a liberal supporter of academic freedom and his
heavy use of intoxicants.

On May 29, 1967,

he stated through-
out the years the employee has gained the reputation in Boulder
as being a user of intoxicants and possessing a liberal
political philosophy; however, he stated he has no actual

b7C

DN 140-1980
-2-

SECRET

b7C
b7D

first-hand knowledge of this
has no
reason not to recommend him on the basis of his character,
loyalty and associates.   opinions
with regard to the employee's liberal political philosophy
stem mainly from public statements the employee has made in
newspapers and he has no specific information which would
cause him to feel that any of these statements were actually
un-American or in support of any foreign government as opposed
to that in the United States.

A sample of censored pages from Higman's FBI Files

2.

THE FBI: BEAUTY AND THE BEAST

When I came back to Boulder as an instructor in the Department of Sociology in 1946, the President had hired a young philosopher from Berkeley, David Hawkins, who had been appointed by Robert Oppenheimer to be the official historian of the Los Alamos Project developing the atomic bomb. When I heard him explaining in a public lecture what went on in Los Alamos, we became very close friends, and I developed an interest in the project. Boulder became a mecca for the people from Los Alamos; I got to know the Oppenheimers, Frank and Robert, and Leo Szilard, the man who did the first chain reaction in England. He subsequently attended World Affairs Conferences over the years. Consequently I knew that the Soviets didn't need the Rosenbergs to develop their bombs because they had captured people who made the original chain reactions in Germany. The originals were made in Germany, not in America. These German scientists were captured by the Russians and closeted in a secret city where they developed their own space program and, in fact, got ahead of us, as Eisenhower discovered to his amazement. They skipped the high octane gasoline stage and went directly to kerosene, and in 1957 they spun around the world with Sputnik, which we couldn't do. So I was aware of the fact that the Rosenbergs were not necessary to them, and I brought it up in my Contemporary Social Issues class.

Meanwhile, by coincidence, Ward Darley, who came to be President of the University, discovered an important fact about the sorority system. A member of a sorority had a younger friend from Moline, Illinois, and wanted to have her rushed by the Pi Phi's. She was required to submit her name to the local alumni club in Moline, even though they had never been to Boulder. There the sorority's alumni club invited the girl's mother to a tea; not the girl, but her mother. If they didn't like her mother, they would not recommend her daughter for membership in the Boulder sorority. It was called, "We couldn't get a 'rec'," meaning a recommendation. President Darley felt that this practice was ridiculous and let it be known that he would ask the Regents to make a rule that sororities and members of sororities could write their own lists of who and what they wanted. If they wanted to have nothing but people with green hair or three legs, it was their business and not their mothers' business. Quite a storm was created across the nation, for the sorority mothers to lose their power over their daughters. An all-day meeting was held in the brand new University Memorial Center, to which a thousand people came and testified on both sides of this issue. An organized Greek letter team brought women in from out of town to live in each sorority house to try to train the girls to be loyal to the alumni.

I did my little speech in the morning around ten o'clock, and I was pretty articulate. At the conclusion, I started across the stage, walking in front of the sorority women sitting there, one of whom was a close friend; whose daughter was in our wedding. Lolita Pouty was national treasurer of Pi Beta Phi. As I went by, she said, "Oh, Howard, I wish we had you on our side."

She didn't know her mike was open, and her remark brought down the house. I was exceedingly embarrassed, and I crept out of the room. I later learned that the man in charge of the opposition was Marilyn Van Derbur's father, Francis Van Derbur, an officer in the Kappa Sigma fraternity. He was a leader of the Greek group fighting President Darley. All afternoon he kept saying, "That Professor Higman....That Professor Higman....That Howard Higman."

I later learned that after I had discussed the matter in the class, in which his daughter was a student, she went home, and like any child, had talked about my class over dinner. I knew then that it wasn't she who turned me into the FBI, it was obviously her father. And it all came about because of the fact that I happened to know David Hawkins, a Professor of Philosophy.

PART ONE

The confrontation began. It was early February, 1960. In my usual way I began my class in Contemporary Social Issues by asking if any student had anything in mind. Miss Van Derbur did. She began reading from *Masters of Deceit*, a book by J. Edgar Hoover, Director of the FBI.

"Please comment on your position regarding the FBI," asked Marilyn Van Derbur, Miss America of 1958 and a senior at the University of Colorado. I smelled a plot but didn't duck the question. In brief I said that I belonged to that group which disapproved of the rise in America of a political police; that I doubted whether the FBI had contributed significantly to the security of the United States.

"The Rosenbergs gave secrets of the atomic bomb to Russia," she insisted.

I said I doubted that any scientist believed that the Soviet Union developed the bomb principally because of the contributions of the Rosenbergs.

I gave credit to the FBI for developing one important and useful thing in America—a system of fingerprinting.

I said that it was my opinion that other agencies of the government were less interested in publicity than the FBI and were often more efficient. Furthermore, I said it was totally inappropriate for a police officer—Hoover— to comment, even indirectly, on the political activities of the President of the United States as he had when he said Mr. Eisenhower had contributed to the rebirth of the Communist Party in the United States by inviting Khrushchev. I said Hoover had grossly exaggerated the strength of the Communist Party in the United States. Many believe there were as many undercover FBI agents in the Party as there were true believers.

Editors Note:

For the reader's ease, we have used italic type and indentation for all FBI material obtained from the Freedom of Information Act.

The debate raged for two days until I closed off the topic and returned to our previous line of inquiry—social changes wrought by atomic energy. The classroom debate subsided.

However, news of this discussion reached the FBI within four days. I am uncertain as to how. On February 17 the *Rocky Mountain News*, a Denver-based Scripps Howard paper, carried the story, "Marilyn, Professor Battle Over FBI," and began the article with, "A head-on clash between a former Miss America and a Colorado University sociology professor over the worth of the FBI spread Wednesday far beyond the CU campus."

Boulder, Denver and Washington were all getting reports, more or less accurate, on the clash. A friend called from Greece and asked, "Howard, what are you up to now?" Another called from London. Calls poured in. I was surprised over the clamor. Amused.

In 1992, through the Freedom of Information Act, I obtained my FBI file, filled with items dated from 1949 through 1991. It contains thousands of pages. Much of the information was censored. J. Edgar Hoover was annoyed with me. I had criticized him and his FBI. For that he spent years having me and my family investigated. Let's follow his trail. The file tells the story.

> *FBI Office Memorandum Urgent*
>
> *To: SAC (Special Agent in Charge) Denver*
>
> *February 11, 1960*
>
> *From: Director, FBI (J. Edgar Hoover)*
>
> *Subject: Unknown professor, University of Colorado. Discreetly interview (censored) and ascertain identity and exact remarks of unknown professor. Check Denver indices regarding professor after ascertaining identity. ...all facts prior to taking any further action.*

The file is frequently censored to remove names of contacts, confidential informants and information considered sensitive to national security or to protect persons who may be harmed if the material is made public. My FBI file numbers are 100-6823 and 140-1980.

FBI Memorandum

From: SAC

Subject: Howard Higman, miscellaneous information.

At 9:15 a.m. on 2/15/60 in connection with this case Supervisor R.E. Wick of the Bureau requested that this office discreetly ascertain subject's background and all information available concerning him. Also to analyze the situation and suggest what type of attack we should take to counteract his lies and propaganda and who we might suggest as the individual or organization to handle such a backfire.

At 10:30 a.m. I called Mr. Wick. He was unavailable.

...I also advised him that a letterhead memorandum was being prepared and would be forwarded to the Bureau and that it would contain background information and derogatory information concerning Higman and this should arrive at the Bureau on 2/16/60. I further advised (censored) that in view of the policy of the University of Colorado which is very liberal and the fact that (censored) would indicate that nothing could be done concerning Higman because of their policy concerning academic freedom. In view of this I felt it would be better and would recommend we depend on our own strength and that we contact President Quigg Newton of this University and advise him it has come to our attention that Higman had made false and erroneous statements concerning the FBI and we felt that we should have an opportunity to present our side of the case. I told (censored) that I felt some speaker from the Bureau, preferably Inspector William C. Sullivan should

come to the University and speak to the entire student body at an open public meeting and advise them concerning this authority, policies and statistics of the FBI in the Internal Security field; the authority, policies and statistics of the FBI in applicant type investigations; a brief but forceful resume on the real purpose of international Communism, the history of Communism in America and relationship with USSR espionage; the history of FBI investigations in protection of Civil Liberties, Civil Rights, etc. I told (censored) this would be included in our background that was being forwarded concerning Higman. (Censored) stated we should do nothing further concerning this matter until we heard from the Bureau. I advised him that we would take no further steps until this advice is received.

Hoover received the news about my classroom comments from a source unknown to me at the time. He wrote the following letter.

February 17, 1960

Dear (censored),

My associates in our Denver Office have informed me of your prompt action in advising them of the unwarranted criticism of this Bureau by an instructor at the University of Colorado, and I wanted you to know of my personal appreciation.

We in the FBI have always welcomed constructive criticism, but when fallacious and inaccurate criticism is voiced against this Bureau, it is necessary to set the record straight. Thank you very much for your thoughtful handling of this matter.

Sincerely,

J. Edgar Hoover

On the same day, Hoover wrote the following letter to my student, Miss Van Derbur.

February 17, 1960

Miss Marilyn E. Van Derbur

890 11th Street

Boulder, Colorado

Dear Miss Van Derbur,

My associates in our Denver office have advised me of your excellent defense of the FBI in recent classroom discussions at the University of Colorado, and I wanted you to know of my personal appreciation.

Your actions in unhesitatingly confronting error with truth are in keeping with the highest traditions of academic freedom.

Students such as you who are ready and willing to challenge fallacious and highly inaccurate criticism are indeed a credit to your school.

*It is a pleasure to send you under separate cover a copy of my book, **Masters of Deceit**, which I have autographed to you.*

Sincerely Yours,

J. Edgar Hoover

February 18, 1960

The SAC Denver began to seek "individuals whom we feel are reliable for purposes of contact and would without question disapprove of subject attacks on [the] FBI." He went on to say:

*" All of Denver, be contacted and advised specifically that Higman has misquoted the Director in the **Rocky***

*Mountain News of February 18, and that such state-
ment is a lie. It is adroitly suggested that they contact
their friends prominent in affairs of the University and
its alumni to write President Quigg Newton, University
of Colorado, calling to his attention the inaccurate and
irresponsible statements made by Howard Higman in
his classes.*

*The relationship of this office and (censored) is excellent
and I feel that a statement could be published by (censored) this office and (censored) here condemning
Higman for his statements concerning the FBI and inviting (censored). The Bureau's attention is called to the
fact that (censored). It is suggested that the Bureau immediately dispatch letter to: Jack Foster, Editor,* **Rocky
Mountain News** *, 400 West Colfax Avenue, Denver, referring to the article entitled, Marilyn, Professor Battle
Over FBI.'"*

FBI Memorandum

February 18, 1960

From: SAC Werner

Subject: Howard Higman

*Mr. Wick stated that he had discussed the matter with
Assis-tant to the Director John P. Mohr and Mr. Mohr
felt very definitely that we should not contact (censored)
for the reason (censored). Mr. Wick stated they were still
considering what should be done in the matter at the
Bureau and among other things made the following suggestions which are to be considered:*

1. Put an article in the student newspaper.

*2. Contact influential persons and sources in Denver,
particularly former graduates of the University who are*

friendly to the Bureau and request them to write letters to the University concerning the article.

3. Also the Bureau wants a teletype today setting forth the names (censored) together with full background on them and recommendations as to whether they should be contacted by me.

4. (Censored) sources, whether or not we can use them to combat this article.

Nothing is to be done, however, by us until we advise the Bureau together with our full recommendations on this matter. I also spoke to Assistant to the Director John P. Mohr who advised we must get something in today, some positive suggestions as to how this matter could be handled. I advised Mr. Mohr we would have a teletype in today.

FBI Memorandum

To: Mr. DeLoach

February 19, 1960

From: M.A. Jones

The SAC, Denver is very discreetly obtaining information regarding university student's newspaper. On receipt of information we will consider having friendly former Special Agents write letters protesting criticism. The SAC will advise of identity of former friendly Agents in the Colorado area.

Action Being Taken Combating Criticism:

Special Agents who are personally acquainted with professors at the University are directing letters of protest to them. The SAC is contacting influential sources and acquaintances to obtain protests regarding the criticism. **We are checking out the background of all teaching** *personnel at the University of Colorado. This is being handled as a special project.*

Observations:

(censored) . Current instructions to our Denver Office are that no contact is to be had with the newspaper except in the course of official business, and then the contacts should be most circumspect. As recently as 7-10-58 the **Denver Post** *published an editorial captioned, "Those Who Stoop to Snoop" critical of the FBI and wire tapping.*

The Denver Office has suggested that a Bureau speaker address the University of Colorado students, pointing out our responsibilities in internal security matters and explaining communist doctrine.

It is believed inadvisable to implement this suggestion at this time. It is believed inadvisable to have the SAC contact Higman for he has already made his "blast" in open classroom sessions and has been interviewed by the press.

The SAC of our Denver office is very discreetly obtaining information regarding the University of Colorado student's newspaper. When this information is received we will consider having friendly former Special Agents who are graduates of the school or reside in that area, write letters to the paper protesting the criticism. The SAC will advise the identity of the former Agents in the area to whom we should consider contacting concerning this matter.

Action Being Taken Combating Criticism: (Censored).

The SAC at Denver is on a first name basis with (censored).

His protest of the criticism, if it can be obtained, will obviously have great weight.

The FBI was not without resources. They were prepared to investigate all teaching personnel at the University. Imagine the cost! I wonder what they could have done if I had passed secrets to the Soviets, or my daughters had.

The furor intensified when an editorial was published in the February 19 issue of *The Colorado Daily*, an independent student publication. The topic, "Academic Freedom vs. the Tabloid Press" took the *Rocky Mountain News* to task for its initial article on this brouhaha.

Academic Freedom vs. the Tabloid Press

It's slightly unusual to find ourselves lined up in favor of any abridgment of freedom of the press, but we feel it necessary to protest violently the recent case of unauthorized publication of the remarks of a C.U professor to his class.

The Denver press has aided in a disgraceful violation of academic freedom by printing a story yesterday about the "radical" remarks of a university professor to a sociology class.

The situation is doubly unfortunate in this instance because the spying was carried out without the knowledge of the professor (or the class).

We hope there will be a curtailment of this type of activity by the press. For, if we are to have free exchange of ideas in the classroom, it is essential that professors and students feel no inhibitions to free speech. They must feel free to take any position, popular or unpopular, for any reason, without the fear that they are making the remarks inside a goldfish bowl. Only then can there be complete academic freedom in the classroom situation. (We might add parenthetically that this argument cannot be extended to the legislative situation.)

It is not hard to predict that the academic process would be considerably inhibited if a student or instructor had the feeling that anything he might say in the sanctity of the classroom could be fodder for the tabloid press.

In this particular case the report was not given directly to a newspaper, but, it seems, to the FBI. The FBI (which should be the last government agency to concern itself with the content of academic lectures) or another Washington source released the report to the press. Then, in a serious breach of good taste, the Denver tabloid yesterday blew the report into a five-column story.

If it becomes necessary to publish anything at all on the matter, as it must if considerable controversy arises, the story (as in the *Daily*) should be limited to the controversy and its after-effects.

To maintain complete freedom of discussion, classroom exchanges must be regarded as privileged communications.

We cannot too strongly condemn the provincial "spy"—or spy system— that found it necessary to "inform" on a professor.

And we cannot too strongly condemn the provincial press that lives off exploitation of such "news" items. In these difficult times, the university classroom is becoming the last citadel of free discussion. Let's keep it that way.

Ron Krieger

When I attempted to learn how the FBI got wind of the classroom discussion, a *Rocky Mountain News* reporter, Jack Gaskie, told me that the *News* had learned of the incident through the Washington Bureau of the Scripps-Howard newspapers. I was mystified as to why or how the story reached Washington. My campus was the scene of great speculation over whether the FBI had released the report of the classroom drama to the press.

In the meanwhile, Miss Van Derbur sent another letter to Hoover, unbeknownst to me until I obtained my FBI file.

Dear Mr. Hoover:

Your letter of February 17, 1960, was of great importance to me. The fact that the U.S. Government is interested in the affairs of college students and that a man of your stature will take the time to write to a student certainly makes me very

appreciative.

*Many students are seeking the truth but are not getting it in our colleges today. Your book, **Masters of Deceit**, gave me many answers to questions I was concerned about. The FBI is a well-known and substantial agency.*

I definitely believe that I am right in my argument with Professor Higman; however, there are still some students who do not know the true facts and think that I may be wrong. This incident has been very stimulating to me. I am not

concerned with newspapers; however, I am concerned with the students and what they think. Although Professor Higman has a right to speak as he pleases, he should never ignore the facts.

Sincerely,

Marilyn Van Derbur

FBI Memorandum

To: Mr. Mohr

February 26, 1960

From: C. D. Loach

Subject: University of Colorado

Criticism of the FBI

Editorial 2-26-60

*SAC Werner of the Denver Office at 10:15 a.m. today telephoned and dictated to Wick the following editorial on page 52 of the 2-26-60 issue of the **Rocky Mountain News**. The editorial is captioned, "We Side With the FBI," a two-column head. The editorial reads as follows: "The stormy debate over the worth of the Federal Bureau of Investigation between Miss Marilyn Van Derbur and Howard Higman, Professor of Sociology at Colorado University, moves us to rise and take the floor. Miss Van Derbur, Miss America of 1958, clashed with Higman in a defense of the FBI. Her action reported in the **Rocky Mountain News** was read by FBI chief J. Edgar Hoover who sent the **News** a logical defense of his organization, a defense printed in the **Rocky Mountain News** Wednesday. We say logical because some of Higman's criticism of the FBI certainly is unfounded. He implied that the FBI is an organization of 'political police.' Hoover's answer was a vigorous protest to the charge. He clearly pointed out that the FBI is constantly under the scrutiny of allied governmental agencies, the Department of Justice and to men who appropriate its budget and the press. Higman said he 'doubted ' the FBI had contributed to the security of the country. In this, and in view of the FBI's brilliant record of wiping out organized domestic crime and in keeping an eye out for foreign espionage, we disagree. The FBI record in World War II in combating spies and sabotage is apparent. Higman implied the FBI is publicity mad. Nothing can be further from the truth. As a newspaper we come to* *grips with the tight-lipped news policy of the FBI. Higman went on to say that he doubted the authenticity of the FBI's estimate of communist strength in the United States. We will side with the FBI in these estimates rather than take the conjecture of the professor. Higman suggested Miss Van Derbur has sprung a 'plot' on him in asking him to review his attitudes on the FBI.*

"We say the beautiful, brainy and courageous young lady did the right thing. We express the fond hope that more undergraduates would spring 'plots' on their professors in their striving for knowledge and truth. A University classroom certainly should be the spawning ground for discussions of a more serious nature than athletics and dating. A university professor has a clear prerogative to discuss with his classroom what he sees fit. He should also be able to stand up to any differences of opinion without yelling 'plot.'"

Recommendation:

*That the attached letter be forwarded to the **Rocky Mountain News** thanking them for this editorial.*

March 2, 1960

Following advice from his staff, J. Edgar Hoover fired off a response to Krieger. He was engaging in what I call affirmation by denial.

Hoover Answers Editorial

Editor, the Daily:

*I have carefully noted your editorial, 'Academic Freedom vs. the Tabloid Press,' which appeared in the Feb. 19, 1960, edition of the **Colorado Daily**.*

All FBI personnel fully join me in subscribing to the democratic policy of free exchange of ideas in the classroom. We hasten to point out, however, that these persons in positions of responsibility who offer criticism are obliged to know what they are talking about.

It would seem to me that this obligation rests particularly upon those who train young people for life in our democratic society. Professor Howard Higman obviously failed in this obligation.

More important than a personal desire to criticize the FBI is the fact that Professor Howard Higman, or any instructor who guides the thinking of young people, should not commit the academic sin of drawing conclusions without first establishing the facts. Such individuals obviously do not live up to the academic responsibility that should parallel academic freedom. The FBI is not a "political police." Such criticism, if true, would associate this Bureau with physical torture techniques, secret trials, secret penal confinements and executions which are representative of a Gestapo or communist police. Our organization has neither general nor local jurisdiction insofar as law enforcement is concerned. We operate strictly within the confinement of slightly over 150 Federal jurisdictional matters which have been assigned to us by the congress. Our every act is under the observation of the Congress, the Federal courts, the Attorney General, and U.S. attorneys, national and local bar associations and, most important, a free press. As a trustee of many years of one of the Nation's respected universities, I would like to once again state that academic freedom should be encouraged, but at the same time our classrooms should not be in the realm of privilege which lies beyond scrutiny by the public and the press. The very nature of the unfounded charges made against the FBI by Professor Higman in a classroom reveals the inherent danger of drawing a curtain of secrecy around our institutions of learning.

J. Edgar Hoover

March 14, 1960

By now, the cast of characters in this investigation had increased and the tone had become nasty. I was labeled an academic punk. W. C. Sullivan wanted to take me on in my own territory. Although I didn't know about the challenge at the time, nothing would have suited me more. I had never met J. Edgar Hoover, but I certainly would have liked to have had the pleasure. The following memo called us to battle.

FBI Memorandum

To: Mr. A. H. Belmont March 14, 1960

From: Mr. W. C. Sullivan

Subject: University of Colorado

Reference is made to the enclosed memorandum from C.D. DeLoach to Mr. Mohr dated March 3, 1960.

As I recall, an invitation was extended recently to the Director to speak at the University of Colorado. Quite properly, this invitation was declined. This is not a suitable place for the Director to appear. On the other hand, it may be that a Bureau representative might profitably appear there and clarify the atmosphere and forcefully present the Bureau's basic viewpoints in the security field.

Without underestimating the capacity of Associate Professor Howard Higman of the University of Colorado, who has been attacking the FBI, I think it can be said factually that Higman is basically an academic punk. There is nothing about this man which the FBI cannot cope with quite successfully. In addition to Higman, it is evident from the enclosed memorandum that there have been other subversive influences at this University.

If the Bureau is willing and it can be discreetly arranged, I have no reluctance at all to going out to the University of Colorado and speaking before the students and faculty members under whatever auspices this University sponsors visiting lecturers. Obviously, it would be walking into a situation where some are filled with animosity for the Bureau and anxious to hurl brickbats at its representatives. What of it? We need to meet some of these academic punks in their own backyards and on their own grounds generally. A lecture presenting the FBI's true role in the security field interspersed with facts concerning the Communist problem would very likely be favorably received by the vast majority of students and faculty members present. If the Bureau feels that too much attention is already centered around the University of Colorado and the FBI at this time, then the lecture could be considered for the fall term of this year. In any event, I think it is well for us to pause and consider the desirability of going out to the University of Colorado either now or in the fall and confronting our opponents directly in their own territory.

ADDENDUM: (3-14-60) (WCS:[CENSORED]) What has been said of the University of Colorado, I think, also applies to the University of California. I certainly would have no objection to appearing out there now or at any time in the future clarifying the Bureau's role in internal security matters and the reality of the communist threat to the existence of this country.

The final volley in the Beauty and the Beast episode came directly from Hoover, who wrote the following letter to Jack Foster. Another case of affirmation by denial. This letter marked a hiatus in my file, but within six years, a new series of investigations began.

Upon examining my entire file, I learned that the Higman dossier contained entries dated back as far as 1940.

February 18, 1960

Mr. Jack Foster
President and Editor

Rocky Mountain News
Denver, Colorado

Dear Mr. Foster:

I have read the article captioned "Marilyn, Professor Battle Over FBI" appearing in the February issue of the **Rocky Mountain News,** *and I want to call your attention to the numerous inaccuracies and distortions in the statements attributed to Professor Howard Higman. We have always welcomed constructive criticism and Professor Higman is, of course, entitled to his opinion, but when his reported remarks are at such great variance with the facts, I feel it is necessary to set the record straight.*

I understand Professor Higman described classroom discussion of the FBI as a "plot." Since this Bureau is a fact-finding agency of the Department of Justice and part of the Executive Branch of our Government, it would not appear that discussion of our jurisdiction and responsibilities would constitute a "plot" unless the instructor so construed his own remarks.

We in the FBI vigorously protest the statement that we are a "political police." This is a blatant falsehood and I challenge Professor Higman to cite examples supporting this unwarranted conclusion. Our activities are constantly subject to scrutiny and examination in the Department of Justice, Bureau of Budget and Appropriations committees of both houses of Congress. The objective of this scrutiny is designed to insure that our work and program conform to established and approved policies of this government. Our contributions to the security of this country have repeatedly been examined in the courts throughout the land and reported by a vigilant press.

In regard to the Rosenbergs, I wish to state that the FBI did not pass upon their guilt or innocence and it must be remembered that they received the advantage of numerous hearings in our higher courts, and every facet of justice in our democratic society was exercised to insure a fair and impartial trial. I would like to point out that the FBI has jurisdiction to investigate over 150 Federal investigative matters, and that the successful handling of the many responsibilities entrusted to us does, of course, frequently make news. We do not seek publicity but have always conducted our operations on the premise that efficiency will bring its own notice to the public.

To characterize my remarks concerning the handling of youthful criminals as belonging in the class of "raving advocates," is inaccurate on its face. I do think, however, that all citizens should be aware of the fact that youthful crime constitutes a serious menace in this country and that the number of serious crimes committed by young persons has been increasing at a rapid rate. If we refuse to be realistic in our concern over their problems, we as a Nation will pay a tragic price.

I must strongly protest Professor Higman's statement that I commented on the political activities of the President of the United States and that I stated the President contributed to the rebirth of the Communist Party in the United States by his invitation to Khrushchev. This statement is not true. It is true I did report what the communists themselves had to say regarding the effects of Khrushchev's visit upon the Party and its plans for future growth. Certainly the public is entitled to this report.

A current fallacy is to measure the strength of the Communist Party in terms of numbers. To do this, as many have experienced, is to dig our own grave. Actually, numbers can never be taken as a true test of communist strength. The communists act as a clandestine conspira-

torial group and the Communist Party has the power of rapid growth in emergency situations. Hence, a Party which numerically on paper may be small, can within a very short time, increase in numbers. Moreover, the Party draws strength from a large number of sympathizers and fellow travelers who, though not actually members themselves, are willing to do the work of the communists. In addition, unfortunately, all too many un-suspecting dupes are often hoodwinked into the communist web. It is not numerical strength alone, but the strategic location of members in industrial and vital defense facilities to which we must be alert. This means that one communist in a key strategic position may be worth more to the Communists than 100 members in other areas.

Sincerely Yours,

J. Edgar Hoover

According to the file, Hoover instructed his agents to compile any materials they might have pertaining to me. They did. I am impressed with their ability to examine my life. Many scholars of Hoover and the FBI under his control believe that personal information collected on those under investigation was used by Hoover to control the situation and gain inordinate power. Since his scatological interest in his prey permeates my file, others believe he stalked Martin Luther King, the Kennedys, Lyndon Johnson, and numerous others for that reason. In fact, some believe that his tenure as FBI Chief was predicated on his power to expose presidents, members of Congress, other Americans by using private, personal information likely to embarrass and weaken them. Here's what they discovered about me.

FBI Memorandum

No investigation has been conducted by the FBI concerning Howard Higman; however; the files of this office contain the following information received during the course of security- type investigations concerning other individuals and organizations:

SAC, New York

August 26, 1949

SAC, Denver New York file 100-74682

Re rep SA

(censored) dated 8-1-49 at New York City, in which a lead is set out for Denver to furnish background information on Howard Higman, care of Colorado University. (censored). A clipping from the Boulder Camera Newspaper in 1940 reflected that Higman that year was the youngest candidate in Colorado for the State Legislature. This clipping set out background information to the effect that Higman had been president of the Sigma Nu Social Fraternity, drama editor of the "Coloradan," and active in other campus organizations. (Censored). Higman's address in Boulder, Colorado, is listed as 930 Eleventh Street, and according to the directory of Colorado University he is an associate professor of Sociology at this institution.

Higman's Selective Service record, made available by (censored) of the State Headquarters of Selective Service, Eighteenth and Wynkoop Streets, Denver, Colorado, confirmed much of the background information obtained from (censored). His full name is Howard Hunter Higman. It further reflected that Higman was rejected for military service because of physical defects in 1942 and 1944. On August 27, 1944, he left Colorado University and went to Washington, D. C., to work for the War Production Board of the U.S. Government. He gave as his address while working in Washington, 34 B Westmoreland Avenue, Tacoma Park, Maryland.

*The Colorado University publication **Silver and Gold** in its issue of March 11, 1949, reported that Howard Higman was faculty sponsor for the "United Nations Week." (censored).*

In 1952 the FBI memorandum stated, "no investigation has been conducted by the FBI concerning Howard Higman." A copy of this memorandum was sent to the U.S. State Department. The FBI agents discovered an article that appeared in the Denver Post in 1950, in which I took on the FBI. They labeled it miscellaneous.

Criticism of FBI

*The February 20, 1950, issue of the **Denver Post** contained the following article:*

"Anti-Red Hysteria Paving Police-State Way", Prof. Says
"If hysteria fostered by anti-Communist fear expands at the present rate, the United States may be in the grip within ten years of a totalitarian rule like that of the Nazis under Hitler. This is the major short-range danger confronting democracy in America," Howard Higman, associate professor at the University of Colorado, declared in a lecture on 'Democracy and the Atomic Age' in the Charles Denison library at the Colorado Medical Center Sunday afternoon. "This short range obstacle must be removed before the whole of democracy can concentrate on long-range problems such as race relations and minority group problems." Bolstering his warning that this country could fall under a totalitarian rule, Higman pointed out that Germany was backing away in fear from Communism so fast that it chose the leadership of one man, Adolf Hitler, as the alternative. "A bill for low-priced housing for the lower income groups would stall in congress unless it were labeled as anti-Communistic in which case none would dare oppose it," Higman pointed out.

Hoover must have hated criticism. I can just see all those agents racing around, collecting newspaper articles in which citizens dared to criticize the police. The article continues:

Higman insisted the best way to fight for liberty anywhere is to practice it. He declared that the Federal

Bureau of Investigation was moving in the direction of a 'police state' type of force. Loyalty checks, he said, catch only the honest liberals who would confess that they had ideas other than those of the status quo reactionaries.

"The Communist party in America backed the Henry Wallace Progressive Party in the last elections because they were actually voting for the Republicans," Higman maintained. "They thought the Republicans would lead the country into a depression and then there would be a chance for their ideology."

July 1956.

By now, FBI agents were searching local police records and talking with confidential informants.

FBI Memorandum

No criminal record Boulder.

Confidential informants acquainted with CP (Communist Party) membership and activity in Denver- Boulder, Colo., area are not acquainted with Higman.

Directories at Boulder, Colorado, as reviewed on July 13, 1956, reveal no Howard Higman in Boulder. Directories do reflect that Howard H. Higman, 930 11th Street, Boulder, is an Associate Professor of Sociology at the University of Colorado. The official program of the "Ninth Annual United Nations Week, Conference on World Affairs, Sponsored by the Department of Social Sciences, Monday Through Friday, April 9-14, 1956, University of Colorado, Boulder, Colorado" lists Howard Higman as Chairman of the Conference.

On July 13, 1956, (censored) Boulder Police Department, and (censored), Boulder County Sheriff's Office, advised their respective files contained no data identifiable with

Howard H. Higman.

Confidential Informants, who have furnished reliable information in the past and who are cognizant of certain phases of Communist Party membership or activity in the Denver and Boulder, Colorado areas, are not acquainted with Mr. Higman.

May 28, 1959.

The following memo demonstrates the logic of those investigating me. I wonder how many others the FBI tracked over and over during the 1950's. The red scare was pervasive and Hoover made it his cause. Guilt by association was used to broaden the net of those he wished to label. This memo was sent to SAC in Denver.

FBI Memorandum

May 25, 1959

The file in this case has been reviewed and there is nothing in it to indicate that the subject is now or was ever a member of the Communist Party or that he is at heart a communist, although he does associate with people who no doubt do believe in communism, at least in theory.

Subject is still on the faculty of the University of Colorado at Boulder, where he serves as Associate Professor of Sociology. He continues each year to serve as Chairman of the United Nations Week held each spring on the University of Colorado Campus. It is a University sponsored affair and is more properly called the "Conference on World Affairs." Confidential Informants who are familiar with some Communist Party Activities in the Denver and Boulder areas do not know the subject. They are listed as follows:

(censored).

In view of the fact that there is no indication that sub-

ject is a communist or takes any active part in communist affairs in this area or elsewhere and since he is a member of the faculty at the University of Colorado it is believed an interview with him would produce no results and might lead to embarrassment. Such an interview is not recommended.

The final memorandum confirms the FBI's knowledge that I was not a member of the Communist Party. I wonder why they didn't drop it at that. I also wonder whose embarrassment they are referring to, certainly not mine. I would have enjoyed exposing their waste of taxpayer's money and their frightening tactics. Why did they retain my name on their Communist Index when I was clearly not a Red?

FBI Memorandum

July 17-August 20, 1959 Howard Higman.

Confidential Informants who have furnished reliable information in the past and who are cognizant of some phases of Communist Party (CP) activities in the Denver and Boulder, Colorado areas are not acquainted with Mr. Higman.

*The **Boulder Camera**, Boulder, Colorado daily newspaper issue of June 14, 1951, contains an article concerning Howard Higman.*

This article states in part:

For the second summer, Howard Higman, assistant professor of sociology at the University, has been invited to take part in the Salzburg Seminar in Austria... "

Higman is one of a limited number of American educators asked to serve for the second consecutive year. He is chairman of the nationally-known World Affairs conference on the Boulder campus.

Lectures to be given by Prof. Higman will be [sic] on the general subject of the structure and dynamics of democratic government in the United States, included in the seminar on 'Control of War.'"

*The **Boulder Camera** issue of November 17, 1955, contains the following information concerning a petition to the U.S. Supreme Court to invalidate the McCarran Internal Security Act of 1950. One of the signers was Howard Higman.*

"Boulder Men Back Petition Against Security Act"

"Thirty Colorado educators, clergymen, attorneys, journalists, and civic leaders—including ten from Boulder—are signers of a statement backing 360 Americans who recently petitioned the Supreme Court to invalidate the McCarran Internal Security Act of 1950.

The amiens curiae brief was filed by the 360 some two months ago when the high court agreed to hear an [appeal] of the Communist Party from a decision of the Subversive Activities Control Board finding that it is a subversive organization under terms of the 1950 Act. "

The Act requires that all organizations found to be 'Communist Action,' 'Communist-front,' or 'Communist-infiltrated' (the latter under 1954 Amendments to the Act) must register as such with the Justice department. "

The Court is expected to render a decision on the constitu-tionality of the Act sometime this winter""

*The **Rocky Mountain News**, Denver, Colorado, daily newspaper issue of February 12, 1959 contains an article concerning a speech delivered by Howard Higman at a meeting of the Denver Forum, a discussion group. This article states in part as follows:*

"My thesis," he said, "is that we need a different kind of American for the future from what we needed in the past.

*The trouble with nice people—those who are well ad-
justed—is that they don't know when not to adjust, or
to whom not to adjust. Thus when McCarthy came along,
each well-adjusted person was waiting for the next well-
adjusted person to tell him how to feel. We hid in moral
futurism, which puts morale above morals. We hid in
committees, in procedures, in false specialization, in un-
needed research, in surveys and statistics, in
self-evaluation projects rather than make decisions.*

*"In short, we abolished the word I. We hid in groups and
in group dynamics—which is nothing but the pooling of
ignorance by people sitting in a circle."*

*During January, 1959, a copy of a petition forwarded to
The Honorable William E. Rogers, Attorney General of
the United States, was furnished to this office. This petition urged dismissal of further prosecution in the Smith
Act case concerning United States vs. Bary, et al. This
petition was signed by Howard Higman, Professor of
Sociology, University of Colorado, among others.*

*It is to be noted that these subjects mentioned above were
convicted in U. S. District Court, Denver, Colorado, on
March 11, 1959.*

Finally, one document was included in my FBI file that shed
light on procedures used by the Agency with regard to CIs (confidential informants). This memo reveals Hoover's determination to trap
persons he feared or suspected. I'm not sure why I was a subject. I'm
not now nor ever have been a confidential informant, to paraphrase
Senator Joseph McCarthy.

*OFFICE MEMORANDUM UNITED STATES
GOVERNMENT To:SAC, DenverDate: 4-13-59*

From: SA (censored)

Subject: Howard Higman

Re Bulet: October 2, 1958, setting forth instructions that due to increased international tensions, the CI (Confidential Informant) should be completely re-examined on an individual case basis. As each case is reopened disposition should be considered in one of the following categories: a) potential informant; b) espionage subject; c) SI subject; d) retention in CI; e) removal from CI. The following minimum investigative steps should be taken: 1) Review file and all pertinent references thoroughly.

2) Contact informants, sources, and defected Communists who could be expected to know the subject. Contact for evidence of current activity and also for the sources' evaluation of potential dangerousness.

4) If the subject has been a CP "drop" or ceased activity suddenly, develop information to show the reason. Many of these "drops" are purely on the basis of theoretical and intellectual differences. The convictions of the persons involved remain unchanged in their hard-core devotion to the principles of international communism, waiting only for what they consider to be a more favorable climate within ruling communist circles. It should also be borne in mind constantly that unexplained cessation of communist activity by a subject may well be based upon a contemplated assignment in espionage or illegal underground activity.

5) Consider interview or re-interview without regard to prior interview results. Bear in mind the Khrushchev revelations of terror under Stalin, anti-Semitism in the Soviet Union and the Hungarian revolt.

6) Secure a current description. The Bureau has been informed that this program must be completed by October 15, 1959, and quarterly reports must be submitted beginning January 15, 1959, reflecting statistics main-

*tained throughout this program. Pursuant to these in-
structions, all Agents to whom cases are assigned are
instructed to designate a copy of all pertinent communications to the control file which is 100-8281.*

PART TWO

Security of Government Employees Investigation:
The Second Phase

Serendipity is defined as the faculty of finding valuable or
agreeable things not sought for. My becoming involved in President
Johnson's War on Poverty in September 1964 was such an experience. A misdirected phone call from the U. S. Labor Department
launched a new dimension to my life. I was to become a poverty war-
rior. The telephone call, intended for the University of Denver, was
inadvertently received by a friend of mine at the University of Colorado Extension Division. Lois Badger informed the caller that Howard
Higman was the man to direct their proposed training program for
thirty-five employees of the U. S. Labor Department. I was to teach
traditional employment counselors how to help young drop-outs and
delinquents find work. I recruited Tom Adams and Bob Hunter to
help me because I was basically ignorant about delinquents, welfare
mothers and drop-outs.

We conducted the training in a completely unorthodox manner. In Chapter Six on the War on Poverty, I'll explain more about the
episodes that brought J. Edgar Hoover into my life for a second time.

Because the University of Colorado received government
funds to operate the War on Poverty programs, and I was enlisted as
principal director, I was subjected to the FBI's then new program,
SGE (Security of Government Employees). I directed a series of programs, at the Washington agencies' request, not mine. I did support
Lyndon Johnson's programs and wanted to help, where I could. The
FBI reappeared in my life in 1966, at first with hesitation; then with

full force, personally directed by J. Edgar Hoover. The following is a chronological presentation of a humorous, at times ugly and intrusive search into my personal and professional life. By the way, the initial grant from the U. S. Bureau of Employment Security was $11,810.

Other grants followed, totaling 11 million dollars, through the mid-seventies; all unsolicited by me. Colorado's poverty training was viewed with favor by many in Washington. We were said to be top flight. Hoover did not share that view. The following entries tell the story.

United States Government Memorandum

To: SAC (140-1980

Date: 10/13/66

From; ASAC

Subject: William H. H. Higman, aka; OEO, SGE

At 9:40 a. m. today, I called Bill Cleveland, Section Chief, SGE matters at the Bureau, concerning Bureau airtel of 10/11/66 which requested extensive investigation of Higman.

I advised Cleveland we had ascertained Higman was Director of VISTA project in Colorado during the summer of 1966 and (censored) advised today Higman is now a full time professor at the University and is not employed now by VISTA. I advised Cleveland, Higman is now on the campus at Boulder.

I also advised Cleveland we had ascertained that (censored) and detailed LHM concerning (censored) is being mailed to the Bureau today.

Since Higman is not now connected with VISTA and in view of the fact that he has been critical of the Bureau in the past, I suggested to Cleveland that they check the current status of Higman in relation to VISTA before

*we do any investigation. Cleveland indicated pursuant
to my suggestion we should continue the file review requested in the Bureau's airtel of 10/11/66 but no active
investigation should be conducted and he would call us
back today concerning the future on this matter.*

*At 2:00 p. m., (censored) Bureau, telephonically advised
that SA(censored) that WFO had just found out from
OEO that agency does not have any plans to employ and
that Higman is not now employed by that agency. He
said that Higman's application had listed an occupation of consultant for the Department of Labor and OEO
found this was not true.*

*SA(censored) advised (censored) that on this date there
were being forwarded to the Bureau the five copies of a
LHM regarding Higman in connection with (censored).*

*(Censored) was advised that this LHM contains back-
ground information and a succinct summary of
derogatory information regarding Higman.*

The special agent in charge, Denver, filed the following recommendation to the Washington office of the FBI. *Since Higman is
not now connected with VISTA as indicated above, in view of prominent position of Higman at University which would entail extremely
sensitive and discreet investigation plus past public criticism of Bureau
by Higman, Denver recommends no investigation of Higman under SGE
program.*

The Denver FBI Bureau submitted a one page secret statement.

*William Howard Hunter Higman
Consultant
Bureau of Employment Security
U. S. Employment Service
Department of Labor
Washington, D. C.
Basis For Investigation*

Donald E. Kelley, then United States Attorney, Denver, Colorado, on January 1, 1959, provided a copy of a petition he had received from William E. Rogers, then Attorney General of the United States, which had been received by Mr. Rogers from a group of individuals in Colorado. The petition urged the dismissal of further prosecution of subjects in U. S. District Court, Denver, who had been charged with violation of the Smith Act. Included on the petition was the typewritten name "Howard Higman."

Results Of Investigation

Background

United States Employment On October 26, 1966, U. S. Department of Labor, Divisions of Investigations and Security, furnished Standard Form 85 for W. Howard Hunter Higman, bearing a certification, dated October 26, 1966, signed Howard Higman, and date of appointment, November 3, 1966, as consultant, to be paid $60.00 a day, and Washington, D. C., as place of duty.

The form contains the following information regarding Higman: Date of birth, April 25, 1915, at Boulder, Colorado; on October 25, 1941, at Denver, Colorado, he married Marion Hackstaff, who was born January 4, 1917, at Denver.

Higman lists his Social Security number as 523-48-9003, passport number, F 373523.

May 16, 1967

Airtel mentioned in the following memorandum was not included in my FBI file. Not only was I to be investigated, but also members of my family. They were, and I include those contacts later in this chapter. So, in May, 1967, the FBI launched a thorough probe, even though the Denver ASAC in charge cautioned that such an inquiry "could be a problem and that such inquiry would undoubtedly be relayed on to him [meaning me] by the people contacted."

United States Government Memorandum

To: SAC (140-1980)Date: 5/16/67

From: ASAC

Subject: William Howard Hunter Higman

Buded: 6/27/67

At 9:15 a. m. this morning,

I telephonically contacted Section Chief William Cleveland concerning the Bureau's airtel of 5/12/67, initiating an SGE investigation of Higman.

I pointed out to Mr. Cleveland that the preparation of the letterhead memorandum requested in the Bureau's communication would be extremely time-consuming and noted the Bureau expected it by 5/22/67. I also pointed out the Bureau expected a report by 6/2/67.

I asked Mr. Cleveland whether the information from the LHM should be included in the report, pointing out this could be a duplication of the work, and in that connection suggested that a report only be submitted. I also mentioned to Mr. Cleveland, Higman is an extremely influential individual at the University of Colorado and any inquiry made concerning him, whether on or off the college campus, could be a problem and that such inquiry would undoubtedly be relayed on to him by the people contacted.

I mentioned that while Higman is a professor of Sociology on the faculty, he in fact is one of the ruling cadres of professors on the campus and wields authority and power far beyond that expected of a professor. I pointed this out to Mr. Cleveland in view of the Bureau's instructions in the last paragraph on page 2 of their 5/12/67, airtel.

The preceding paragraph on page 2 indicated Denver should insure during the investigation that the employee's relatives are fully identified.

Concerning the preparation of the LHM, Mr. Cleveland said that a concise LHM should be forwarded to the Bureau by 5/22/67, in view of the deadline and the volume of information available for it, and it need not include all data in the files concerning Higman.

Concerning my suggestion of preparing a report instead of a LHM, Mr. Cleveland said both should be submitted but the report should include all detailed information not placed in the LHM.

Concerning the contacts to be made in relation to the investigation, he authorized us to conduct whatever investigation is necessary, including interviews of (censored) and no contacts should be made on the campus, including (censored) checks, except with prior specific Bureau authority. He said if any problem arose in connection with the investigation I should contact him concerning it.

Airtel Registered

To: SAC, CHICAGO 5/25/67

From: SAC, DENVER (140-1980) (P)

William Howard Hunter Higman

Buded: 6/2/67

Basis for investigation of employee is that the name of Howard Higman appeared on a petition to the Attorney General urging dismissal of further prosecution of Colorado subjects under the Smith Act.

Employee's daughter, Ann Higman, approximately 24 years of age, attended Pomona College, California, and is presently graduate student in Anthropology at Uni-

versity of Chicago. Bureau instructed that employee's relatives be fully identified and that the indices of appropriate field offices covering their residence be reviewed.

Chicago and Los Angeles review indices on Ann Higman and if any information contained therein report same in SGE report. If any indices negative, advise Bureau and Denver.

To: Mr. Gale

Date: 5/24/67

From: W. V. Cleveland

Subject: William Howard Hunter Higman

SECURITY OF GOVERNMENT EMPLOYEES

Purpose: To set forth request of Denver Office for authorty to conduct an investigation on the University of Colorado campus consisting of interviews of (censored).

Background: Higman, Professor of Sociology, University of Colorado since 1946, is subject of full field investigation under Federal Employee Security Program which was re-instituted on May 12, 1967.

In February, 1960, Higman made highly critical remarks against Bureau in one of his classes, which incident received wide publicity in Colorado, and Bureau forwarded letter to Colorado newspapers refuting his erroneous remarks. He has been affiliated with various peace organizations, interested in world peace, the United Nations, and equality of races. He allegedly signed petition to halt prosecution of Communist Party leaders (censored). In December, 1966, he was member of delegation visiting the Soviet Union sponsored by the American Friends Service Committee.

The Denver Office believes of the following (censored, Denver does not anticipate any problems in connection with such interviews.

ACTION: If you approve, the Denver Office will be advised authority granted to interview (censored) and that arrangements should be made to interview (censored).

May 26, 1967.

Hoover became directly involved in determining who should and who should not be interviewed concerning me. However, the subjects interviewed were not limited to Colorado.

Airtel To: SAC... (censored) 5/26/67

Washington Field (140-24088)

From: Director, FBI (140-33577)

William Howard Hunter Higman

Re Denver Airtel 5/23/67

A number of individuals acquainted with Higman will be interviewed during the course of this investigation. In view of this, the Bureau does not consider an interview of (censored) or (censored) necessary. Bureau authority is therefore denied for interview of such individuals by (censored) and Washington Field.

(Censored) and New York will subsequently be advised regarding other requests contained in referenced airtel.

June 2, 1967

A synopsis of the interviews was filed on June 2, 1967. I gather it was based on the reports of those who met with informants and persons approved by Director Hoover.

FBI Memorandum

Report of: (Censored)Date: June 2, 1967

Office: DENVER

Field Office File #: 140-1980

Title: William Howard Hunter Higman

Character: Security Of Government Employees

Synopsis: Investigation of employee based on information that name "Howard Higman" appeared on petition to Attorney General 1/1/59 urging dismissal of further prosecution of Denver Smith Act subjects. Employee resides 930 — 11th Street, Boulder, Colorado, and is Professor, University of Colorado (CU), and has been employed at CU since 1946. Employee's wife, Marion, and daughters, Ann and Elizabeth reside with him. Employee's sisters are Winifred Bengston of Boulder, and Josephine Day, of Fort Collins, Colorado. Employee's father, Joseph Henry Higman, died in 1935, and mother, Clara Higman, died in 1961. Employee rejected for military service in 1942 and 1946 because of physical defects. Employee worked War Production Board, Washington, D. C., and resided at 34 B Westmoreland Ave., Takoma Park, Md. In 1946 employee was Acting Deputy Chairman, Shipbuilding Stabilization Committee of Department of Labor. Employee has written publications including those with titles "Theories of the Effects of War," "The Effect of the McCarran Act on the U. S. —European Relations," and "The Salzburg Seminar on American Studies." (Censored). President Johnson complimented CU World Affairs Conference April, 1965.

(Censored). In 1950 employee said that FBI was moving in direction of a police state. In 1960 employee made critical remarks about FBI in classroom which were challenged by a student.

(Censored). In 1955 a petition to the Supreme Court to invalidate the McCarran Internal Security Act contained the name Howard Higman. (Censored). Employee wrote

an article for student publication recommending admission of Red China to UN. In 1963 employee reported as a sponsor for a Preparatory Congress for a World Constitutional Congress. Employee purported to have signed a petition in 1964 to abolish the House Committee on Un-American Activities. Employee purported to support Committee to Aid the Bloomington Students.

(Censored). Employee purported to attend conference in 1965 regarding national security problems at West Point. In Oct., 1965, employee stated he supported President Johnson's policy in Vietnam. (Censored). In May, 1967, employee reported to have stated he identified himself as a member of the "Antiwar Intellectual Community." Employee traveled to Austria in 1950, 1951, and 1957 to participate in the Salzburg Seminar; to Germany in 1965 to help plan a German conference similar to the CU Conference on World Affairs; to Russia in 1966 to participate in a seminar on world peace.

Employee, upon return from USSR, said that Russia is still a police state with a controlled press. A source reported Higman picks committee members of Conference and dominates selection of participants. Source reports that because some of the participants of the Conference have been controversial, Higman has been subject of controversy.

Source reports Higman has a shallow scholarly background, is a good organizer but uses his friends and has built up considerable publicity for himself.

Another source reports employee has said he is anti-Communist and that employee has said that academic freedom does not involve responsibility. Another source reports that Higman is a controversial figure and has been criticized for the type of people he has invited to the Conference on World Affairs. Another source reports that Higman is a lover of publicity and advocates dis-

sent. Several sources report that Higman is a heavy drinker and was involved in and possibly the cause of divorce between (Censored). (Censored) declined to comment as to employee. (Censored) as well as (censored) recommend employee for position of trust and confidence, U. S. Government.

All consider him controversial, outspoken individual, but loyal to U. S. Government. States employee heavy user of intoxicants, although such does not interfere with duties at CU.

Another source said (censored) knows nothing of any attendance of any meetings by Higman which he would consider Pro-Communist or Pro-Soviet. (Censored) stated that he under-stands that (censored) is aware of this situation and the only question is whether or not he would be willing to discuss the matter. He stated that there is no secret around Boulder that Professor Higman "likes boys." He stated that he has no personal knowledge concerning this situation and that he feels that (censored) knows nothing which he feels should be included in the signed statement nor does he have any personal knowledge in which he would testify in a hearing. The Denver Office will conduct appropriate interviews concerning the foregoing if the indicated individuals have not been interviewed previously.

June 7, 1967

In a long memorandum from Director Hoover, Special Agents in charge in Denver, New York and Washington were given assignments. In this memo, Hoover points out that Denver SAC should attempt to discover why I was rejected for military service in 1942 and 1944. He says "information might be pertinent in view of allegations… indicating employee's associates possibly involved in homosexual activities."

Hoover also asked that agents investigate my life in Washington, D. C., twenty-five years after I left the nation's Capitol to return to Boulder. He asked that the Washington Field be alert for any information bearing upon my moral character."

Hoover's preoccupation with homosexuals is explored in several books about the Director. His interest in my sexual preference is noteworthy; I imagine he wanted to know if I "like boys," as one unnamed source suggested. I wonder about J. Edgar myself. Hoover was obsessed with detail and intrigue as the following memo demonstrates.

Airtel

To: SACs,

Denver (140-1980)-Enc.Date: 6/7/67

New York (140-17031)

Washington Field (140-24088)

From: Director, FBI (140-33577)

William Howard Hunter Higman

Labor

SGE

Re New York report 6/1/67, Denver report 6/1/67, Denver airtel 5/23/67 and New York airtel 6/1/67.

Denver refer to Chicago airtel of 5/31/67 which indicated Higman's daughter, Alice Eaton Higman, is a graduate student at the University of Chicago and no Ann Higman is in attendance. Referenced Denver report in the synopsis and on page 11 indicates Ann Higman now at University of Chicago and Alice Eaton Higman employed at Colorado University under sponsorship of the Office of Economic Opportunity. It is also noted Alice Higman now residing at employee's residence address.

Denver should immediately furnish Bureau clarification in order that referenced Denver report can be corrected at the Bureau and disseminated.

Following clarification regarding the identities and location of the employee's daughters, Denver should attempt to obtain further information regarding the reasons for the employee being rejected for military service. Such information might have pertinence in view of allegation furnished by (censored) indicating employee's associates possibly involved in homosexual activities.

Washington Field should conduct neighborhood investigation if not previously handled at 34 B Westmoreland Avenue, Takoma Park, Maryland. For your information, his Selective Service records as reviewed by Denver in 1949 indicated employee in 1942 and 1944 rejected for military service for physical defects. It was also indicated that on 8/27/42 Higman left the University of Colorado to work in Washington, D. C., for the War Production Board and furnished the above as his residence address.

Enclosed for the information of Washington Field is one copy of (censored) airtel 5/31/67 which contains information received from (censored) regarding the allegation that Higman's associates possibly involved with homosexual activities. Washington Field should be alert for any information bearing upon employee's moral character.

For the information of Denver, in the event subsequent newspaper articles are copied and included in supplemental reports, the copy should be prepared after clipping has been placed on plain paper which should bear only the name of the publication, the city of publication, and the date. It is also suggested that if additional newspaper articles are forwarded with supplemental report that the details of the report indicate that a copy is attached as Exhibit A, B, etc. This is considered a more desirable practice than incorporating copies of articles within the report.

A series of memos responding to Hoover's June 7, 1967 directive provide interesting answers.

Report of: (censored)Office: Denver

Date: June 9, 1967

Field Office File #: 140-1980 Bureau File #: 140-33577

Title: William Howard Hunter Higman

Character: Security Of Government Employees

Synopsis: Supplemental Report

(Censored) reported in 1949 that Howard Hunter Higman had been rejected for military service in 1942 and 1944 during World War II because of physical defects.

(Censored) reported 6/8/67 that information regarding employee's rejection for military service has been destroyed.

On August 26, 1949, (censored) reported that Howard Hunter Higman was born April 25, 1915, and that he had been rejected for military service in 1942 and 1944 during World War II because of physical defects.

On August 17, 1942, he left the University of Colorado, Boulder, Colorado, and went to Washington, D. C., to work for the War Production Board. He listed his address while working as 34 B Westmoreland Avenue, Takoma Park, Maryland. On June 8, 1967, (censored) advise that the records containing information concerning the rejection of Howard Hunter Higman for military service were destroyed a number of years ago and there is no information available concerning this matter.

June 12, 1967

Hoover did not relent in his personal pursuit of knowledge he wanted and hoped to discover.

Radiogram Urgent

To: SAC (censored)

From: Director FBI (140-33577)

William Howard Hunter, Labor, SGE

Information regarding story alleging possible homo-sexual activities involving employee has been received from (censored) individuals, however, all state no per-sonal knowledge.

(Censored) may well be individual who could furnish information from personal knowledge.

In view of (censored) desiring no involvement (censored) should not be advised of (censored) identity. Mail copy to Denver.

Note: Higman is University of Colorado professor.

Allegations received regarding homosexual activities of people (censored) reportedly has additional informa-tion and Denver requested Bureau authority for (censored) to interview.

June 16, 1967

The following memorandum suggests additional interviews regarding the charge of homosexuality as requested.

FBI Memorandum

To: Mr. Gale

Date: 6/16/67

From: W. V. Cleveland

Subject: William Howard Hunter Higman Purpose;

To advise request by (censored) for authority to interview (censored) in effort to resolve information possibly relating to morals of employee.

Background: An established source of the Denver Office has furnished information regarding his recollection of hearing a story involving (censored).

According to the story (censored), additional inquiries have determined that other individuals recall a story regarding a party in approximately 1959 which involved (censored) and at which abnormal sex acts were committed. Such individuals have no personal knowledge and will not testify and have indicated they cannot recall whether Higman mentioned in connection with the story. One individual suggested (censored) may possess information regarding the alleged incident. It was noted that (censored). Bureau files contain no information regarding (censored).

(Censored) indices negative and no indication he has previously been contacted.

Recommendation:

If approved, (censored) will be instructed to interview (censored) regarding his knowledge of Higman which interview must be handled other than (censored). Instructions will also be issued that most circumspect inquiries be made in an effort to determine if (censored) can furnish information regarding alleged incident and whether Higman involved.

July 14, 1967

Hoover persisted with this line of inquiry. He gave his staff three days in which to reply.

Airtel

To: SAC, Denver (140-1980)

From: Director, FBI (140-33577)

William Howard Hunter Higman

Re airtel 5-31-67,

Denver airtel 6-7-67 and subsequent communications relating to investigation regarding employee. It is noted established source of Denver Office furnished information to the San Francisco Office regarding a story indicating possibly employee associated with homosexuals. Denver promptly review investigation conducted this matter.

Advise Bureau whether you have any confidential informants who are familiar with homosexual activities in pertinent area who might possess information regarding any homosexual activities on part of the employee and whether such individuals have previously been contacted regarding employee. If not previously contacted and no reason known by you why they should not be contacted, you should do so and furnish Bureau results by radiogram by close of business 7-17-67.

July 17, 1967

Three days later the Special Agent in Charge in Denver sent this required radiogram to Director Hoover.

Radiogram Urgent Date: 7/17/67

To: Director

From: Denver William Howard Hunter Higman

Re Bureau airtel July fourteen, last.

Denver Office has no confidential informants familiar with homosexual activities in Boulder, Colorado, the residence and location of occupation of employee.

Attention is directed to report SA (censored) June eight, last, wherein (censored) Boulder, advised Higman not engaged in activities which would subject him to arrest or questioning for violation of laws of city of Boulder and state of Colorado and that files of Boulder Police Department contain no information regarding Higman.

As I examined my lengthy FBI file, I discovered a number of interviews by FBI agents with sources unnamed and possibly unknown by me. I include a few, both pro and con, to illustrate the nature of these inquiries and the contents of my FBI file. These reports are dated from May 18 to May 31, 1967. The agents were busy. I was called everything from a "muddlehead liberal" to a "good American," and one source said "he probably drinks more than the average university professor." A stranger might deduce that I'm complex.

DN 140-1980

(Censored) advised on May 18, 1967,

(censored) stated that the employee is a controversial professor at CU primarily because of his connection with the Conference on World Affairs. (Censored). The source stated that the employee basked in any type of publicity.

Source stated that employee has a reputation in Boulder, Colorado, as being a "muddleheaded liberal" who has championed the causes of individuals with unorthodox opinions and issues.

Source stated that you cannot buy Higman, he has too big an ego.

Source reported that the employee has a reputation in the City of Boulder as being a heavy drinker but source has no knowledge that the employee has ever been arrested because of this activity.

(Censored).

Source questioned Higman's loyalty to the United States because of employee's reputation of inviting individuals to attend the Conference on World Affairs who have expressed pro- Communist and pro-Soviet sympathies. Source recalls that Higman has made the statement that academic freedom does not involve responsibility and has also made the statement that he is anti-Communist. Source stated that there are a number of people in the community of Boulder who disagree with the views expressed by the employee. (Censored).

Source reported that the employee has been a moving figure in back to the Conference of World Affairs and has been the individual to select the personnel who participated in the Conference. Source reported that (censored) the personnel who participated in the Conference on World Affairs have been heavily weighted to the "left." Source explained that source means there have been more participants who advocated ideas which were out of step with the foreign policy of the United States than there were individuals who supported the policies of the United States.

Source stated that the employee is a good American who is very popular with his students but is one of the most controversial professors at CU.

Source reported that the employee had created trouble for the University with the State of Colorado Legislators because of some of the individuals the employee had invited to the Conference on World Affairs which resulted in bad publicity for the University.

Source reported that the employee, to the source's knowledge, has never been linked with the CP (Communist Party).

Source stated that five or six years ago an article was written in the "Reporter" magazine which described Howard Higman as "half genius, half mad." Source would recommend employee for a position of trust in-

volving war on poverty matters but would not recommend him for a position of trust where he would have access to matters pertaining to the security of the United States.

(Censored).

Source advised that the employee was an inconspicuous professor at CU until he organized and developed the Conference on World Affairs which is held yearly at the University.

Source explained that the employee is appointed each year by the President of the University to be the chairmen of the committee which organizes the Conference. The employee then appoints a committee of his personal friends to serve on the committee. The employee selects those individuals who are to appear at the Conference and runs the committee like a dictator. The employee selects the topics to be discussed and secures the assistance of other professors to participate in the Conference.

Source reported that many faculty members refuse to participate at the Conference. Some individuals who have served on this committee in the past resented the dictatorial manner in which the employee ran the Conference. Some of the committee members resented the fact that the employee did not set up any ground rules so that there could be fair representation from each side regarding any particular issue discussed at the Conference.

The former President of CU, Quigg Newton, promoted Higman to the position of full Professor in the Sociology Department primarily because of the employee's success in the operation of the Conference.

Source said that Higman has a shallow scholarly background but is considered a good organizer and originator of ideas.

Source reported that within the past two years the employee has taken an active interest in the War on Poverty Program known as VISTA."

Source said that the employee has originated several of the VISTA projects in the State of Colorado.

Source stated that source did not think employee was ever a member of the CP nor could be considered a communist.

Source was of the opinion that the employee formerly was pro-Russian in sympathy but that employee is so totally undisciplined he could not be captured by any idea or action for a long period of time.

Source stated that the employee went to Russia in the latter part of 1966, and is of the opinion that this trip opened up the eyes of the employee regarding life, ideas, and practices in the Soviet Union. Source reported that the employee has loyal friends and bitter enemies; that the employee has a reputation of using people; that he is a "name dropper." (Censored).

On May 31, 1967 (censored) who declined to sign a statement or appear before a security hearing board, advised that source knows of Howard Higman and knows that Higman is not now, and has not been for the past ten years, a member of the CP in Colorado. On May 29, 1967, (censored).... favorably commented upon their character, loyalty, and associates. He stated that the employee is a native of Boulder, Colorado, having attended grade school, high school, undergraduate and graduate school in the city. He is very well known in the community and during the past 15 or 20 years has developed the reputation of being an extremely heavy user of intoxicants as well as being an outspoken individual on many controversial issues. He stated he feels the employee actually likes making "rash statements" in order

*to lead people to believe that he is taking a very unpopu-
lar stand on a particular issue whereas he actually feels
entirely to the opposite. He stated that most people who
know Higman know this and accept his statements as a
facet of his personality rather than taking him seriously.
(Censored) considers both the employee and his wife as
extremely good Americans whose loyalty to the United
States he would not question. (Censored) that although
the employee and his wife do associate with what he
would term a "heavy drinking crowd," they also social-
ize among the more conservative element in the City of
Boulder, particularly with regard to the professors and
their wives at the University. Conference On World Affairs University of Colorado (Censored). The April 16,
1965 issue of the* **Denver Post,** *reported that a telegram
was received from President Johnson complimenting
CU's World Affairs Conference. The telegram reads as
follows: "The frontier of our knowledge and our concern
is no longer defined by oceans. We have taken on great
responsibilities as a nation. If America is to remain great,
we must develop a new generation of young people interested and involved in the world beyond our borders.
The Conference on World Affairs at the University of
Colorado is helping to meet this important challenge. I
congratulate you."*

GENERAL EMPLOYMENT

*(Censored) the employee is well read in Marxist-Leninist
theory and engages in frequent discussions concerning
Marxism- Leninism in the Soviet Union. He stated that
this has caused many individuals to believe that the
employee is imbued with communist doctrine but that
he knows from many discussions with the employee on
communism that he actually does not believe in this sys-*

tem of government. He pointed out that recently the employee has publicly stated that he is in favor of participation of the United States in the war in Vietnam which is in specific contradiction to most liberal thinking people and the communists throughout the world. (Censored).

On May 25, 1967, (censored). . . . there is no question in his mind whatsoever that the employee is entirely loyal to the United States Government as he always been outspoken in his support of the democratic way of life as opposed to the totalitarian, and he has always been particularly strong in his support of the Democratic Party of the United States. In this regard he pointed out the employee has recently taken an open stand in the participation of the United States in the war in Vietnam which is entirely contrary to the views of the majority of the liberals at the University. He stated he has always been publicly critical of the way of life in the Soviet Union, having recently completed a trip to this country. He stated he feels the employee is entirely loyal to the United States and would give this country his undivided support in the event of any hostilities with any foreign power. He pointed out that he most certainly does not consider the employee an alcoholic or a problem drinker of any type as his drinking has never interfered with his teaching duties or as a professional sociologist. (Censored) recalls having read newspaper accounts of Employee having been chairman of annual Conference on World Affairs at the University of Colorado. He stated that he recalls that several years ago Employee had at the Conference the First Secretary of the Soviet Embassy and on another occasion, the Bulgarian Ambassador, the names of whom he does not personally recall. He also recalls that employee had as a guest (censored) who showed films on Red China which he had taken in Red China.

After reading their dazzling array of opinions and gossip, perhaps even J. Edgar Hoover may have been confused. I am. I never knew I had so many loquacious friends and enemies. I also realize I have no private life. Hoover engaged in much ado about nothing. Think of the time and money this vendetta cost American taxpayers. Finally, a summary report of this witch hunt was sent to the Civil Service Commission. Remember, I was only a part-time, infrequent consultant who never sought any consultancy from the U.S. government.

Before I provide the summary report, let's look at the botched investigations of my daughters, Anne and Alice. Even J. Edgar, in several memos, tried to straighten out their identities.

Anne and Alice Higman

During the FBI's investigation of me in the Security of Government Employees background search (incidentally, for work I was requested to do by the United States Department of Labor), two of my daughters were also the subjects of searches. Perhaps Hoover thought communism was inherited—all in the family. However, the Bureau Agents were mixed up. They investigated Anne at Pomona College while it was Alice who attended that California school. Anne attended Barnard College in New York. Regardless, time and money were no barrier to Hoover.

> To: SAC, Chicago
>
> From: SAC, Denver (140-1980)
>
> Buded: 6/2/67
>
> Employee's daughter, Anne Higman. approximately 24 years of age, attended Pomona College, California, and is presently graduate student in Anthropology at the University of Chicago. Bureau instructed that employee's relatives be fully identified and that the indices of appropriate field offices covering their residences be reviewed. Chicago and Los Angeles review indices on Anne Higman and if any information contained therein

*report same in SGE report. If indices negative, advise
Bureau and Denver.*

The basis for investigation was the fact that I signed, in 1959,
a petition urging the Attorney General to dismiss further prosecution of several Colorado activists. At the time, Alice was nineteen years
old.

Results Of Investigation

Credit and Arrest

*On June 1, 1967, the files of the credit Bureau of Pomona,
California, were caused to be searched for information
concerning the employee's daughter, Anne Higman, who
reportedly attended Pomona College, Claremont, California, dates not shown. No record was located. On June
1, 1967, the files of the Claremont Police Department,
Claremont, California, were caused to be searched concerning Anne Higman. No record was located. The above
files were caused to be searched by SA(censored).*

*On June 1, 1967, the files of the Retail Merchants Credit
Association, Los Angeles, California, were searched at
the request of IC (censored) contained no record identifiable with Anne Higman.*

*On June 1, 1967, the files of the Los Angeles Police De-
partment and the Los Angeles County Sheriff's Office,
Los Angeles, California, searched at the request of IC
(censored) contained no record identifiable with Anne
Higman.*

Miscellaneous

*Confidential informants, who are familiar with Com-
munist Party membership and activities in the
Claremont, California area, advised in June, 1967, that
Anne Higman is unknown to them.*

At the same time that Anne, who never attended either
Pomona or the University of Chicago, the FBI received a field report

on Alice, who was in Chicago. The correct field report also finds no evidence of Communist Party activity on Alice's part. She gave no secrets to the Soviets.

Results of Investigation

Relative

On May 31, 1967, (censored) University of Chicago, Chicago, Illinois, advised SA (censored) that Alice Eaton Higman, 5430 South University Boulevard, Chicago, Illinois, whose home address is 930 11th street, Boulder, Colorado, is enrolled at this school as a graduate student in Anthropology and is due to graduate in the summer of 1968. Credit and Arrest On June 1, 1967, (censored) Chicago Credit Bureau, Inc., Chicago, Illinois, advised IC (censored) that the files of this agency contain no information concerning Alice Eaton Higman.

On June 1, 1967, the files of the Bureau of records and Communications, Chicago, Illinois, Police Department, were reviewed by IC (censored) and no arrest record was located concerning Alice Eaton Higman.

Now for the final report of this intrusive search to find out about the man a *Reporter Magazine* article described as "half genius, half mad."

United States Government Memorandum

To: Mr. GaleDate: 7/24/67

From: W. V. Cleveland

Subject: William Howard Hunter Higman

Purpose: To advise that investigation of Higman under the Federal Employees Security Program has been complete, the results have been furnished to the Civil Service Commission(CSC), and to note that a nonspecific allegation received regarding Higman was not disseminated.

Background: Higman is the University of Colorado (UC)

*Professor of Sociology who, in February 1960, made criti-
cal remarks against the Bureau in one of his classes at
which time Marilyn Van Derbur (Miss America 1958)
contradicted his remarks. Incident received wide publicity in Colorado newspapers. Investigation of Higman
was based upon his name appearing on petition to Attorney General which urged dismissal of further
prosecution of Smith Act subjects at Denver.*

*Results of Investigation: Investigation determined that
in applying for position Higman admitted that in 1954
he was arrested, place not shown, for driving under the
influence of alcohol and was fined $75. No arrest records
were located regarding Higman. In 1949 and 1951 he
was sponsor or faculty advisor to two student activities
(censored). He reportedly signed a petition to invalidate
the McCarran Act of 1950; urged admission of Red China
to the United Nations; signed a petition demanding abolition of the House Committee on Un-American
Activities(HCUA); and supported Committee to Aid the
Bloomington Students, a group indirectly controlled by
the Socialist Workers Party.*

Memorandum to Mr. Gale

Re: William Howard Hunter Higman

*(Censored). One reference signed a statement of protest
regarding HCUA and another reference urged revision
of United States policy toward Cuba and (censored).
Several (censored) described Higman as a heavy user of
intoxicants, however, recommended. Others would not
recommend or would not comment regarding a recommendation. One individual described Higman as having
loose morals in addition to being a heavy drinker, and
would not recommend for access to information regarding the security of the country. Information also*

*developed regarding Higman's alleged extra-marital re-
lations several years ago with (censored) which resulted
in divorce of (censored). One individual questioned loyalty due to his inviting to Conference on World Affairs
persons who expressed Red China and pro-Soviet sympathies. (Censored). Allegation Not Disseminated:
(Censored) furnished vague, nonspecific, information he
recalled hearing from persons now unknown regarding
(censored). This source had no personal knowledge, but
had vague recollection Higman may have had some connection with the incident. Other sources recall hearing
several years ago of a party involving (censored) but do
not recall that Higman involved or his name mentioned
in connection with that story. Other persons interviewed
as noted above were aware of employee's reputation for
loose morals and that information has been disseminated. However, none indicated any knowledge of
possible abnormal sex practices on part of employee.
Since the source's recollection was vague and since investigation has disclosed no information which would
indicate Higman ever involved in any alleged abnormal
sexual practices, it is not believed such information
should be disseminated.*

*Action: For your information. With regard to Higman's
critical remarks concerning the FBI, the attached editorial and newspaper article which appeared in the"Rocky
Mountain News" in February, 1960, will be disseminated to CSC, if approved. These two newspaper articles
present our vigorous answer to Higman's unfounded remarks.*

From 1982 to 1989 the FBI continued to collect information .
The final two entries are letters sent to FBI Director, William Webster,
inviting him to speak at the 1982 World Affairs Conference and the
1989 World Affairs Conference invitation to Judge William Session,
FBI Director. Each declined the invitation. I imagine my file will continue to grow until my demise.

Higman is the only man I know who has turned bad temper into an art form. Higman is a rare example of a disappearing breed, the Great American Curmudgeon. These days US academics are becoming so bland you can't tell them from lawyers or PR men. People like Higman, who can stand in the middle of a room wearing a jacket that looks as if it was run up from the drapes in a Turkish seraglio and bellow about the fate of the United Nations, or the shortage of salad dressing, are what the Japanese call 'intangible cultural assets' and should be preserved at all costs.

—Simon Hoggart
London Observer Magazine
April 23, 1989

3

TWO NOTED LECTURES

RINGS AND THINGS:
Cross Cultural Communication

Rings and Things could be called, *Some Elements in Cross-Cultural Communication*. It is an heuristic. I use the word *heuristic* to refer to an idea that is put forward, not because it is correct, but because, by thinking about it, you might arrive at something that is correct. I am fond of teaching students that, if you approach a problem with an open mind, you are likely to end up with an empty head.

The particular heuristic I have in mind is a dichotomy. The word *dichotomy* refers to a division of a continuum into two mutually exclusive parts. The difficult word in that last sentence is the word *continuum*.

I guess the most obvious continuum with which we are familiar is light on the surface of the earth. Leaving clouds out of it, it is the lightest it ever gets at twelve noon, when it immediately proceeds to become darker slowly until four, five or six, depending on the sea-

---

Editor's Note:

Howard Higman delivered countless lectures during his years as a Sociology professor. We have selected these two as exemplary. They were wrought from his knowledge of sociological theory but mostly from his firsthand experience as an action sociologist during his poverty program years. Always the consummate observer, he was able to flavor an heuristic with example after example gleaned from the lives of the poor or the powerful. Although these lectures were given twenty years ago, they are largely relevant today.

son, when it continues to get darker rapidly until seven, eight or nine, when it continues to get darker slowly until midnight, when it is as dark as it ever gets. Then it starts to get lighter slowly until four, five or six in the morning, when it continues to get lighter rapidly until seven, eight or nine, when it continues to get lighter slowly until twelve noon, when it is as light as it ever gets. Thus, it is always either getting darker or lighter, and that is a continuum. The dichotomy, of course, is *day* and *night,* and the only cruel question you can ask is when *day* stops and *night* begins...and that is not polite.

My students' favorite dichotomy is sex. They have the notion of there being two sexes: males and females. Males are not females, and females are not males. As those of you who have studied biology are aware, however, even sex is a continuum. Males are also females with rudimentary mammary glands and female hormones, and females are also males with rudimentary penises and male hormones. It is, indeed, a matter of degree.

If one could find male things and female things and arrange them in a row—very male, slightly less male, and more slightly less male; more female, slightly more female, and more female, to the extreme female—as you marched along the row you would have a continuum. In inspecting this array of events you might say it started out *male.* Actually the extremes are not as healthy as you might think. Some creatures are too male for their own good, and some are too female for their own good. But, as you marched along the row, you would say, *male, male, male, probably male, maybe male,* and then, *it doesn't matter.* These last individuals have an option.

What we tend to do with regard to sex is to ask individuals to choose sides and stay with it. We do this because of architecture. It is easier to have two doors marked *Men* and *Women* than *any men, men,* and *sort of men.*

The dichotomy we are going to deal with today is the dichotomy between what I will call the *Contemporary American Middle Class* and *everybody else.* This is Aristotle's way of making a dichotomy; just take anything, and then everything else is the opposite of it.

Who are the people who are not contemporary American middle class? Some people are not contemporary American middle class because they are not contemporary; for example, my mother. My mother died at the age of ninety-four with certain views about the world which were the same views that she had when she was twenty. She had ideas about up and about down that had absolutely nothing to do with Houston, Texas, and the guidance system in space flight. There are lots and lots of persons around America like that. They are little old men and little old ladies in Chippewa Falls, Missouri, La Junta, Colorado, and in the centers of cities like Detroit and Chicago. They are not contemporary American middle class because they are not contemporary.

Then we have persons who are not contemporary American middle class for the obvious reason that they are not Americans. They are Asians, Africans, Germans, Englishmen, Europeans, Latin Americans.

And, finally, there are persons who are not contemporary American middle class for the reason that they are not middle class. This raises the difficult word—*middle class*. What does the word *middle class* mean?

I first ran into the word, *middle class* in English Literature about the British system of *working-class roughs* and the respectable, middle class, *establishment, nobility, royalty* and *queen*. Later I ran into the word *middle class* in George Bernard Shaw's plays, in such expressions as *middle class morality*.

Psychologists like Richard Centers, anthropologists like Warner and Low, and sociologists like Hollingshead at Yale ran around devising little boxes. They asked questions and then put a subject in a little box where he was *lower, lower middle, middle, upper middle, lower upper, upper,* and *upper upper* . I learned in 1936 that *upper upper* class persons use distillation dishes as ashtrays. I dashed out and bought distillation dishes, but it did not help.

The word *middle class,* however, is a new word — about twenty years new. It is largely used pejoratively by your nephews and persons who are not members of it. The word is contained in sentences such as, "Yeah, that's your middle class hang-up."

I said, *persons who are not part of it*. Who are they? They are everybody who has a name. Some of these names were pejorative: *wop, coon, dago, kike, honkey, nigger, mex* and *chicano*. Today *Chicano* is no longer pejorative. Twenty years ago it was a very biting word.

We have all kinds of abstract words in this category like *minority group, racist, nationality*. We used to have all kinds of nationalities. "What is your nationality?" "He doesn't like my nationality." That word is still used by a lot of people who have not been to college, since *nationality* is a high school word.

It is hard to realize that you are what the word is, and the word is derived largely from the contrast of not being in it. We trained Black VISTA volunteers not to react negatively on an Indian reservation when a chief says, "We want you Whites to get out of here."

It may come to you as a surprise that aristocrats are just the same as poor people, but they are. Neither one is contemporary middle class. To start with, neither is preoccupied with employment. Phrased another way, they both are the only people who own their own automobiles. The rest of us subscribe to them at $356.35 a month.

I am now going to take up the idea of privacy. Some things are more private than others. Sometimes your name is private. I remember being on a Pullman train when the conductor came along and asked, "What's your name?" I was furious. "What's it to you?" thinks I. Later that day I was on an airplane and the stewardess came along and asked, "What's your name?" I replied, "Howard Higman," I wondered about it all evening—why my name to me was private on the train and public on the airplane. But it was.

What you have been; where you are going; whether or not you are married; how much money you make; whether or not you like your wife; what you plan to do with your wife; of which child you are most afraid—these things get more and more private.

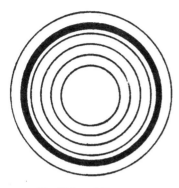 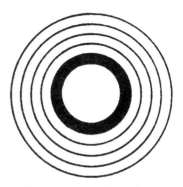

Traditional Persons   *Contemporary Americans*

The rings above represent layers of increased privacy. If we had all day and a very large blackboard, we could draw thousands of layers; the second circle being more private than the first, the third more private than the second, the fourth more private than the third, the fifth more private than the fourth and so on. The proposition is that with traditional people—the poor people, the rich people, the Europeans, the Asians, the Africans, the old people, the minority groups, the nationalities—everybody with a name—the barrier is right near the surface. You run into a barrier right away, and you are not included if you are a stranger. In the case of the contemporary American middle class, you can get very far into the person before you run into a barrier. That is the first assertion.

The second assertion is that the barrier in the case of the contemporary American middle class is impermeable. You cannot permeate it. There is no way to get in. No one has ever gotten in. My European friends ask me, "Is the reason we cannot get in there with Americans that there is nothing in there anyway?" I will not answer them. Partly because I do not know why, and, if I did know why, and it was true—that there is nothing there—I do not want to admit it.

In the case of traditional people, although you run into the barrier on the surface, it is possible to go inside of it. Some people do. What is inside is what is called by some groups *soul.* They use the word *soul* to refer to something in their personalities that they find missing in our personalities.

Now, let us take up a barbarous term—*proximities*. One of the two advantages of being a sociologist is that you can make up barbarous words for absolutely ordinary things. The other advantage is that if you are apprehended coming out of a brothel, you can announce that you are conducting a survey. *Proximities* are simply persons who are in proximity. Two people go into a hospital to wait for bulletins about friends in intensive care. All they have in common is a dirty ashtray and last year's *Time* magazine.

Traditional people sit there and exchange almost no information with each other. There are hours and hours and hours of tapes of non-talking traditional people who are in proximity. On the other hand, with contemporary American middle class persons in proximity, it is merely a matter of time before they have shared all of their experiences. We have hours and hours and hours of tapes of middle class Americans doing just that.

We have another word called *friend*. One cannot define the word *friend*, except with profanity. A friend is a person for whom you are willing to go to hell. Traditional people have friends. There are only a few friends—five, six, nine for whom a traditional person is willing to go to hell. My mother had five friends. Her best friend was Mrs. Rowe. You should not let the fact that she called her Mrs. Rowe mislead you, because my mother called my father Mr. Higman.

We in the contemporary American middle class say we have friends. Often I say, "Sure, he's a very good friend of mine." I have 2,067 very best friends. If we draw a diagram of my middle class relationships with friends, it oddly enough looks just like a bunch of lines sharing the outer core, because they run into the barrier, and there is no way to permeate the barrier. One of the conclusions that can be drawn from this picture is that members of contemporary American middle class have no friends. Now, the reason one can draw the conclusion that members of the contemporary American middle class have no friends is that members of the contemporary American middle class have no friends. But since they do not know what it is they do not have, they do not miss it particularly. They are unaware of it.

A friend is a person for whom you are willing to go to hell: Tommy Chavez is arrested for a misdemeanor which Danny Archuleta committed. Say to Tommy in the Peublo jail, "That wasn't you, Tommy. It was Danny." He says, "Shhhhh." He does not care which half of him is in jail. He will go to jail for the other guy. I would not cut a class for my sister.

So we speak of having friends, but what we do actually have is allies. You cannot function in the contemporary American middle class without alliances.

For example, you cannot get a telephone call without alliances. If the phone rings and somebody asks for Charlotte, in the middle class a non-ally says, "Charlotte? Sorry, she's not here," and hangs up. If your ally answers the phone, she will run upstairs and downstairs and look in the shower and under the bed yelling, "Charlotte! Charlotte!" And finally come back to the phone to say, "Gee, she was here just a minute ago. Can I tell her who's calling? Herb? Sure, Herb, I know she'll be back at four-thirty." When Charlotte comes home, she says, "Charlotte, Herb called." This is a tape of the conversation of allies.

If you do not like that example, I will give you a different one. You cannot hold a job without allies. If you go to work at nine o'clock and at nine-thirty you go to the coffee shop, and at ten-thirty you are still in the coffee shop and someone comes in the office looking for you, your non-ally says, "Miss Stenchfield? I haven't seen her all morning." Not your ally. Your ally says, "Miss Stenchfield? She just stepped out of the office. Do you want to see her, Sir?" And she races down to the coffee shop and says, "J. B. is looking for you."

I call Washington and ask for Dr., Harper, and the woman says, with victory in her voice, "I'm sorry, Dr. Harper just stepped out of the office." I have an image of a nation from coast to coast where everybody has just stepped out of the office. But it works, because of allies.

I remember when I went to Washington for the War Production Board. The first day I looked around and saw a very dangerous man. I certainly did not want to get mixed up with him. Then I saw another guy looking at the same guy, and I decided the other guy also thought the first guy was dangerous. So I made an alliance right away with the guy who shared my view. We went out for coffee, out for lunch, out for coffee. When I got home that night, I said to my wife, "Gee, I got a best friend." "Who's that?" I said, "His name is Red, he's from Kenosha, Wisconsin." "What's his last name?" "I don't know, but he's my best friend." That weekend he brought his wife to my house for dinner and the next weekend I took my wife to his house for dinner. We decided to rear our children together in a kibbutz and buy a ranch in Michigan jointly. Actually, we ended up jointly owning a floor waxer.

Suddenly one day Red was moved out of our office. We no longer had Charles to talk about, but we said to each other that we would never let this interfere with our friendship. "We'll have lunch together every day at the place across from Constitution Avenue." After a few lunches, we stopped. One or the other of us called and said, "I'm sorry, but I can't make it for lunch today." As a matter of fact, the last lunch we had together was very unsatisfactory. As I was talking about Charles, Red's mind wandered and suddenly he looked up and said, "You know, I think we overestimated Charles." I said, "We did not." "Oh, you ought to see the threat in my office—a woman named Priscilla Buttons." Well, I could not get excited about Priscilla Buttons whom I had never met and about whom I did not care a whit. So we did not lunch together anymore. Whenever we ran into each other we were embarrassed, and one of us would say to the other, "Gee, we ought to get together." Or the other one would say, "Why don't you give me a ring sometime."

We can examine contemporary American middle class persons' friends by examining their Christmas card lists at five year intervals.

In the days of Dwight Eisenhower when he wanted people from NATO countries to exchange students, there was a *People to People* Program. Students from Norway and Sweden came to our university and vice versa. In our town one sorority house, Delta

Gamma, offered free board and room to a Swedish girl. Near the end of the first semester she confessed to me that she was going back to Sweden. She said, "I can't make any friends in the Delta Gamma house. They don't like me." I said to her, "They do too like you." She said, "No they don't." She had a particular relationship in mind, and she was unable to effect this relationship. I said to her, "You just don't know contemporary American middle class kids. They don't have this kind of relationship." I happened to know what she did not know: that the Delta Gammas had met the night before and voted to do an unprecedented thing. They had voted not only to award her a second year room and board scholarship, which they had never done before, but they even had voted to allow her to be a Delta Gamma, wear the pin, come to the meetings on Monday nights, and play with magic. They really did like her. So I said to her, let's do an experiment. You go back to the house and get a list of girls that run around together— Abigail and Arlene, Betty and Barbara, Chris and Charlotte, Daphne and Doris, Elizabeth and Elsie,— and bring it back and show it to me." She did, and then I said, "Get a little notebook and every time you see Abigail without Arlene, interview Abigail about Arlene, and Arlene about Abigail, and interview Betty about Barbara and Barbara about Betty. Use code names in the notebook in case you drop it. Come back in three months with your findings, and I'll give you three hours credit." She did, and she came back absolutely delighted. She said, "It's fantastic! I know more about those girls than they know about each other!" She overcame her sense of loneliness when she discovered that, by her Swedish definition, the contemporary American middle class does not really like each other.

What happens when we get a collision between the two: an individual who is traditional with the barrier on the surface and an individual who is contemporary American middle class with a far deeper barrier? There was a young German boy who came over from Frankfurt on his way to school in the States. In New York he got on a greyhound bus, and onto that bus got a middle class American woman. When he got on that bus, he saw what he knew he was going to see: that he had no friend on the bus and was thus going to travel alone. She got on the bus and saw four available seats. She chose to travel with him. So we have a case of a woman who is traveling across America on a bus with a young man who is not traveling across America with her.

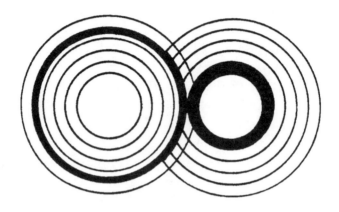

The German boy opened up his knapsack and got out a Walt Disney comic book because he was studying English. She, in turn, started to talk. She said, "My goodness! Isn't it hot on this bus." He did not pay attention to her because he did not know her; therefore, he knew that she was not speaking to him. She continued, "I wonder if they have air conditioning on this bus? With the prices they charge nowadays carrying you across the country in the summer, the least thing they could do is to have air conditioning on this bus." He looked around to see to whom it was she was speaking. He could not find anyone. He said to himself, "I believe that woman is speaking to herself." She went on, "I'm going to Chicago. Well, not actually Chicago, I'm going to Huntington. It's not in Chicago. It's near Chicago, but it doesn't matter, they're going to meet me at the bus station. My daughter—her husband—was up in Schenectady in the electrical business and they just move these people all around. So they moved them to Huntington. My daughter is going to have a baby, and I thought the least thing I could do is to go out there and be with her at this time."

Unfortunately, their eyes met, so she continued, "Are you going to Chicago?" He didn't say anything. "I said; are you going to Chicago?" He said, "No." "You're not going to Chicago? Where are

you going? Are you a businessman?" "No." "You're not a businessman?" "No." "Well, what are you? What do you do?" "Student." "You're
a student. Where are you from?" "Marlborough." "Marlborough? I
don't recall a Marlborough in New England. Where's Marlborough?"
"Germany." "Oh, you're a foreign student!"

We will stop there. We interviewed both of them. She claimed
that he had very serious character defects. He reported that he did
believe that she was employed by the Federal Bureau of Investigation.
We did not hear her yelling. He did. He said, "That woman screamed
at me." We did not hear any screaming at all, but from his point of
view, she was yelling.

This tells us something, and you will discover it. People who
are engaged as we are in the hampering services and hindering professions tend to be described as *yelling*. Social workers are referred to
as *yelling*. "Everyone yelled at me!" A bill collector who calls on an
overdue person to try to get some money will be described as having
yelled at the person. This has a lot of message in it. And the message is
that there is something peculiar about us in the American middle
class that is different from other people; we are covered with scar
tissue, and we do not know it. We have been assaulted so violently
and so constantly as members of the contemporary American middle
class that we are pretty well insulated. Traditional people are not insulated.

I remember an incident when a Dr. Klendermann of
Johannesburg came to the States to study some of the effective new
techniques in TB therapy. She stopped at the Waldorf Astoria Hotel
enroute to the West Coast. That evening she put on a kimono and sat
around resting and listening to the radio before she went to sleep for
the night. Suddenly, there was an appeal. She got up, dressed quickly,
picked up her doctor's bag, went to the elevator, rushed downstairs
and said, "I've come to volunteer." "About what?" She said, "I heard
the radio message, 'Go immediately to your physician and check for
six signs of cancer.' Of course the lobby floor of the Waldorf was exactly as she had left it when she had checked in. Later, she said to me,
"If that broadcast had come through in Johannesburg, everyone would

have been on the streets in five minutes!"

If you want to test this for yourself, listen—if you really can—and I'm not sure that any of us can—to a commercial and literally hear it.

Back in 1948, after the Czech revolution, a young refugee came to Boulder. Being an alien, he could not get a real job, so he worked his way through school in my house. One Sunday we were painting a bedroom, and he kept bursting out laughing. I said, "Otomar, what are you laughing at?" He said, "Did you hear what the man on the radio said!" He had been hearing the commercials, which I could not begin to hear.

In reality, we cannot take a population census because if we go into the ghetto or barrio or anywhere traditional people are living, we find the questions on the census form are very, very aggressive and abrasive. They ask all kinds of secret information, about income, what you do with your money, a name of the father of each of the children. This is not likely to be gotten from these persons.

Once we had an aristocrat for Secretary of State, Dean Acheson. There was a young man who found himself attacked as a traitor to this country. When Dean Acheson was asked to testify against Alger Hiss, he said, "I can't testify against Alger Hiss. He is my friend." Now that was a total violation of the contemporary American middle class ethic. "How does that man dare to defend a traitor!" Instantly there was pressure from coast to coast on Truman to fire Acheson. A Frenchman would never have been bothered by this criticism. If a French high official walked down the Champs Elysees arm in arm with dirty Pierre, and someone saw him and said something, a Frenchmen would say, "Oh, yes, didn't you know that he is his friend?" "Oh."

Sometime at the end of World War II there was an interesting book written by Graham Greene, an Englishman, called *The Third Man.* I'm sure some of you have read it. In it, an American named Holly discovers that his friend, Harry Lime, was engaged in crimes in Vienna at the expense of children's lives. Holly uses his friendship to trap Harry Lime in the sewers of Vienna and have him shot dead by the British police. For the United States contemporary American middle class, Harry Lime was a villain and Holly was a hero. In Europe, on the other hand, Holly was not a hero at all. He was a villain. He turned in his friend. And that attitude arises because they have such things as friends.

It would be logical for me to suppose that persons who have spent a significant amount of time in our Peace Corps abroad would have found themselves unconsciously acquiring this sort of *traditional* personality and, thereby, finding it very difficult upon returning to the States to feel clean and good and wholesome and honest with the kind of role which is required for membership in the contemporary American middle class. We should seriously test this.

Normally, we have two words for almost everything: one that compliments the thing and one that puts the thing down. You can say about a young man that works for you that he has initiative, is energetic and is a self-starter, or you can say that he is irascible and has problems with authority. In a like fashion, you can say that traditional persons have integrity and that members of the middle class do not. In fact, minority group persons do say about us that we do not have integrity. And it is a good idea for us to recognize this. It is true.

There is a kind of unconscious presumption that integrity is good. It isn't necessarily. Integrity merely means integrated oneness. It is true that traditional people are integrated and do have oneness. It may be good or it may be bad. The person that I have most despised in my life had the most integrity of any politician with whom I am familiar: Adolph Hitler. He was horrible, but no politician more nearly wrote exactly what he was going to do than Hitler did. Nothing more logically hung together than Hitler's Nazi movement. One of my heroes had no integrity: Franklin Roosevelt who ran on a ticket in 1932 promising to abolish the federal payroll.

Another word for integrity is rigidity, or, to sound less pejorative, we can say some persons are rigid and some are flexible. I am thinking about a woman named Martha who went to a meeting of the missionary society of the Methodist Church. They were studying Biafra. The Methodist Church in this town is against alcohol. There was a motion before the town council to legalize the sale of liquor, and the church had a petition out against it which Martha signed. She then left the meeting, got in her station wagon, went to Stoiber's Liquor Store, and bought scotch, gin, vermouth and bourbon to take to the Kappa Kappa Gamma alumni committee meeting. She then went to a Democratic caucus where she stuffed envelopes for a candidate for Congress and told anti-Republican jokes. She then went home, packed her suitcase and went with her husband, a vice-president of a bank, to a banker's convention at the Broadmoor Hotel in Colorado Springs where everybody was a Republican, and she sat around laughing at anti-Democratic jokes. Some persons would say that Martha has no integrity. I would not. I would say Martha is flexible. If she took her gin to the Methodist Church or her anti-Republican jokes to the banker's convention, or her alcohol petition to the Kappa house, then I would say, "What's gotten into Martha!" That would be inappropriate behavior.

People in the middle class do not have shared values. Let me illustrate. A few women go to the PTA meeting at Baseline Junior High on Thursday night where an item on the agenda is to buy blue velvet drapes for the end of the gymnasium before the junior class play an May 18th. One woman's husband paints houses; one woman's husband is a ne'er-do-well public relations man who has never had a contract and lives on money supplied to his wife by her father; one woman's husband is a totally successful left-wing lawyer who has made a killing on civil rights cases; another woman's husband is an internist in medicine and treasurer of the John Birch Society. They do not have shared values. But you know what they do at the meeting? One husband asks, "What did you do?" "We bought blue velvet drapes for the end of the gymnasium before the junior class play on May 18th." "Were you for it?" She says, "Not particularly." He says, "Well did you vote for it?" "Oh, yes." "How come?" "Oh, it was unanimous."

On the other hand, there is a meeting of Chicano groups in the city of Denver. One leader is talking, and he is not more than half-way into the strategy when it becomes perfectly clear that an-other leader is not going to buy that line. He is interrupted by a second leader who states that the entire content of the speaker's body is feces. He then starts to outline an alternative, at which point the third leader gets up and says, "You're both full of (that material)!" And they all stomp out of the meeting. What is read in the paper is that the meeting broke up "in disagreement."

What we learn from that sort of painful experience is that traditional people cannot cooperate with strangers and they cannot cooperate because they have integrity. Cooperation involves corruption. To cooperate you have to vote for people you do not like, and smile at people at whom you want to frown and agree with people with whom you disagree. By and large, traditional people are characterized by conflict and cooperation; by love of friends and hatred of enemies: the kind of dichotomy wherein *you are with me* or *you are against me*. Middle class types do not give total commitment to anyone or total hostility to anyone, either.

In our society we engage in a phenomenon called *competition,* and, by and large, traditional people do not. Traditional boys do not play basketball because it does not end in death or total victory. In a Spanish barrio, for example, the taller, bigger boys will always pick teams so that the littler boys are on one team and lose the game. If, by any fluke, the littler boys might start to win, they would change the rules of the game, because the idea of competition is illogical to a person with integrity.

Towards the end of the 1968 primary campaign, Nelson Rockefeller went around making violent attacks on the personality of Richard Nixon. Some of you remember it. The minute, however, Nixon was nominated, Rockefeller was shown hugging and kissing Nixon and joining the campaign train to elect him. My minority friends were absolutely astounded. They said, "How could Rockefeller say on Monday that this person is a heel and on Wednesday that he is a hero?" Well, the fact is that something happened in the meantime; Nixon had been nominated.

I can give you some illustrative phenotypic vignettes. One is a black seventeen year old girl in Denver who was a prostitute. She had a baby, was not married and was not going to get married. She wanted a new kind of work. We got her a job in a dirty hotel. She was in the kitchen one afternoon and someone knocked over a gallon jug of mustard which formed a big pool on the floor. The girl was standing near the pool not doing anything. Her supervisor walked in. He looked at the pool of mustard on the floor, looked at her, and said, "Martha, clean up the mustard."

Two different things happened in that room that day. His version was, "Here we were. We work eight hours a day for four hours of pay. We leave at five o'clock to go do our thing with the little money we make in this hellhole. We go around leaving microbes on spoons and glasses, but we certainly can't leave a skating rink of mustard in the middle of the linoleum floor and get away with it. She ought to know that. You would have thought she would have cleaned it up automatically. Well, she didn't. I'm her supervisor. It's my job to tell her to clean it up. So I did. To hell with it."

Her version is, "There I was standing there; I hadn't done nothing to nobody. In comes this bastard, and he is race prejudiced. He didn't ask me whether or not I had spilled the mustard. And I say, he who spills the mustard, cleans up the mustard. I'm not taking that kind of crap off anybody. And I wrote a manifesto, *He who spills the mustard cleans up the mustard.*" She quit that job.

There was a kid who came to a remedial reading class with a new automobile. His counselor, Mr. Reese, said to him, "Tommy, I see you got a new car." "Oh, yeah, Mr. Reese, didn't I tell you?" "Tell me what?" "I got two checks for this program. They got me down twice. I registered as Chico and my mother registered me as Raymond, so I get fifty bucks a week now," That's a felony, and he told this to his counselor who does not have an M.D.'s immunity. If he doesn't report Chico, he's guilty of a felony too. If he does report him, Chico is lost to him for sure.

Take a case wherein there's a victim. Someone dropped a check on the floor. It was thought that Danny picked it up and forged his signature to the check. The head of the program called him in and said, "Danny, we caught you. You forged your signature on this check," Danny turned to the head of the program and said, "You may take your program and with it do something anatomical." And he left. Everyone went around bemoaning the sad fate of Danny. Mr. Hicks said to Tommy, "It's too bad about Danny." Tommy looked at Mr. Hicks and said, "No, it's not too bad about Danny. Nothin's bad enough for that bastard." "Oh, come on, you don't want to feel that way about him. We're all in the same boat." "No Sir, Mr. Hicks. You don't know what he done to his sister." Then he grinned, looked up at Mr. Hicks, and said, "You know something. Danny didn't forge that signature. I did."

There are two things to learn from that. A middle class kid would not, for one minute, have confessed to his counselor to having committed two crimes. Tommy had committed the crime of forging, and he had committed the crime of having another boy punished for it. But in terms of his value system, it was a good deal. It had settled some kind of vendetta. What is more, Mr. Hicks was his friend, so why should he let a little thing like a crime interfere with their relationship? A middle class boy would know that if he confessed to committing a crime, he would lose a friend. That's because he did not have the friend to begin with. He had an ally. So the fact that Tommy confessed attests to his traditional group membership.

We also learn something from Danny. It was claimed that Danny confessed by leaving. He did not confess at all. He left because he was brokenhearted. He was brokenhearted because the program had accused him of the crime, and traditional people do not accuse their friends.

We parents in the middle class may not be aware of it, but we rear our children by accusation. From the minute they're born, we start right off saying, "You broke the cookie jar, didn't you?" Then we watch their reaction to see if we came anywhere near the truth. It is a form of investigation. By the time they are six, they have been taught to defend themselves when they are guilty and they have been taught to defend themselves when they are innocent. They have, in fact, been taught to defend themselves totally.

Here is another case in point. Into a potato cellar full of anglo workers came the boss, screaming little telegrams of hate at everybody: "Jeb, get that rake off the floor." "Harry, you left the barn doors open again. If I've told you once I've told you twice, don't leave the barn doors open!" Nobody seemed to give a damn. In a few minutes the boss would be gone and everything would revert to the nice, happy rhythm that was there before he came into the room. He did leave. I left with him, got into his car and we sped away.

Suddenly, he slowed down the car and, looking sort of sheepish, said to me, "I've got to stop here a minute and talk to one of my men." He came to a slow stop in front of this house, out of which came a Spanish-American irrigator. He walked over to the car and said, "Hi, Mr. Brown. How are you?" "Pretty good, Fred. How's your wife?" "Oh she's all right. Say we sure want to thank your Mrs. for sending over that hot water bottle. Don't know what happened to ours. Your wife's okay, eh? Good. How are the kids?" "They're all right. Sammy's got the croup." At this point Fred kicked the earth and a pile of dust came up. "Beats me. Rained day and night around here for two solid weeks. Thought it was going to wash this ranch into the Rio Grande River. Look at it now, you'd think it had never rained at all. Guess it's about time, maybe, we start irrigating." Mr. Brown said, "Yeah, Fred, I think so." "Well, when do you want me to start, Mr. Brown?" "Oh, whenever you're ready." "Well, I ain't doing anything now so I'll start this afternoon." "Fine." "Where do you want me to start?" "Where are the pumps?" "They're over on the west side." "Why don't you start there?" "Okay."

Now this grower may not know the theory, but he certainly knew the practice. If he had talked to Fred Archuleta the way he talked to those Anglo men in the potato cellar, Fred would have packed his things and gone to Colorado Springs.

On the other hand, several years ago we had a group of medical students from Rochester, Chicago and Berkeley who formed a

Student Health Organization in which they volunteered to work in barrios and migrant labor camps during the summers. A group of them were over on the Western Slope in Colorado when I arrived there. I was met at the airport by a Spanish American and I asked him how the medical students were doing. He said, "Well, they're fine, but they sure are mad." I said, "What do you mean—crazy?" "No, no, angry." "Angry? That can't be. They're volunteers devoted to their work." He said, "Well, you'll see when you get there." We arrived at the scene, and here they were with organized lines of children marching along, in an assembly line, with parts of their bodies bared to be inoculated. One student dabbed on alcohol, the next student inserted the needle, the next held the cotton. It was efficient, and it did get the job done, but there were no expressions of friendship or kindness. Just, *Let's-get-this-job-done* kind of attitude. The Spanish Americans saw this as *anger*.

In a summary phrase, the language of traditional people tends to be affective, whereas that of the middle class tends to be instrumental. Traditional people talk about how they feel—*feel good, feel bad, feel better than worse, what's good,* and *what's not good.* We talk about *who, when, where* and *how to, what will and will not work.* There is very little content of how we feel about it in the process. It is what we call *instrumental speech.*

Another illustration is the case of a French professor from the Sorbonne. In 1951 he came out to Colorado for a visit and we went up into the mountains to Central City to hear a performance of the opera's *Tosca.* When it was over, we all came out of the opera house with our guest absolutely ecstatic about the performance. He was glowing. We went around the corner to a place called *The Glory Hole* where some poor amateuristic students were doing a bad version of the *Can Can.* The place was full of smoke and the smell of scotch. We went in laughing, and the Frenchman disappeared. After he was gone longer than we thought he should have been, had he gone where we thought he had, I went to find him. I found him outside cooling his heels with his arms behind his back, puffing air out of his mouth, I said, "What's the matter, Stanley?" He said, "How could you!"

You see, he just could not turn off *Tosca* and turn on the *Can Can* like a faucet. I could. He could not. The glow of that high-level aesthetic performance was not something that could go away or be transformed in one second to a barroom brawl.

We had another empirical case of the same phenomenon on the Indian reservation in Uintah, Utah. The VISTA trainees had been trained carefully not to show any disrespect for religious services of the Indians, which ended, they were told, at sundown. When the sun went down, the volunteers immediately took off their religious manners and began whooping it up. The Indians regarded this as an insult. They said it showed a lack of respect. The volunteers defended themselves by saying, "Yes, but the sun went down!"

The question becomes, "can one go back and forth between cultures?" I would say that, by and large, in the United States, you can go from traditional to the middle class, but that you cannot do the reverse.

The attempt to go in reverse may account to some degree for the hippie movement. People went around doing opposite things. They turned cleanliness into dirty long hair; they cut little holes in their bluejeans and sewed bandanas over the holes. Incidentally, we did some research to see what happened to them and you may be interested to know that nearly all of them cut their hair, shaved, washed, married the woman with whom they were living, moved into high-rise apartment houses and have jobs with the Metropolitan Life Insurance Company. Meanwhile, they left their dirty clothes on the streets and teeny boppers came along and put them on. They are currently out fooling policemen.

One can suspect that the attempt to experiment with drugs and chemistry may have been an attempt to permeate this barrier. The evidence is that drugs do not really get you with anybody; they just make you less aware of the fact that you are not.

Choice is revealing. You never know about anyone until he has to make a choice. It reveals one's values. If I'm on a mountain with my daughter on one cliff and my wife on another and suddenly they both shout for help, and I go over to get my wife, my daughter dashes to her death; if I go over to get my daughter, my wife dashes to her death.

There are obviously only three things I can do. I can save my daughter with the rationalization that she still has her life ahead of her, or I can save my wife with the rationalization that children are easily come by, or I can let them both go through indecision. It is always painful to choose. So we try to avoid choosing if at all possible. Therefore, because we see very few choices actually made, we know almost nothing about anybody.

For instance, a young Spanish-American from La Jara in his high school career was brought to the attention of the track coach. The coach recruited him for the professional athletic system which we run in our undergraduate colleges, and the next thing he knew he was playing football at Nebraska. Whether or not you know it, it is illegal to play football at Nebraska for four years and not receive a degree. So he did, much to his surprise. This forced him to be eligible for recruitment into an Educational Opportunity Program for law school. Whereupon he graduated with a law degree. At that time, about eight years ago, a Chicano lawyer was of great benefit to a political party and the Nebraska Republican Party picked him up. One day he was to appear live on television with the governor. By coincidence, this live performance was to occur at the same time that his cousin Isabella's wedding was scheduled. There was an extended family of one hundred and eighty-three people in that community. Under normal circumstances, he would have died before missing Isabella's wedding. But he chose to appear on TV with the governor. He said, "I am doing this for my people." Then he rented a Piper Cub and flew back to Colorado for the party. He missed the ceremony, and consequently the eyes and faces of his cousins and uncles and aunts were taut. And at the celebration that night there was hostility.

The ex-traditional person does not understand this behavior. When he does not understand, he returns the insult with what I call *punitiveness*. I can demonstrate this to you by citing that there are many ex-Black policemen who are more brutal with their own people than Whites are, or ex-Chicano school teachers in Denver's West High School who are rougher on their own people than Anglos are. Sometimes persons do understand and are able to maintain relationships and a balance between the barrio and the middle class, but it is very, very hard to do.

Let me say now that what I have been presenting to you is not reality. It was not billed as reality. It is called *an ideal type*. It is a model from which all reality varies. This is even true in the physical sciences. Physics is not *the physical world*. A description of uranium fission in a book is not what goes on in uranium fission. It is what goes on in the book. In the book it says that uranium fissions split into approximately two halves, emitting three free neutrons. In reality, an actual atom of uranium may not fission at all when hit by a neutron. It may fission into seventeen parts. It may emit one, three, five, eight, thirty-eight free neutrons.

In large numbers we have what is called *a cross-section*. The first time I ran into a 2.7 reality was when I learned that the people in Massachusetts in 1928   had .7 of a child. The name for this is *statistics*. What I am saying here is that this talk is not a description of reality, but a model. This is true of even maleness and femaleness. Although as humans we are very profoundly forced into these roles, we are not as different in reality as are the roles themselves.

I also say this: that we might even construct situations in which we find people who work in the traditional world and play in the middle class world. Other people might play in the traditional world and work in the middle class world. Their work and play roles therefore are in conflict, and they get embarrassed if they are caught in the wrong place. They might even discover that they have what Freud would call *regressions*.

For example, I know a professor at Dartmouth who is absolutely the most traditional man I know, but he made a conscious decision after getting out of Nazi concentration camps to learn absolutely the middle class role. It is as false for him as the part of Rex Harrison in *My Fair Lady*. One can tell it is just a role he plays twenty-four hours a day. He has become very good at it, so he goes about being contemporary American middle class. But just scratch his skin slightly, and there is a traditional guy seething inside this superficial skin.

Much of what I have said is fairly easily substantiated by recorded, analyzed behavior. Two questions we can ask ourselves are: "So what difference does it make?" and, "How did we get this way?" For volunteers who actually meet real persons out there in the life, it is far more important for them to understand this than it is for you and me. We tend to be dealing with middle class persons; they tend to deal with traditional persons.

I have come to the conclusion that the most effective group of American persons working with people in the United States today are public health visiting nurses. This is an hypothesis subject to being tested. The reason I have this idea is that I have presented the Rings and Things working scheme to social workers who come back a year later and say, "Oh, yes. That was a very interesting description." I have presented the same scheme to visiting nurses who come back a year later and say, "You've no idea how that changed my world. It's just overwhelming." I therefore have the feeling that visiting nurses actually go into real houses where there are real people in a chair or a bed or a room. I have the sense that social workers call on the telephone or operate out of their automobiles, filling out squares on pieces of paper. They appear not to have the faintest idea of who these people really are. This is worth checking out, for it is no mere coincidence that, over and over again, visiting nurses show an enormous educability compared to other groups.

Now I am going to give you two derivative ideas. One is the necessity of dealing with traditional people who live in the world of certainty while we in the middle class live in the world of probability. Our grandparents lived in the world of certainty. Our language remains the language of certainty, although we have learned that even though the word structure is certain, it does not mean it. It means probability. We talk probability talk with certainty language. We are always absolutely misunderstood, and are, therefore, held in low regard. The reason that our language is the language of probability is that we have become interdependent. We are no longer our own bosses. Therefore, we cannot speak with certainty, yet we continue to use those words. My grandmother in Racine, Wisconsin, thought that she was her own boss. It doesn't matter that she really was not. She thought she was. She thought that there was only one person in the whole world who could interfere with her. Only one. When her friend said to her, "Clara, you will come over Sunday afternoon, won't you?" She said, "Yes, Emma, I'll be there, God willing." God could stop her, but nobody else.

With me, that is not so. I make an appointment with Bob Hunter for ten o'clock in his office. At a quarter to ten the phone rings. The secretary in the office of the President of the University of Colorado calls my secretary and says, "Betty, President Thieme wonders if Professor Higman could come to his office at ten o'clock." I wonder if he is wondering.

We say we keep appointments and that they, traditional people, do not. That is false. They do not make appointments. If they do not make them, they do not keep them. Why would you make an appointment if you are not doing anything? If you are unemployed or not in school? Would you say, "Oh, here it is Tuesday at eight o'clock. I'm not in History. It's nine o'clock. I'm not in English. It's ten o'clock. I'm not in French. It's eleven o'clock. I'm not in Sociology. It's twelve o'clock. I'm not in the lunchroom. It's one o'clock. I'm not in the gym....Here it is Wednesday, and I'm not in."

If you do not have a steady job and have not worked for years, you would not make appointments either. You would not say, "It's Tuesday morning, and I'm not going to work at nine o'clock."

I asked a Chicano boy if he wanted to mow my lawn. He said, "You want your lawn mowed?" "Yes." "Okay, I'll mow your lawn." I said, "Monday at eight." He said, "I'll mow your lawn." I said, "Monday at eight?" He said, "Sure, I'll mow your lawn." Monday he did not show. Tuesday he did not show. Wednesday morning I got someone else to mow the lawn. Wednesday afternoon he came to mow the lawn. I said, "I said Monday morning!" He said, "I'll mow your lawn." He didn't hear "Monday at eight o'clock."

We say we keep appointments but we do not. I am giving all of my friends this Christmas little red *disappointment books*. We are not judged by appointments we keep, but by the graciousness with which we renegotiate them, because our time is constantly pre-empt-ied by others. We are not free to make appointments, really.

I am now going to give you two illustrations of what I call *shared planning*. First, I once went to Kansas City with a Black friend of mine. I had to see two persons in the Labor Department on two projects, in one of which my Black friend was involved. We finished the meeting on the one project with which he was involved, and then he sat out in the lobby while I negotiated with the fellow in the office. When my negotiations were done, the Kansas City man opened his door to see me out while we continued remarking about what had gone on. He said to me, "Goddamn it, Higman. That is a good idea. We'll fund it." My Black friend and I walked out and I made a phone call to Boulder to Bob. I said, "Hey, Bob, I just talked with Neil, and I think he looks with favor on this project." And I hung up. My black friend turned to me very upset and said, "Why did you lie to Bob?" "I didn't lie to Bob." "Yes, you did." "I did not. I told him that Neil looked with favor on it." He said, "That's not what he said." I said, "Yes, he did. Look, you weren't at the meeting. I got the feeling that he's really going to go along with it." "But that's not what he said." "Well, what did he say?" "He said, 'We will fund it.'"

At that moment I realized that I was going to have to do a most terrible thing. I looked at him and said, "Frank, the words 'we will fund it' do not mean 'we will fund it.'" He looked at me and said, "You mean to tell me the words 'we will fund it' do not mean 'we will fund it?'" "Yes, the words 'we will fund it' do not mean 'we will fund it.'" "What do they mean?" I said, "You're not going to understand this, Frank, but I'm going to tell you anyway. Neil said all he could say because he couldn't say anymore. All he could say was, 'Look, Higman, if after you leave, I look at this thing again, and I decide you did not con me, I'll show it to my friends; and if they don't think I'm an abject ass, I'll show it to my boss; and if he doesn't notice it and gets on the list and goes into Washington, and if it gets a priority, and by the time it's to be funded, the funds haven't been impounded; there is an x amount of chance that there might be such a project.' That is all the words 'we will fund it' could mean."

If you listen to yourself and other middle class persons, you will notice that we know these things, so we do not get trapped by our words. But they do.

Here is a second example. I went to Sterling, Colorado, on Migrant Council business once. We were at Mrs. Archeluta's house and her young son came dashing in. I asked where he was in school. She said, "He's just graduating from Sterling High School." I asked, "What's he going to do in the fall?" "He's going to barber school in Denver. His uncle is in Denver and got him into the barber school." I asked if I could see his high school records, which turned out to be very fine records. I said, "He should not go to barber school. He ought to go to the University." "Oh, no, he can't get into the University." I said, "Sure, he can. There's a whole new program called EOP recruiting Chicano students. In fact, if he does well enough, there's a special program recruiting for medical school." She said, "We don't have the money." I said, "I know, but there are scholarships for kids now and tutoring help for remedial English for lack of access to reading materials in the past." I said, "He can go to the University, be admitted and get a scholarship. You won't have to pay anything."

Next day I was in a coffee shop in town and someone said, "Did you hear about the Archuleta kid? He's been admitted to the University of Colorado with a scholarship." I said, "That's fantastic! What a coincidence! Would you mind going to their house and finding out if it's really true?" She said, "Not at all." In about thirty minutes she came back and said, "Yes it is. Mrs. Archuleta said that there had been a professor there yesterday, Howard Higman, from the University of Colorado, who had admitted their son to the University and had given him a scholarship." Mrs. Archuleta was not lying. I am a professor at the University of Colorado and I was in her house and I did say, "He could be admitted to the University of Colorado. He can have a scholarship." What happened is that she didn't hear me right. What I thought I had said was, "Look, there's a certain statistical chance and possibility that, if you go through the following procedures, make the right phone calls and write the right letters, that in the competition, it might work out."

One last point on this subject is that we train our middle class kids to be failures. We start right off teaching our kids to fail immediately. We have two wonderful middle class phrases: "There's no harm in trying," and "it doesn't cost anything to apply." Consequently, my children have applied for so many things it is unbelievable. The minute they apply, they forget it, because they know they are not going to get it. A middle class child applies for admission to Harvard, Michigan and Berkeley law schools. "What did you get in the mail today?" "Oh, I got turned down by Harvard." "Oh." It is not bad for a minute because he did not expect to get in. It is not a personal insult to apply and not get in. A person is a fool to apply to only one university. You apply to a minimum of three or four. "There's no harm in trying" and "It doesn't cost anything to apply."

With traditional people that is not true. There is a great deal of harm in trying, and it costs a lot to apply. What it costs is another insult, another slap in the face. And they do not have the scar tissue to avoid taking it personally. What I am saying is that it is almost impossible not to insult a traditional person.

People who have names are traditional; people who do not have names are not. If you ask a person on the staff of ACTION, who perceives of himself as middle class, what he is, he says, *American*. If you said to my mother, "What are you?" She would say, "A Presbyterian."

One person I know said to me, "You know, I've been getting something for years in the mail and I always throw it in the waste basket, but I'm beginning to think maybe I ought to join. What do you think?" The thing he had in mind was called *German Americans*. It had been a long time since he had thought of himself as German. He did not have a name; he was anonymous.

It was very difficult for Americans in 1973 to deal with what I am going to deal with right now. A computer cannot deal with it, it is non-unilinear. It is not a division into two mutually symmetrical opposites. There are words like *nationality, race, religion, creed, color, ethnic, minority.* There are questions like, "Who am I?" "Who are they?" Reality in the human world is verbal. It is words. The only real answer to the question, "What is a Jew?" is "A Jew is a Jew." *Jew* is a word. What is a dog? A dog is a word. A dog doesn't have weight, it doesn't have color, it doesn't have height. It doesn't have any of the physical characteristics of a thing, because it is not a thing. But things are things. They are black or brown or big or little. But a dog is a dog is a dog is a dog. Even though no dog is dog.

If I asked all of you to draw a picture of the front of a house right now, you would not draw the same thing. Does a house have two storeys, one storey, four storeys; does it have a door in the middle, on the right or on the left; four windows in the front or two windows in the front; is it birch, wood, adobe, or canvas? None of the characteristics of a thing are present in the word, *house.* But the word *house* is nevertheless very useful in causing people to relate to misunderstanding together comfortably. So these things are actually words. *Honky* is a word. *Kike* is a word. *Wop* is a word. *Bitch* is a word. *Englishman* is a word. *German* is a word. *German-American* is a word. And *Italian* is a word. You can ask questions like, "How are these words used?" The accurate answer is, *variously.* Different people use them differently.

In order to communicate with persons, it is terribly necessary to realize that the persons with whom you communicate probably do not use words the way you do. They therefore probably do not hear you, and what is more, you probably do not hear them.

Furthermore, words are not *either-ors.* There are all kinds of *races.* A long time ago scholars had lots of races; they were thought to describe species of animals, such as the difference between zebras and donkeys or horses and mules, The idea of *race* is controversial now. A conservative position would be that there are three or four races like Caucasian, Black, Yellow. The more liberal position is that there is only one human race, that the groupings which have been called different races are created by selective mating such as that which produces purebred dogs or horses. The thoroughbred is weaker than the mongrel—a result of somatic differences which have occurred as deselection of parts of the germ bank through isolation and breeding.

The opposite view of this, of course, would be that there are different *stems* of people. Some people use *race* to cover any of the differences in groups that they can identify.

I grew up in the world in which there were no *Jews*. They were not there. The reason that they were not there is that my mother and father did not have a word for them. Therefore, they were not there. We had something horrible called, *Catholics*. We had words for them. "I seen you playing with Roland and Steve. Don't you know they're Catholics!" That was real. The words are the things that are out there.

There was a Spanish-American foreman in a meat packing company in Colorado. They cannot do this—have a Mexican-American in the buying field. The ethos and philosophy of everybody in that part of the country is *redneck*. They are cowboys and they are violently anti-union and violently anti-Spanish-American and violently anti-Catholic. A cowboy cannot go around successfully having a Spanish-American foreman. It does not work. I asked the foreman, "Why do you have so much trouble?" He said, "Well I hate to tell you, but I'd like out. They hold my nationality against me." He used the word *nationality*. He is a traditional person.

Normally, in the United States, religion refers to Jew versus Christian. At the time of John Kennedy's election, *Catholic* was an entity. This may be a surprise to you, but there were more column inches on the subject that John Kennedy was a Catholic than on any other issue in the presidential election that year. Eight years later it was not even referred to.

People are what they say they are. You cannot say to someone, "But you are really a Jew." "You are really a Black." I accurately described my staff at one time by saying, "I have a colored woman, a Negro, and three Blacks on my staff."

At a dinner party in Indianapolis one night, a deputy director of the Peace Corps, later the Ambassador to Ghana for the United Nations turned to the cook and said, "We Blacks...." She blew up. "Don't you call me Black. I'm a colored lady!" She was. She was not a Black.

You cannot say to someone, "You are a Chicano." He can say, "I am a Chicano," but you cannot say it. I would never go to East Los Angeles and say, "You Chicanos" or "You Mexican-Americans" or "You Spanish-Americans" or "You Hispanos." No matter which word I used, it would be wrong. And I would tell them just this, so that I would not be misunderstood.

In the university world, *ethnic* has come to be a *safe* word. If you want to work in a big administration like this, you have to have a big vocabulary. You have to know lots of peoples' languages. Do not fight over the way people use words, understand how they use words. In the university setting, *ethnic* derives from 1906 when we discovered that the interesting things about people are learned. It comes from *ethos* or *idea*. You cannot be *ethnic* in the womb; you turn *ethnic* at birth. When people asked me, "What is a Jew?" I used to say, "A Jew is defined by the religion in which he does not believe." It has to be learned.

A basketball player came to see me one day and asked if I would talk to his parents because they were interfering with his marriage. They did not like mixed marriages between Catholics and Jews. I asked him where he met his Jewish girlfriend. He said, "You got it backwards, Professor. She's the Catholic. I'm the Jew." I said, "You're wrong, Mr. Baskin, you are a Catholic." He said, "I'm not. I'm a Jew." I said, "That's nonsense." "Where'd you grow up?" "Chicago." "Where'd you get the idea that you're a Jew?" "Once a year, my father told me I was." I said, "Where were you born?" "Wisconsin. My father was a doctor of medicine and we moved to Chicago for his practice." I said, "Who were his clients?" "Catholics." "Where did you live?" "In the Catholic community." "Did you go to the Synagogue?" "I've been twice." "You didn't go to religious services?" "Sure. I went to Mass." "How come?" "I was on the Catholic basketball team."

Here is a young man who acquired a Catholic ethos. He is *ethnically* Catholic. He grew up in a Catholic neighborhood. He played with Catholics. He beat other Catholics on the basketball teams. He related to the priest. Once a year his father would say to him, "Oh, David, don't forget you're a Jew." "Sure, Dad." He fell for a Catholic girl and they were married. He had a noninterdenominational marriage. They were both Catholics! I explained to his father that he could not have his lad go around being a Jew when he had not bothered to *Jewify* him.

In the main, the uncles and fathers are traditional and the sons are contemporary American middle class. This is the conflict we see in Jewish homes in America today.

Ethnic, generically, is the idea of an individual who has learned the meaning of the words, *we* versus *they*. And the *we-ness* versus the *they-ness* is determined by the *they* more than the *we*.

I did not know I was an *American* until I went to Europe. I did not feel slightly American. I did not feel patriotic, chauvinistic, nationalistic or anything else American. I was in a beer stube in Salzburg with a bright young Netherlander sociologist from Lieden University by the name of Jan Glastra Van Loon. We were alike professionally— above it all, *worlders*. Lo and behold, a G. I. from Colorado came into the bar. His hair was short, and he sat there getting drunk on cognac. A young lad from Helsinki who was the president of the *Hooray for the USA* club in Finland was gathering American slang in a book. He had gathered wonderful words like *Oh, you kid!* and *Cake Eater*. This boy from Colorado used language about as colorful as you can hear, provided you stay in the latrine, and the lad from Helsinki was gleefully copying it all down in his notebook. Of course, the drunken G. I. got mad at the Helsinki boy because he thought he was making fun of him. So he took a bottle, knocked the bottom out of it, and started to swing at the Helsinki boy. Some of us thought this should not happen, so we interfered. My friend, Jan Glastra Van Loon said, "I'll get the MP's." I said, "No. He did not understand what was happening. He thought he was being insulted." Jan Glastra Van Loon said, "You can't let him get away with a thing like that. Why, he threatened that boy's life with that bottle!" I said, "But you didn't understand. He thought he was being made fun of." I took the G. I. into the latrine and asked him where he was from. He said, "*Canon City*." That's a penitentiary. We went back to the bar and what happened was that I had a fight with my friend from Holland. I discovered I was an *American*. I identified with that abject ass, not the cultivated, intelligent, juridically correct Dutchman! That is when I began to understand *nationality*, which is the possession of a person's mind by a myth.

You, therefore, cannot be rigid. You have to allow Mexican-Americans to be perceived of as White in Texas, just as you have to allow Negroes to be perceived of as White on an Indian reservation where the dominant *we* is red and the real dichotomy is *Red* and *not Red*, whereas in Texas it is *Black* and *not Black*. The human animal is somewhat like a computer in that it has a preference for binary systems like *Christian-Jew, Protestant-Catholic* and *Black-White*. It is a vast array of complexity. Nearly everybody can go off in some corner and settle down in his own playpen with a teeny-weeny vocabulary and get away with it. You cannot, because in every direction you look, you are perceiving people who do not have an agreed-to vocabulary and an agreed-to definition of what is and how it is that is.

The prestige hierarchy in America used to be a matter of churches with Episcopalians at the top, then Presbyterians, Baptists and Methodists, and Catholics at the bottom. It roughly corresponded with the *years-ago* that these persons came to America, except for Blacks and Irishmen. Except for Blacks and Irishmen, prestige came in layers. If your father was born in England and you came over here, you would be an *Englishman*, but if he came over and fathered you, you would not be an *Englishman*. However, if your father was born in Italy and came over here and fathered you, you would be an Italian. We have studied this empirically and have found that it keeps changing year after year through time. In other words, back in 1933, if your father was born in Italy, you would definitely be an Italian—an *Ital-*

ian, a Dago, a *Wop,* depending on the degree of mis-education. Now college students do not say, "Roosevelt is Dutch." "Eisenhower is German." "Truman is English." Half of them do not say that LaGuardia is Italian; half of them do. Thirty years ago all of them would have said that. Present trends indicate that in another generation none of them will.

Empirically people tend to lose their ethnicity through time. However, at any given moment in any given segment of society, there are ethnicities in groups. These considerations may prove helpful as we attempt to construct some useful mechanism for mitigating the possibly surmountable obstacles which we will inevitably encounter in our efforts to build cross-cultural communication.

GENETIC SOCIETY

There is one thing about which there is almost universal agreement at the present time. There seems to be general consensus that things are very strange: "It isn't like it used to be." "I don't know where we're going." "I don't understand people anymore." "Why can't people be more like me?"

My purpose here is to step back from the immediacies of our everyday current experiences to look for some perspective. Let's call it a clinical, empirical and inductive look with a didactic component. That's my job, so the first thing I'll do is make a moral statement which you may challenge.

Because we do not understand, problems frustrate us, other persons' behaviors and utterances anger us, and we are inclined to try to solve problems by an angel-devil theory. According to Quincy Wright, "The community of nation's must be built by a continuous development of the principles, institutions, and laws of the world as a whole, not by an organization of angels, with the hope of ignoring, excluding, converting or destroying the devils." I am not identifying devils. I am going to try, however, to take a strong, stretching, intellectual look, in which maybe we see to some degree how it is that things that we don't like, or don't understand, *are*. If we see this, we may not do too much about it other than feel less bad about it and, thus, have less of a need to be punitive.

First, I happen to live in an exceedingly unusual time. When my father was my age he did not live in a world that was exceedingly unusual. In fact, his world was somewhat different from his father's world, but not all that different; and from his grandfather's world, but not all that different. Whereas my world is *all that different* from the world in which my father lived when he was my age.

In a quick phrase, I call this *discontinuity in history.* There are continuity and discontinuity in history. Change is gradual and slow, but sometimes when we look back upon it, it appears exceedingly abrupt, and we date a break in the continuity of history by saying that everything that went before is different from everything that came afterwards.

When I was little, I was taught that Rome fell in 429 A.D.; and I had visions of persons going to bed in Rome that night, that there was a terrible clatter, everybody rushed to the windows, looked out to see what was going on, and yelled, "Rome's falling!" Well, I'm told that if I had been there at the time, I would not have noticed the fall of Rome. In fact, I've been told that there is still one man there who has not noticed it.

Because I want to cover a great deal of ground, some of which will be of interest to some of you, but not all of it to all of you, I deliberately will be disjointed. Being a college professor, I am capable of taking an extra hour in weeding transitions so that you would not see the disjunctures, but I'm not going to bother you with that.

In the Western World since a Greek named Anaximander came along, we have had a thing called the dichotomy between spiritual and material. Some of you know that most of the people in the world have not looked at it materialistically. That is why some of the young are interested in Asian religions today. By and large, the young look at the world spiritually as do the contemporary Native American Indians. But the Greeks, the Western Europeans and most of us tend to be materialists.

The materialist who has the most fame was a German in England by the name of Karl Marx. But I submit to you that the greatest materialists who have ever existed on earth are contemporary members of American Rotary Clubs. The alternative to the materialist's view is the idealist's view, or the notion that ideas dominate and that material is secondary. Being an opportunist, I shall not choose between these views, but rather choose them both.

There are several revolutions in our history. The first revolution introducing discontinuity in the experience of life occurred about a million years ago. It marked the break between the first billion or two billion years of pre-human life on earth and the last one million years of human life on earth. We say that life has been on earth about a billion or two years and that we human beings have been on earth about one million years, but we continuously take a longer view because we have anthropology departments with graduate students who invariably dig up older graves or find other fossils. We say normally that non-human animals do not have funerals or cook eggs so when we find fire places or burial ground we refer to them as human.

The first revolution, in its spiritual aspect, was the invention of symbolic or abstract language. Pre-human animals do not use abstract language. They have language. We may call it signals. Signals have to be *here* and they have to be *now*. Let me summarize it by saying that dogs do not make appointments.

We understand that there was a collection of chickens at Cornell University with a thirteen-word vocabulary. They had a word for "the trough is full of water," "the bowl is full of corn," "jiggers, here comes a hawk," and "goodie, goodie, here comes the rooster." This is not abstract language. Abstract language is neither here nor now. Possibly it isn't at all, like success and honor. I can say to you that I will meet you in Dallas tomorrow, the thirtieth day of August, at four-thirty p.m., and that is not *here* and that is not *now*. It is abstract, symbolic language.

The first revolution in material aspects was basically the invention of tools. Pre-human animals basically do not employ tools. The things they used to manipulate their environments are parts of their bodies; hawks don't have telescopes, they have eyes that see very far; bears don't have vices, they squeeze you to death with their arms; skunks don't buy mace, they have their own.

In each case, the human animal is, by and large, weak and mediocre compared to the non-human animal that can do something — not everything – but something – swim, fly, hold, pinch, leap, run – better than a human. In fact, Wes LaBarre tells us that you and I have bodies equivalent to a fetus of a chimpanzee in the womb: a great big head with a little body hanging down and little tiny masseter muscles that cannot bite through the branch of a tree. Human beings are too underdeveloped to establish a mechanical sexual periodicity, being in heat, which means that they can learn to attach themselves sexually to a wide variety of times, places and things.

Tools can be thought of as missiles and levers. The missile is simply a rock grabbed by an ape and thrown into the air which accelerates in energy, and by the time it reaches the lion, has enough force to knock him dead. The human fist could never do that by itself in a confrontation with a lion. The lever is merely a log over a log and under a log and, if you put a hundred pounds down on the ten times longer end of it, you exert a thousand pounds up. This multiplies by tens of times the energy factor which the human animal has to bear in manipulating his physical environment – in peace or in war.

With language and tools, life was monotonously repetitious for almost a million years. The life of a daughter was identical to her mother and grandmother and great-grandmother. Then, about ten thousand years ago – a tiny end of a million years – we had another revolution. We call it the invention of civilization. We say it occurred somewhere between the Tigris and Euphrates rivers. This revolution was the invention of writing and, thus the phrases; historic and pre-historic, literate and pre-literate, and civilized and primitive.

Writing makes two things possible; two things that are impossible without it. One is the enlargement of the human group to *any* size. Without writing no group can be larger than the distance over which one man's voice can be heard. Those of you who know the first book of John know "that in the beginning was the word and the word was (good) God," depending on how you spell it. It's a pretty small group that can hear one person speak. Any group that gets bigger than that would break down from internal incohesion. With writing, on the other hand, you could write the word on identical scrolls and yeomen could go to the Upper Kingdom and the Lower Kingdom and Egypt or Phoenicia or Assyria and the *word* could be spread. The other main thing that writing made possible was the permission of deviance. Most of us might not have thought about it, but, without writing, the rules for survival can be preserved only in conduct. The only way we can know how to behave is by seeing it.

I had this actually happen to me once. There was a telephone fastened on the wall with a telephone book fastened on the wall beside it, but the telephone did not work. So I marched across to a telephone that did work, but there was no telephone book. I had no pencil. I returned to the first telephone, looked up the number, kept saying it, walking across the room – "788-3121 - 788-3121 - 788-3121," and somebody looked up and said, "738-8211." At that moment I lost the number and I turned to that person and said something unattractive and went back and looked up the number. But suppose there had been no telephone book in which to look the number up again; then I would not have said something unattractive, I would have killed him. And that discourages deviance.

Next came a revolution in energy – the horse and the wheel. Whether or not that horse is an elephant, a camel, a dog or an ox, it is an explosion in biological muscle of animals under the direction and control of a human will. You put a horse before a cart with wheels bearing an Assyrian with a spear, and that man is now thousands of times more powerful than his primitive enemy on foot.

This was *civilization* and it ran along essentially uninterrupted, with writing and the horse and the wheel, until about four hundred years ago.

About four hundred years ago we had a revolution of equal magnitude, disconnecting that which went before from that which was to come after it. This revolution in energy you may call gunpowder or chemical explosions or jet airplanes or cannons or hydroelectric power or electricity – things going on inside engines instead of inside muscles of horses. (Even though we use the word horsepower to describe it, very few bits of horse power are provided by horses anymore.) Engines represent hundreds of thousands of times more energy directed by human will than that directed in the world of the horse.

The concomitant revolution in communications was printing. What printing the Gutenberg Bible did was to make universal literacy possible. Prior to printing, the word was written, but it was written in longhand and was unbelievably rare and expensive. Every book up to four hundred years ago was written by hand, and it took a college boy four, five, six, seven, eight years of taking courses at the University of Bologna in Italy to acquire one copy in his own longhand of Aristotle's *Poetics* or *Politics*. In fact, the word *college* entered the language as a labor union against professors. It was a collegium of students forcing professors to read their copy of their book so slowly that one could get his own copy by taking a course no more than four times. If you had a copy of a book, you were a professor and you ran around reading your copy. You may have noticed that this is still going on.

Printing, on the other hand, is cheap. Although librarians don't know it, books are very, very inexpensive. We have a lot of librarians who feel that everything is in the right order if every book is in the library on the shelf in the right place locked up.

Anyway, we can say that four hundred years ago, with gunpowder and printing, came democracy. A stupid individual at the corner of Thirteenth and Wazee in Denver with a gun pointed at my temple is remarkably my equal. Printing and gunpowder are democratizing. When printing came into England four hundred years ago, people wrote political tracts and tacked them on lamp posts, and people stood around and said, "hmmm, yes," and "hmmm, no." It was called public opinion and gave rise to the House of Commons.

Well, that's life some of us have known; a life my mother knew, my mother's mother knew, my mother's mother's mother knew, and the life into which I was born. I am a person who was born into a world of books and gunpowder. I was reared on *The Little Lame Prince* and Louisa May Alcott's *Little Women* and *Little Men* – that's why I am a little man.

Now has come another revolution; the revolution in energy from sources other than sunlight. Oil, fossil fuel, wind, and coal, hydroelectric power come from sunlight in some form or another; but we now have energy coming from the center of the atom: helium fission, uranium fission, nuclear, thermonuclear energy. It multiplies by millions of times the energy factor that man has to bear for peace or for war – not hundreds of thousands of times, but millions of times.

If you want to date that theoretically, you would use the date 1905, when Albert Einstein at the University of Berlin made the observation that mass and energy were equivalent: the equivalency of energy equals mass times the speed of light squared, and that parallel lines do meet in space, and so on. If you have an engineering point of view, you might use the date of March 1, 1954 when the Americans detonated their first hydrogen bomb in the Pacific, the ash of which fell upon a Japanese fisherman seventy-five miles away and killed or maimed him.

Another revolution in communication obviously is electronic communication: radar, television, computers, Telstar. I will make the argument that, when human beings around the world on one day saw live on television one man shoot another man dead in the second floor jail in Dallas, Texas, that united the human race spiritually in a fantastic way. We studied editorials written in Russian, Romanian, Portuguese, French, German, Mandarin, Swahili, and they had a strangely similar identity. They created that dead American President almost into a symbol of man on a tiny, tiny, tiny little earth with shared problems and shared values. The live Kennedy was one thing; the dead one was a totally different thing in terms of the meaning around the world. Anyone in Africa in the Peace Corps saw signs that went up immediately in the most remote places about Kennedy. These people were speaking for themselves – the human race – and it is the result of instant communication with vast consequences for us.

If you look at the military or engineering side of this thing, theoretically, we now can say we have the capability to fabricate electrical energy sufficiently to light the earth at no cost of the power. We have built a breeder plant in Tennessee which will produce more fuel than it can consume.

When I was little, we heated our house with coal. My dad would send me down to take out ashes and clinkers to the back yard and put them in a square box, and somebody would come and take them away once a month. If I had a breeder plant, I would not be taking out clinkers and ashes, but coal, to the back yard. And finally the back yard would be full of coal. I'd call my friend and say, "Hey, guess what, I've got a back yard full of coal you can have," and he'd say, "Hell, no, so have I." This is a technical fact.

Looked at materially, a payload of a World War II bomber (the kind of bomber that leveled Tokyo, Dresden and Coventry) would be the equivalent of about four tons of dynamite. If you let four tons of dynamite be represented by four cubes of sugar standing on a table, the bomb that we dropped on Hiroshima (which was of uranium fission) would be a column of sugar cubes extending into the air as high as the Empire State Building. The difference between the Empire State Building and the four cubes of sugar is a quantitative difference that is really qualitative. The March 1, 1954 bomb would be a column of sugar extending into the air as high as sixty-three miles. That is fourteen megatons.

The explosion of that March 1 made Mr. Eisenhower and Mr. Churchill totally aware of the total obsolescence of warfare, often referred to by Mr. Churchill as "the mutual balance of terror." Mr. Kruschev understood it, too. He went before his authoritarian council and repealed the communist constitution which had in it the proviso that World War III was an inevitable war. Kruschev learned from that explosion that there could not be an inevitable war.

At this point, Senator Everett Dirksen and Senator Russell accepted the advice of Stanislaw Ulam over the objections of the monomaniacal physicist named Edward Teller and engaged in what came to be called the *Test Ban Treaty*. This started because of the world of Dr. Strangelove which is not fiction, but is, indeed, a documentary. Even though a majority of our college students did not list the avoidance of the coming of thermonuclear Armageddon as a top social problem, it nevertheless was.

Television is instant communication and information. By and large, the young today derive their views of politics in forty-seven seconds. Anyone who seeks to run for office and can't put himself across in a forty-seven second statement cannot win. That is unlike my grandfather who spent hours reading the Lincoln-Douglas debate in the newspaper before setting out to vote. We now have instant people with instant views. We say this about the young; but what we are discovering is that those of us who are decrepit, arthritic and old (meaning me) are not reading either, because we, too, pick it up from Peter Jennings, Tom Brokaw and Dan Rather.

The difference between television and books is that television doesn't have boundary lines. Books start with chapters, have margins, start at the beginning, like *Alice In Wonderland*, go to the end and stop. But that's not true with TV news.

Looking out of that window I see half of a building right now. I wouldn't say to you, "I see half of a building." I'd say, "There's a building outside." I see half of it, and I presume that the other half is also there, out of sight. I'm not an empiricist like Professor William James. He was riding in a carriage with a friend who happened to look out the carriage window remarking, "See, Professor James, the sheep on the hill. They've just been sheared." Professor James replied, " Well, on one side, anyway."

Do not suppose that your political leaders are as stupid as the things they say. They are not. But no political leader can remain a political leader saying anything brighter than his audience.

Mr. Eisenhower called up C. D. Jackson from New York and

said, "Wise up the people of America as to what they're up against."
C. D. Jackson set out on what was called "Operation Candor." But
who ruled the day? Not C. D. Jackson, not Dwight Eisenhower, but a
Senator from Wisconsin, Joesph McCarthy, with his devil-angel theory.
Simultaneously you and I went running around looking for communists in a high school journalism class or under the bed. You may not
remember 1955, 1956, 1957, but it was not a time of preoccupation
with the realities of the world in which we lived at all, but a completely fantastic avoidance of anything real.

Some of you are old enough to remember in 1961 when John
Kennedy came along and said, "All right, I think I've got a way to
make them understand." So he said, "Okay, if you want to have your
Cold War, go out and dig yourself a little hole in the back yard in
which to hide." We did. We spent a couple of months talking about
what to put into that little bomb shelter. Then we talked about how
to ventilate it. Then a Methodist Bishop authorized us to shoot our
neighbor's daughter dead if she tried to get into our bomb shelter.
Then my friend, Willard Libby, of the Atomic Energy Commission,
built a bomb shelter in Santa Monica. We read that it burnt down in
a brush fire. He fixed it, and the next month that same bomb shelter
went down the drain in a flood. Then we learned that our bomb shelter was of no use if we were more than seventeen minutes away from
it at any moment. Then we discovered that we were never within seventeen minutes of our homes. The last straw was when we discovered
that 87.6 percent of Americans do not have back yards.

If three-year-olds, four-year-olds, five-year-olds look through
the television tube and see an irate African leader talking about American imperialism in the Sahara, it doesn't have a beginning nor an end
like a book or newspaper does. It goes on and on.

To get off this subject quickly, let me say simply that it is symbolized for me and you by the difference in my music and the young's
music. My music is baroque. I like Vivaldi, Bach, Corelli and Mozart.
I'll never forget how pleased I was when I learned when not to clap.
What use would that information have been at Woodstock or on MTV.

Let us turn to poverty.

Poverty as a problem is twenty-five years new. Poverty as a fact is as old as the human race – a million years or so. The difference between a problem and a fact is that a problem has a solution and a fact does not. We live in a world that has lots of facts with no solutions. Americans have more problems than people do. For example, in America marriage is a problem. In France marriage is a fact. No Frenchman would think of regarding marriage as a problem. He knows marriage is hell—something with which you put up, a fact. When he lands at Kennedy airport, he's totally startled to see all kinds of books on *How to Make Your Marriage Work.* Don't Americans know that that is impossible?

Though poverty as a fact is as old as man, some of us are likely to recreate the past. There is nothing to be found in the 1960 campaign about poverty except a slight reference to Appalachia, the solution to which was a bank called EDA, if you remember. The New Deal was not a poverty program. It was for the entire population. Most of us were flat on our backs in the world of economic collapse after 1929. Poverty was never a problem to my father. He'd see poor people. He noticed poverty. He would say, "Mr. Tompkins is just poor, that's all." "And the poor ye shall always have with you." That's a fact.

The cause of poverty has had three explanations in the course of time which I'll explain: my father died believing in explanation number one; my mother died believing in explanation number two; most Americans (about 87.6 percent) believe in explanation number two; and finally there is explanation number three. Explanation number one came into being one million years ago; explanation number two came into being one hundred years ago; and explanation three is coming into being right now. Or you might date it 1906 if you're theoretically oriented. Or 1962 if you relate to a person like Michael Harrington who wrote *The Other America*, when at the same time, Kenneth Galbraith embarrassingly published a book without reference to poverty called *The Affluent Society.*

What are these explanations or causes of poverty? Cause one

of poverty is God. Most people throughout most times have been animists. They have believed that the world is animate; that everything is spiritual – that every blade of grass, every grain of sand, every drop of rain has its own will. It is the job of the shaman or witch doctor to propitiate those wills. If a coconut falls from a tree and kills a neighboring tribesman, someone *told* that coconut to fall and kill that person. There's a spirit in both the coconut and the person. That's animism; millions and billions of spirits. I must confess to you that I caught my daughter, Alice, who is a teacher of Anthropology at Regis College in Denver, practicing animism. I once heard her speak to a hammer.

About ten thousand years ago the Greeks came along and reduced these billions of spirits to a measly thirty-six or so. These spirits lived on a mountain called Olympus. One of them I rather liked. He was a drunk by the name of Bacchus. If you remember, you read Sophocles, Euripides and Aristophanes who told you that the Greeks knew that life was in the hands of the gods. What people did down on earth was the will of the gods.

Then along came the Jews with Jehova and the Christians with Jesus and Mary and, finally, my father, the Presbyterian. He believed in predestination; *Con de favor de Dios*; "God moves in mysterious ways his wonders to perform:" God's will. If Mr. Tompkins is poor, that's between Mr. Tompkins and God.

I didn't know until I was grown up that my Presbyterian father and Marx's communists were just alike: they both believed in predestination. The only difference was the Russian accent of my friends. "According to historical development…" As I said, my father died believing *that there isn't anything you can do about it*. And you know people who believe that now: what people are is between them and God.

Cause two of poverty is heredity. This explanation of poverty came about one hundred years ago when we had a revolution in England. The names connected with this revolution are Lamarck, Mendel, Charles Darwin and a man named Wallace, who oddly enough was not a governor. Today, words for this are chromosomes, genes and physical inheritance. Genetics. *Genetic Society.* These biologists came forward and said that behavior was the consequence of little things that we inherited. We ran around seeing people doing things, so we'd say they inherited them. We had a little gene for running, walking, sitting, stealing, giving, eating, laughing, crying, associating, disassociating; this was inheritance. Charles Darwin had a museum in which he had a hierarchy of skulls from superior to inferior. He had monkeys, chimpanzees, gorillas, Negroes, Orientals, Europeans, Caucasians, and at the tiptop, Englishmen. He had a Rodgers and Hammerstein singing their glory; two men by the name of Gilbert and Sullivan. They sang, "For he is an Englishman,and it's greatly to his credit, for he himself has said it; he is an Englishman." He had a poet named Rudyard Kipling who sang the songs of the white man's burden.

Across the English Channel there was a Frenchman who tried the same thing. The French always do. His name was Gustav LeBon at the City College at Paris. He, too, had a museum with monkeys , chimpanzees, gorillas, Negroes, Orientals and Caucasians. At the top, however, there was one difference: DeGaulle. That comes down to us today as the Common Market and The European Community.

Now the point is that these things are related to the cause of white supremacy; colonialism around the world, and Little Rock, Arkansas, as well. These are the intellectual bases of the racist society in which we live. They have a basic, fundamental, universal, elite, intellectual, scholarly basis. My mother had racist notions which had this intellectual basis and scholarship. She thought Negroes were innately amorous, musical, beautiful and indolent. Therefore, if you invented a job for an amorous, beautiful, indolent person, you were doing the right thing. She believed these things to be inherited, and a great number of Americans believe that the characteristics of peoples' behavior are something they inherit.

You hear people say, "Yes, Billy plays the violin real good. He inherited it from his Uncle Ben in Philadelphia." He's never seen his Uncle Ben in Philadelphia! Another belief to be mentioned is that the virtuous things tend to be inherited through the germ plasma of the female strain of the family.

The idea that personality characteristics are inherited is a racist idea. It is widely held and widely believed – either virtuously or adversely. I can speak of Germans as having an inherited tendency to understand science; Italians to have an inherited tendency to be musical. These are the ideas of the dominance of chromosomes and genes.

We had two very foolish Americans in the 1960's: one named Shockly and one named Jensen. Shockly did a proper job in inventing the transistor; he knew something about physics, nothing about sociology, but he was famous for running around having there be a genetic deficiency in Black Americans. Jensen was another person of the same variety.

We have a professor of Anthropology on my campus who is under the delusion that the American Indians have a gene for drunkenness. Our biology department can't find the gene, but the professor can find the Indians.

Cause three of poverty is the current view. It rejects heredity as a cause of poverty. Cause three can be attributed to a book by William Graham Sumner, *Folkways*. Everyone in this room knows the words *folkways* and *mores*. But not everybody in this room knows that those words did not exist in those meanings until eighty years ago. They are not to be found in the thinking of Karl Marx or Herbert Spencer or Auguste Comte, let alone Socrates or Plato, or anywhere in the Koran or the Bible. Sumner collected all sorts of missionaries' diaries, and from them he discovered that the European idea that Europeans had morality and other people were without it was not true. In 1870, you could go around the world and teach all of the immoral natives to wear dinner jackets to dinner. Actually, these missionaries were the first anthropologists. They were sent out from their home church to remake the natives. When they found that the natives were delightful people, they wrote wonderful diaries, but they didn't write home about it because they would have lost their funding.

Anyway, we can summarize the work of Sumner in his book as saying that "the interesting things about persons are learned." That is a very carefully constructed, heavy sentence: *the interesting things about persons are learned.* It is a new idea, and though it is probably only coincidence, it is hard to believe that the time lapse between that thought and its translation into action is the same as the gap between the development of the theory behind the hydrogen bomb in 1905 and its detonation on March 1, 1954.

In 1954, the Brown Decision of the Warren Supreme Court said that if it is not true that personality differences are the result of learning, then it is illegal to provide alternative learning styles: places where you can learn to be dumb and places where you can learn to be bright. But, the illegal kind of school system we had in 1954 we still have in the United States of America right now.

In summary, the third definition of the cause of poverty is that poverty is the result of an unfair, uneven opportunity to learn.

Three of you will say, "Higman says there's no such thing as heredity." I do not. There are some things that are hereditary. Some of our friends and relatives have had children born who happen to have physical defects: they're born blind, without a voice, without hearing, with a defective nervous system or heart murmurs. They are physically-retarded individuals who will have to have special care as long as they live. But we are not talking about them. We are talking about the idea that there are inherited characteristics called "Chicano characteristics" or "German characteristics."

There is no difference in children whatsoever until we get them into the school. Then begins systematic retardation. The language in the school has nothing to do with their lives. We know there is a language called *Chicano*. It is not Spanish. There is a *Black* dialect (*Ebonics*) in the ghetto.

A child is born without language and culture. In 1964 we went into Lariat, a Spanish-American ghetto in Southern Colorado, and there was a little boy named Herman, living in a room with thirteen people. When he was six months old he rode around on the back of his thirteen-year-old sister. We picked him up for Head Start and to our amazement we discovered that at the age of four he had no name. There was no response to our calling him Herman. He had never seen a paper clip or a crayon. He couldn't conceive of red, white, or blue. He didn't know what color was. But he could learn his name. A the end of the week he was beaming when the bus rode up: "Hello, Herman." "Hello, Mrs. Hunter." We discovered he didn't have a face. He had never seen a mirror. We took a picture of him with a Polaroid camera. He couldn't find himself in the picture. We put a mirror on the wall where he could see himself: "Oh, it's me, Herman!" He could learn it.

Given this psychological perception, we now say that the cause of poverty is an unfair, uneven opportunity to learn. That is the reason why Justice Warren found it is illegal for American children to have unequal opportunities to learn. This profound philosophical point is not controversial in the world of behavioral scientists or in law, in spite of the fact that large numbers of Americans presently do not understand it.

Secondly, I will admit that there is a game you can invent in which heredity is crucial, such as professional basketball in which a short center is six feet six inches tall. So I will admit that heredity is involved. There are some people here old enough to remember a woman by the name of Jane Russell about whom something hereditary was interesting.

However, that is not the main thrust of this presentation. I go back to the statement that the interesting things about persons are *learned*. You can test this for yourselves because almost anything you say this week about somebody, I bet it will be about something that is interesting – *interesting* – it will be something that Mr. Brown learned or did not learn. It will not be genes or chromosomes. They are there, but they are not interesting. They are fantastically homeostatic. Heredity is vastly more stable than the weather. Thomas Jefferson and Thomas Paine were right when they said, " All men are created equal." They are – equally stupid. As far as I can see everyone in this room has two nose holes. I admit that that is hereditary, but I assert that it is uninteresting, and I am not going back to Colorado and say that everyone here has two nose holes. Of course, if anyone has one or three, that I'll report.

The term, *heredity*, has given rise to words like Chicanos, Blacks, Whites, Honkies. We believe these personality characteristics are learned. We have observed what we call systematic retardation on Indian reservations. For instance, during projects in which we worked with Indians in Pine Ridge, South Dakota, we tested a method developed by Professor David Hawkins for intellectualizing a child which involved the use of water, icicles and mud – non-verbal things. The Indian children were the absolute equals of the white children whose parents worked for the Bureau of Indian Affairs.

The entrance intelligence test given to soldiers in World War I ranked White northern males tops, Black northern males second, White southern males third, and Black southern males bottom. There is a high correlation between that ranking and the opportunity to learn as provided by the local schools at that time in those places.

Politics is who gets what, when, and where. We can put under three headings what you can get. First, there are goods and services which are obvious; your salary or your monetary emoluments. It's back rubs, beer, beds, theater tickets, college tuition, airplane tickets, coats, clothes, hi-fi sets, gasoline, everything you buy with money. And obviously some people have more than others.

Secondly, we can classify political values under the word, security. Security is the illusion that that which is will continue. It is a very, very powerful drive. The human animal is unbelievably conservative. All of us are. The less we have, the more conservative we are. It's terribly hard to explain to affluent middle-class college boys from Shaker Heights why the poor don't want to rush around, throwing away the little things that they have. It's hard for college students to understand that the peasants fought not for the revolution; not for Cromwell, but for Charles I; not for Tom Paine, but for George III; for Louis XVI, and for Nicholas II. Having very little, there was much to lose.

Nobody wants to lose anything. Walk into an office and find an old Woodstock typewriter that hasn't been used for fifteen years. It's covered with dust, sitting in the back corner. Walk in and pick it up – "What are you doing?" "You don't use this thing." "I know, but it's mine." People want to keep bits and pieces of their domains and turfs. There is no difference between a welfare mother with her welfare check and a vice president of General Motors with his bailiwick. Take anything away from either of them, and they'll yell, "It's mine!"

Security. Some people are more secure than others. In military affairs armies were for the purpose of preventing foreign people from entering a country; or, if they did enter, they were used to drive out the foreigners, as the Russians drove out the Vikings in the eleventh century, the Tartars in the thirteenth century, the Prussians in the fourteenth century, and Swedes and the Poles in the seventeenth century, Napoleon Bonaparte in 1812, Kaiser Wilhelm in 1914, Woodrow Wilson in 1918 (although I didn't realize it at the time) and Adolph Hitler in 1941. That, of course, is why we call the Russians aggressive.

The third value is deference. Deference must be described because we never speak about it. We don't because it is divine. Security and goods are profane. Everyone talks about them. If I get a job to do and have some jobs to offer, persons will come in and say, "Okay, how much will you pay me?" Then they say, "Is it soft money?" "Sure." "How long will it run?" "A year." "Okay." That is security. But they never say, "Oh, by the way, will you show me deference?" Deference is so precious that it is not referred to.

However, being profane, I will refer to it. Deference is the right not to know that you're not loved, not wanted, not admired. We think, ideally, we'd like to be loved, wanted and admired by everybody. Dr. Freud tells me I would not, that it would make me tired. But that doesn't matter, since there's no chance I will be. So the point becomes if you're not loved, wanted, admired by somebody, the next best thing is to *not* know it.

Deference – the right not to know you're not loved, wanted, or admired – is wonderful. There's a professor who does not like me at all. One day he came home and his wife said, "Honey, here's the dinner guest list for this Saturday night: the Browns, the Jones, the Mannings, the Higmans, the Simpsons…" He exclaimed, "Higmans! They're not coming to my house." So I was crossed off that guest list. But I did not know it. Again, I was crossed off a list to be chairman of the Search Committee for a new dean of the Graduate School; I was crossed off a list to be one of three members of the State Civil Service Commission to pick the new director for a poverty program; I was crossed off lists all day, but I did not know it.

I have news for you. So were you. The point is: what a hell of a life it would be if in the morning when the postman came, he brought me a list of my disinvitations. I would sit down, open the mail, and find that I wasn't going to be going to the Browns, to the Jones, to the Simpsons. It would be very depressing.

Suppose that professor I told you about hired a billboard and put on it a sign: "Howard, Marion, Anne, Alice or Elizabeth Higman will not enter my house." My kids would ask, "Daddy, how come we can't go in his house?" I would have to say "Well, that's very complex; wait until you grow up and I'll try to explain it to you."

What I am pointing out is that there are millions of Americans today who do have to rear their children with just such billboards scattered around, announcements that these persons are not desirable.

We were running a training program for Negro college administrators in the South to teach them how better to deal with their Black student bodies. The most poignant story I heard came from a Dean of Women at Bishop College in Dallas. She described to us what it was like as a little girl in Dallas, Texas, to wonder how White water would taste. When she was a little girl, there were public fountains: by law and convention one was for Colored and one was for Whites. She was not allowed to put her little orbicularis oris around that jet of White water. That is not deference. This is not freedom from not knowing you're not loved, wanted or admired. It is rubbing it in.

As late as the election of John Kennedy after World War II, it was against the law in parts of the United States for Black urine to mix with White urine in a public urinal in a bus stop restroom. That is not deference, or as the minorities often refer to it –"dignity." You can't legislate love, but you can legislate deference, because deference is how one *acts*, not how one *feels*. You can make it against the law to *act* certain ways. I agree that you can't make it against the law to *feel* certain ways. Ask a high school student, "Didn't you have a teacher you didn't love, didn't want, didn't admire?" "Yeah." "And did not tell?" "Yeah!" "Did not tell" is the point.

Last year, I went into a bar in Shreveport, Louisiana, where two men were sitting not being waited on. The waitress said, "What do you want?" "Service." "You've had too much service already. See the sign: 'No Niggers, Mexicans, or dogs allowed.'" U.S.A. 1972. That is not deference.

And this has something to do with the reason for militancy in America today. The Civil Rights Act was passed before Black militancy occurred, just as the equality of the Asian Indian to the Englishman was described at Oxford and Cambridge before the activism of Ghandi. The sit-in in the Woolworth stores by White northerners awakened the Black community of the South. The militancy came afterwards, not before, and therefore was not a cause of the civil rights movement, which was supported by the ethnic groups and the labor unions. What turned the ethnic groups and labor unions off was Watts and Detroit and "U" Street in Washington, D.C. – burning, violence and looting.

You and I are, by and large, Puritans. Puritanism is new – four hundred years new. The real good Puritans were a bunch of hippies from Amsterdam, who, in 1620 headed for North Carolina. They misfired and landed at a teeny, weeny rock off the coast of Massachusetts where it was too cold in the winter, too hot in the summer, surrounded by hostile Indians and covered with rocks. And there they discovered the turkey.

Puritanism was a European invention, but we carried it to its real extremes.

Puritanism has four main characteristics. The first is individualism. Most people throughout most times have been cooperative, communalistic, groupie. "You are your brother's keeper." But not with the Puritanistic Luther, Calvin and Knox. One looks out for Number One. It's individualism, and we have all kinds of words for it: private enterprise, self-reliance, do-it-yourself, ask-what-you-can-do-for-yourself. Individualism is continuously being reinvented by the young; the newest name for it is "Doing your own thing."

The second Puritan characteristic is work as an end. Most people work as a means: work to get enough food and quit; work to get enough shelter and then quit to love, live, laugh, play and revere. Not Puritans. Puritans work to get enough food, then they work to get more food and more food, and work to get shelter and then more shelter. They work to work to work to work.

There are two brothers. Bill helps old ladies across the street, plays with little children, plays the mandolin, writes poems. He's a lovely fellow, but doesn't hold a job. His brother, John, a bastard, gets up before dawn, holds down two jobs, beats his wife. He closes down the bar at 2:00 A.M., but everyone says, "Well, you'll have to say this about John, he works anyway." It is a virtue.

Having worked, you then keep it. This is called thrift. You save everything. My father and I saved nails. In fact we saved used nails. We saved bent, used nails. We saved rusty, bent, used nails. On Saturday afternoons we would classify them by degrees of bentness and rustiness in Mason jars. String was saved, and the ball got bigger and bigger and bigger. Wax, tin foil, and old National Geographic Magazines were saved. I had an aunt, and when she died, we discovered a little box. It said, 'String too short to save."

Fourth and finally, having done it, having worked, and having kept it – I don't understand this – you then wash it. Literally, I heard a first grade school teacher on the Pine Ridge Reservation say happily, "I always say there isn't a thing wrong with these dear little Indian children that a little soap and water wouldn't fix."

In New England there were two families. One family, the Hopkins (my relatives), had eighty units for survival, while the Tompkins only had forty. I don't know why the Tompkins only had forty. Maybe they fell into groups talking, stopped working to play, or someone came by who was hungry so they gave it away, or maybe they didn't wash it, and it fermented and they drank it. If the Hopkins had been Spanish Catholics and communalistic, when winter came along they would have said, "Oh, oh, the Tompkins are running out of food. Run over with a casserole, dear." The winter would have continued and they would have run over with another casserole. The ratio became sixty-sixty – communalism. That winter it took sixty-five to survive, so they both would have gone down the drain. Fortunately for me, however, we were Puritans and not Spanish Catholics. So, when winter came, ten-twenty-thirty-forty units were used up. We looked out the window and said, "Oh, oh, there go the Tompkins."

David Ricardo recorded in the *Iron Law Of Wages* that the crust of the earth was stingy. The Englishman, Robert Malthus, recorded it in his *Essay On Population* in which he said that the passion between the sexes will remain a constant and, therefore, food will decrease arithmetically and population will increase geometrically, and soon there will be gasping hunger, and excess population will be controlled by vice, famine and war. Malthus was caricatured by Charles Dickens as a person called *Scrooge* who at Christmas refused, to his nephew, alms for the poor, saying, "I'll let them die to decrease the surplus population."

My favorite quote from Malthus was the one he made on the floor of Parliament in England when he got up to propose the abolition of OEO. He said, "As you all know, I am in favor of the postponement of marriage, but even with marriage postponed to the late age of twenty-eight, however badly the deprivation may be born by the males, there is still time for a devastating torrent of children."

The facts are that the Green Revolution, in spite of peripheral setbacks this year in wheat sales and bad weather, has provided an abundance from the crust of the earth. Ever since the days of Franklin Roosevelt, in order to maintain a price, we had to create an artificial scarcity of agricultural goods. A few years ago in the Mississippi Delta, Mrs. Senator Eastland received a check for $185,000 to *not* grow food and fiber. Six million dollars went to other non-growers to not grow in the Mississippi Delta. Five billion dollars went out across the country to non-farmers to not farm.

When Mrs. Eastland doesn't grow cotton in the Mississippi Delta, Negroes do not pick cotton in the Mississippi Delta. They move to Detroit, and turn Black. Some persons think that if we can pay Mrs. Eastland something not to grow cotton, perhaps we could pay Negroes not to pick it. But that may be radical.

Last year in the Pacific Northwest the earth coughed up more potatoes than could have been eaten. If they had hit the market, today they would have been free. Fortunately for me, we didn't let them hit the market, for if they had, the farmers would not have had enough money to pay the tuition for their daughters to attend my classes.

So it is not the natural scarcity of the earth anymore, it is the system. The year before last in the sub-continent of Asia the Indians grew more cereal due to new hybrids than they could have eaten had it been delivered to them. It was not, but it was a social and political thing, not a chemistry thing. The cereal was eaten by rats or rotted because it was not delivered. But that was not due to the stinginess of the crust of the earth.

On April 24, 1972, I read an article in *TIME* magazine. I never read *TIME* except on airplanes and then only if I cannot get *Better Homes And Gardens.* The article was supposed to show me why I would be paying more for beef. But the significant thing about the article was that it describes the disappearance of agricultural America in a period from 1950 to 1970. Farmers decreased from 10,000,000 to 2,000,000. The years can be projected in which there will be more employees in the U.S. Department of Agriculture than there will be American farmers. And it is before 1990.

I was told by Timothy Findley of the *San Francisco Chronicle* that last year in the Imperial Valley of California there were ten thousand ex-agricultural workers who were no longer needed because of the modern technology we use to produce food in America today. They are receiving eight million dollars in welfare checks, not because they are unwilling to work, but because there is no work for them to do.

At the same time that the ex-agricultural workers in the Imperial Valley are receiving eight million dollars, ten million dollars are being given to five hundred farmers in soil bank checks to *not* farm. That, of course, is not called welfare because that supports the system. It comes out of the U.S. Department of Agriculture instead of Health, Education and Welfare. Once more, these farmers don't have names like George and Charley; they have names like Gates Rubber Company.

In the San Luis Valley in the 1940's thousand of potatoes were grown. Then along came machines for planting them; then along came machines for irrigating them; in 1965 I saw the first harvester which dug the potatoes and then separated the potatoes from rocks, graded them by size, washed them, and packed them. Farmer Limon said to me as he pointed to a sack of potatoes, "Look here. No human hand has ever touched one of these potatoes." I replied that when I got home, I would go to the Safeway store, open a sack of potatoes, and say "Look, Potato, here's a hand!"

What impresses me the most about the charts in *Time* is not what is on the chart but what is off the chart. I want you to think about this. Here are all these people who are *not* used – not growing cotton, not picking beets, not harvesting tomatoes. They exist now largely in the vacated centers of American cities. I refer to this as the de-ruralization of America, not the urbanization of America at all. These persons are rural persons with rural views and rural skills sitting in an abandoned part of Denver, Kansas City, Chicago, Los Angeles, Detroit.

We speak with abhorrence about drop-outs – children dropping out of schools. Dr. Elliott made a longitudinal study of

Spanish-American kids leaving a San Diego school which showed that their brush with the law occurred not after they dropped out, but when they were *in* school. The contemporary American urban public school is at odds with these people. To reiterate, their first brush with the law comes when they are *in* school. And it is not because they don't get to be doctor of medicine, it's because they don't get to play football, read a poem, or have a pom pom, or the teacher says, "Dance with someone of your own kind." In fact, we are finding that dropping out is not a cause but a solution to the problems of the youth. Those who solve their problems do so largely by dropping out, getting a job and a woman. A woman seems to be the essential ingredient to making it in the world. A strong, beautiful woman of sixteen.

These studies show an enormous need to rethink totally the impact of what we think of as schools as solution to the problem that nobody caused. You see, I am not speaking of the public school as a devil or the Whites as racists. Nobody designed this system, but it exists and lots of persons are suffering from it. Fifty years ago not twenty percent of the population thought of going to high school. There was no reason to go. Women learned what they learned from role models – sewing, cooking, punching plugs in switchboards in telephone offices. Males learned carpentry, masonry, mining, lumbering, butchery from role models, not schools. A handful went to high school, and most of those went to learn to be computers, if you will, for the establishment. They learned to keep accounts and send bills. And even fewer persons went to college. Henry Ford didn't get a degree from Harvard Business School, nor did John D. Rockefeller. Those who went became lawyers, ministers, doctors, and college professors. They were a handful of intellectuals. Suddenly, all kinds of persons who previously did not go to school are installed in large, irrelevant, urban schools where they become brutalized and end up in court.

We've been inclined to turn our courts into churches and art galleries. Nine out of ten kids who are incarcerated are incarcerated for something ugly or something sinful. It need not also be criminal. In one city, Twin Falls, South Dakota, I talked to a probation officer who said that recently eighteen out of twenty boys sixteen-to-twenty years-old had been picked up for having an open bottle of alcohol in their possession. That problem could be solved by shipping them all to France. Whether you know it or not, $22,000 a year is spent in the state of Massachusetts on one incarcerated kid. That is vastly more than it would take to put him on a Greyhound bus forever.

I'm going to give you two stories that I think have a bearing on what I'm trying to say. I was on a TV talk program six or seven years ago. I hadn't bothered to rehearse or think much about it. I was not going to speak first because then I could take a position different from the first speaker. But I was out-foxed because the interviewer started talking to me right off. The camera was cranking away. "Professor Higman, what is the cause of the riots in the cities?" I said, using the voice a Republican Senator from Illinois whom I admired terribly, "The concept, cause, is not a scientific concept; it is a moral concept and it has to do with what it is you want to blame…" By this time, I'd thought of an answer, so I said, "The basic cause of riots in the cities is television." The host ducked and said, "Surely you don't mean that all of the arson and violence and warfare on TV is making people violent." I said, "Of course not. It's not the fairy tales on TV; it's the truth."

My grandmother lived in 1870 in Racine, Wisconsin, in poverty, and did not know it. She got up before dawn, packed water, rendered lard, made sugar cookies, bore seven children, saved the lives of five, went to bed at night exhausted and hoped God hadn't found out.

Today, there's a woman in a rocking chair on a porch in Watts in Los Angeles staring out at a freeway with cars going past her in both directions, but none for her. Her mother had come up from Mobile, Alabama, in the days of patriotism to help Henry Kaiser build liberty ships to sink Hirohito and Tojo in the Sea of Japan. Suddenly the defense industry requires calculus, and there's not anyway in the wide, wide world that this Black woman is going to be able to get a job. Her tooth aches and her government doesn't have enough money for a health clinic, but she turns on her television set and sees two fellows spending fifty billion dollars dancing around on the way to the moon, picking up rocks. I know. You say, 'Well, I see she has a TV set. How come she doesn't spend the money for clothing for her children?' You can get a television set for fifty cents down. It costs two thousand dollars to get a flush toilet.

At this point in the show, the host said, "We'll have to stop for station identification." The next day I received a call from the Governor's office which said, "You sure used those commercials to prove your point." I said, "I didn't see them. What were they?" It turned out that the first was a gal by the name of Ethel Merman who sang the glories of the Red, White and Blue where everybody on this side of the Iron Curtain had everything. The other commercial was by a loan company called The Associates. The message was; "Now you too can have up to ten thousand dollars on your signature." Well, that woman on the porch could not cash a check at a Safeway store, even if she had the money in the bank, because of the gestalt of her lifestyle in the society we now have in American cities in 1973. And you know that. And it makes her angry.

The second story is about a young man who had made the error of coming to Seattle because of relatives. He was a Black from Alabama, and there was no way, given the job opportunities we currently provide and given the education he had, for him to make a legitimate living. Nor, it may come as a surprise to some people, but the human animal when it cannot make a legitimate living prefers to make an illegitimate living than none at all. Fortunately for him, at that time the State of Washington had a law against the sale of wine on Sundays, so our hero found he had a job. He bought wine on Saturday and sold it on Sunday. He did this rather well, until, unfortunately, one day he tried something else at which he wasn't as good. Herein is a lesson for all of us. One Saturday night came an employee of Boeing Aircraft Company down to the streets of Second and Yessler. He was in search of amatory athletics. Having consummated his desire, he passed out under the steering wheel of his car under a street light. His jacket was open and his wallet visible. Our hero spied him and the wallet, and he relocated the wallet. Unfortunately for the people of the State of Washington, the wallet had seventy-six dollars in it, and because grand larceny in Washington is seventy-five dollars, he was sent up to the state penitentiary with a sentence of nine years in prison. This meant a cost of $22,000 a year, more or less, for the taxpayers of Washington.

Now, your brains and mine can take that figure, multiply it over and over and over and over, and even if you haven't got a streak of humanism in you or the tiniest bit of compassion for a human being, you can realize coldly and rationally that there is no way for a society operating like this to continue into the future. There is no way for us to have prisons from coast to coast in America for the ejectees of our broken-down agricultural economic system.

Ernest Manley

4.

VIOLENCE, WAR AND ORDER

By Ernest Manley

The other night, Ernest Manley said, at a rendezvous at The James Pub in Boulder; "Howard, I know that you know all of these various, disconnected facts I have said to you, but I do not think as I listen to you that you have ever bothered to put them all together. You seem to maintain your calm by successfully compartmentalizing what it is you know and thus you do not have to put it together and come to the inevitable conclusion." The following is a statement of essentially what he said to me.

This essay will be of interest only to persons who accept the truth of two statements: first; there is no possibility of preventing a conventional war from escalating to the inclusion of every other weapon available to the combatants; second, there is no possibility of the survival of human society following the unlimited exchange of thermonuclear weapons.

Violence

In the formation and evolution of Earth, all processes, organic and inorganic, always have involved and always will involve violence

---

Editor's Note:

Ernest Manley was an imaginary figure created by Higman in order for him to hold discourses. Ernest Manley, an alter ego, received his education in various settings and related them to others when Higman chose to display his friend rather than himself.

or the threat of violence. At the creation, the Big Bang was violence. Organic evolution involves continuous violence which is politely called the food chain, and each form of life represents a reorganization of simpler forms of life which provide the food for higher forms of life. Biological life is one continuous, never-ending slaughter and dinner, whether it is of simple vegetables or complex proteins in the form of cattle.

Violence, or the threat of violence, is involved in child rearing, in disorderly confrontations we speak of as fist fights, or in the more orderly form of confrontation we speak of as duels. Violence or the threat of violence is involved in the maintenance of order. In its highest form, we call the maintenance of order police action. Violence is a necessary but insufficient characteristic of war.

Order

Approximately 10,000 years ago, probably somewhere between the Tigris and Euphrates Rivers, after several million years of human existence, the human race invented law and civilization. Law differs from regulation in primitive societies, which were regulated by folkways and mores or customs, by virtue of man's consciousness of his use of reason in stating what the law shall be. Law renders the consequences of conduct predictable, thus enabling persons or societies to hold individuals responsible for their conduct, and while law inhibits or restricts the liberty of an individual on the one hand, it enhances freedom for an individual by the application of this restriction on the conduct of others. Although law prevents me from using violence against my neighbors in pursuing my goals, I gain more than I lose by the application of that restriction to their use of violence against me. Therefore, I freely accept the idea of individual freedom under the law. Order is the direct result of law, whether that law is established by an authoritarian dictatorship or through the process of democratic negotiation and the coercion of consensus.

Whether the order that is established is just or unjust depends entirely upon the perception of the population at a specific time. When in the course of events a population feels that order is unjust, that population may resort to violence or the threat of violence in order to change the rules. But whatever the rules are at any given time, just or unjust, they nevertheless produce order. In the long run, the efficacy of order is attested to by the continuous growth of the longevity and thus the numbers of the human population inhabiting the crust of the Earth.

Police action is order whether it is the resulting clean-up of a child's room in response to the parent's injunction; "Police your room before you leave the house," or whether it is the restraint of a citizen by local authorities in acts of traffic, property and financial management or interpersonal relations. Police action is maintenance of order even though it is the sending of the Marines into South America by Teddy Roosevelt in behalf of the order that benefits the United Fruit Company, or the use of the American military by Franklin Roosevelt to put down a sit-down strike in San Pedro, California, during World War II. What makes the action police action rather than war is the use of the threat of force by an overwhelming power against deviant, doomed and comparatively weak others.

War

The word war refers not to the use of that word in expressions such as *The War on Poverty* (which would better be called a political struggle), the *War Between the Sexes*, or labor-management warfare. We are referring to war as the event we would all recognize as going on during the Peloponnesian Wars, as that going on during the religious wars in the 14th century, as the wars between Napoleon and Wellington, the wars between the British and the Dutch called the Boer War, the war between the Allies and the Germans in 1914, the war between Abraham Lincoln and Jefferson Davis in the 1860's, or the war between the Allied and the Axis Powers in 1938.

War has been defined very carefully in the most monumental and extensive study of the institution of war, conducted under the scholarly supervision of an international lawyer, Quincy Wright. Entitled *A Study of War*, the research was carried out at the University of Chicago over a long period of time just prior to the outbreak of World War II. War is defined in Wright's study as the simultaneous conflict of popular feeling (people), national cultures (nations), armed forces (governments) and jural dogmas (states) so nearly equal as to lead to the extreme intensification of each conflict.

A word like *France* in the Wright study may be referring to the French people; the study of France at that level includes economics and psychology because people have material needs, engage in barter and exchange and consumption and production. Persons have feelings, goals, attitudes, prejudices, anger, loyalty and love which may be studied by psychology and medicine. *France* may, however, refer also to the nation, the nationality, which is an abstract as opposed to a concrete thing, and consists of the language, tradition, history, ideals and culture which we call French. Thus France is distinguished at the level of nationality from England. France may refer to the French government when we say, "France has decided to disassociate their country from NATO." Lastly, France may refer to the legal fiction called the French State which obtains as long as international law honors conventional beliefs and constructs of sovereignty relating to boundaries which are arbitrary. The people and the government are concrete, can in fact be photographed; the nationality, the nation and the State are abstractions. The nationality can be studied by the disciplines of anthropology and sociology; the government can be studied by the disciplines of the military arts, public administration and political science; the State can be studied by such abstract disciplines as law, theology and philosophy.

Returning to the definition of war, the conflict of popular feelings occurs at the level of persons. The conflict of national culture occurs at the level of the nation. The conflict of armed forces occurs at the level of government. The conflict of jural dogma occurs at the level of the State.

Hard as it may be to understand, the United States was not engaged in a war in Southeast Asia against North Vietnam. It was rather engaged in an attempt to establish order which, had it been successful, would have been called a police action from the point of view of the Americans. From the point of view of the North Vietnamese and the South Vietnamese, there was obviously a war. The four requisites for war obtained for the two sides of the Vietnamese. The conflicts between both sides were so nearly equal as to lead to the extreme intensification of each. The fact that the Americans were engaged in a futile attempt at police action and not in a war is evidenced by the fact that the North Vietnamese, the enemy, did not defeat the United States and thus occupy Washington and set up its government here, as was the case with the occupation of Hitler's Germany, Mussolini's Italy and Tojo's Japan at the end of World War II.

So, we see that war has several characteristics which can be deduced from Quincy Wright's study. When a war occurs, it is unclear at the beginning of the war which side will win. It was not known until Waterloo whether Napoleon would win or Wellington would win. It was not known at the outbreak of the American Civil War whether the North would prevail. It was not known at the beginning of World War I whether the Germans would win or the Allies would win. It was not known at the outbreak of World War II whether Hitler would succeed or whether Hitler would fall.

The second elementary and simple fact is that, in addition to the question of who will win, there will in fact be a victor. As long as it is possible through the use of violence in the form of war for someone to lose and someone to win, war is available as an instrument for the solution of political problems and has repeatedly changed the course of history. Had the South won instead of the North, our history would have been different. Had Hitler won, our history would have been different. Had Napoleon won, our history would have been different.

Because of the first of the two assumptions made at the outset, there is no way to prevent the use of conventional weapons in war from escalating to the use of nuclear weapons. No antagonist would impose upon himself a limitation on the use of whatever violence is available in the face of certain defeat. A person armed with a baseball bat and a gun, who is engaged in a fight with another person whom he sees is going to win by crushing his skull with a crowbar would not say, "I could save myself if I would shoot that person, but I will not use the gun." We have no examples anywhere in which persons have limited the use of violence available to them in the face of their defeat. When any combatant realizes that he has lost and cannot win, but can take his opponent down with him, he will do so. "If I cannot win, you will not either." When Hitler committed suicide, he would certainly have taken us with him if he had had that capability. One's final act is to go for broke. The limitation on the use of violence in a police action where one decides to withdraw does not constitute an example of war because there is no defeat in the sense of the defeat of Hitler, the defeat of Jefferson Davis or the defeat of Tojo.

For the first time in the history of the cosmos, the technological revolution in weapons commonly referred to as nuclear weapons, has rendered war as an institution for the determination of political controversies absolutely obsolete. We will slowly become conscious of the fact that there cannot be a World War III. There can be violence, thermonuclear violence, ending in the termination of civilization, but it would not fit the definition of war, for it would not adjudicate the conflict between alternative ideas about social organization.

The problem is that officials of democratic governments cannot appear to know more than the persons who vote them into office. The fundamental problem, therefore, is not leadership in the sense of Congressmen, Senators and Presidents, but rather the leadership of the business, academic, journalistic and religious establishments to whom the population turns for information in the expression of human values. We cannot look to democratically elected officials either to state the problem correctly or to propose its solution. Democratically elected officials are inherently limited in their rhetoric by the notions in the minds of their constituents surviving from the world of the past.

It is interesting at this time to notice that few persons see the fallacy of the language of the East-West conflict. They speak of defense; they have even renamed our military establishment the Department of Defense. Throughout the long history where war was used successfully to adjudicate political differences, at no time did leaders speak of themselves as engaging in defense. Napoleon did not speak of defense when he invaded Warsaw or Moscow. He said that he was there in the name of the establishment of order. He perceived of that act as police action, not as war; he called it order. Our military establishment throughout time has been referred to as the Department of War, the Department of the Navy, not the Department of Defense. National defense is not in the language of Woodrow Wilson. Rather his idea was to make the world safe for democracy which means order. Abraham Lincoln did not go to war to defend the North, but to *Preserve the Union*. The idea of defense is a fallacy. It is only thirty years old in a million years of human experience and ten thousand years of human civilization.

The policy of defense through deterrence was invented by the Americans with the formation of the North Atlantic Treaty Organization at the end of World War II when the only power that came out of that war materially stronger than before it went into it was the United States of America. Thirty years ago, when the Americans created the nuclear-military establishment, it was a monopoly, not a superiority. The rationale was our fear of the vast body of successful Soviet troops which Hitler had been unable to defeat. It is very plausible from the Soviet point of view to see the growth of the Soviet nuclear capacity as merely an attempt to remove their vulnerability to the American monopoly on nuclear weapons. It is not that the Americans have lost their capability to destroy the world; it is simply that the Russians now have that same capability themselves. In 1946, it could be argued, the balance of power in the world of the 1920's and the early 1930's was destroyed by the uncertainty of the direction and the magnitude of the power of the democracies of Britain, France and the United States.

The balance of power formula contains four elements: One, the number of states in the system; two, their relative parity; three, the degree of separation by the physical barriers between them; and four, the certainty of their direction and their magnitude.

After World War II, the only variables available to statesmen to use to enhance the balance of power was the fourth element, the certainty of the direction and magnitude of American power. Dean Acheson began this strategy with the North Atlantic Treaty Organization and John Foster Dulles carried it on with brinkmanship and pactomania. So, the material nature of the world has rendered the John Foster Dulles mentality useless at best and mortally dangerous at worst.

The problem of civil rights and human rights pales into nonexistence when faced before the problem of creating world-wide disarmament with the right to the use of violence and the threat of violence held only by international and world-wide institutions authorized to engage in police actions.

Although violence and the threat of violence exercised by the British Navy were involved in the 19th century *Pax Brittanica*, the actual successful balance of the British Century was primarily the result of their educational, professional, industrial and economic institutions. It was not primarily the result of the predominance of their military establishment. The struggle between the different ideologies of the different cultures of the world will continue. If they are indeed resolved on a higher dialectic, they will be resolved by the same processes that have resolved the differences between Georgia, Virginia, Massachusetts and California since 1865 on the continent of North America, which was in material terms, given the technology of 1870, a vastly larger place than is the whole Earth in 1980, given contemporary technology.

That being the case, the two strongest superpowers, the NATO Pact nations and the Warsaw Pact nations, are actually allies on the Earth whether they know it or not. They cannot win, one over the other, through the use of war.

The Real Problem in the World

The fundamental conflict on the crust of the Earth today is not an East-West conflict. It is not a conflict between atheistic Communism and theistic Christianity, Buddhism, Judaism or Islam. The basic potential conflict, the real conflict, is between North-South, rather than East-West.

For a long time, the industrialized nations have accelerated their greedy consumption of consumer goods by means of a very unequal distribution of goods, deference and security in return for labor and in return for the use of the material resources of the Earth's crust. This pattern of distribution, like any other pattern of unequal distribution, lasts as long as, for one reason or another, the individual human consciousness of those who benefit most and those who are most deprived do not see or feel injustice.

The course of history is the course of the continuous growth of the claim that every individual human being is the measure of all value and has, as such, civil rights and human rights. Human rights include not only freedom from torture and exclusion, but also the right to have a fair share of the bounty of the Earth. The rights of the middle class of American toilers were well-stated by the formation of the Lady Garment Workers in New York. The labor movement in America will obviously be replicated in the rest of the world as the past isolation in the absence of communication characteristic of geographical distances are destroyed by electronic communications and the inexpensive cassette recorder. To save itself, the affluent North must find ways—faster rather than slower—to deal with the problem of hunger. The problem of unrest and disorder in Latin America and the Caribbean is not primarily the result of the obvious exploitation of unrest by the rulers of the Soviet Empire, but rather derives from the objective awareness of the people of those areas of the unfair share that they receive in their exchange behavior.

Worldwide electronic communication rapidly destabilizes patterns of unequal distribution of goods and toil and security and creates the conditions for the rapid rise of terrorists to positions with access to the instruments of blackmail. Terrorists-turned-leaders of groups of informed or semi-informed persons are a clear and present danger to the survival of the human race.

Conclusion

Quincy Wright's *A Study of War* reveals: "The great society can be integrated only by the acceptance of common ideals, myths and symbols. These symbols must represent the world-society as a whole. But conception is an analytical and comparative process that balks at uniqueness. Persons or groups of persons attempting to achieve practical ideas have usually proceeded by analyzing persons into those favorable and those unfavorable to the achievement. The latter tend to become symbolized as the opponent, enemy or devil to be struggled against. An enemy or antithesis thus appears to develop from the very nature of an idea amidst imperfect conditions. Such an opposition has usually been an essential factor in integrating those holding the ideal into a society, but at the same time has made that community less universal." These words, published in 1942, were acted out by Dean Acheson and John Foster Dulles in 1948 and in 1952, and tragically resurrected again by the Weinberger-Haig-Reagan administration.

To finish by again quoting Wright's *A Study of War*: "To avoid this paradox, if peace is to be achieved, the ideal should be conceived not as a grouping of favorable persons from which the unfavorable should be expelled, but as a reorganization of all persons in groups. Unfavorable persons should not be treated as evil, but as a consequence of the inadequate organization of all. Thus, a community of nations must be built by a continuous development of the principles, institutions and law of the world as a whole, not by an organization of the angels with the hope of ignoring, excluding, converting or destroying the devils."

The elected leaders of the Western democracies cannot conduct affairs in a manner that will avoid worldwide genocide any more than Neville Chamberlain, Edouard Deladier and Franklin Roosevelt could spare the world the catastrophe of 1938.

Only an independent, informed and fearless intelligentsia, medical, industrial, religious and media establishment can raise the level of public consciousness to understand Quincy Wright's words.

TUESDAY, April 5, 1994

- 2:00 p.m. (continued)-

SERIES XVII:	*Politics in the U.S.A.*
Memorial 157	**FAILURE OF NEO-LIBERAL ECONOMICS**
Chairman:	Cal Jillson
Speakers:	Blase A. Bonpane - Molly Ivins
	Ralph Keyes - Martin Walker

SERIES XVIII:	*Families*
Memorial 235	**IS CHILDHOOD EXTINCT?**
Chairman:	Mary Wolff
Speakers:	Myrdene Anderson - Helen Mary Caldicott
	James C. Howell - Robert E. McClendon

SERIES XIX:	*Places*
Memorial East Ballroom	**JAPAN**
Chairman:	William Wei
Speakers:	Mizuho Fukuda - Simon Hoggart
	Anne Parker Luzzatto
	Karl Spence Richardson

- 4:00 p.m. -

SERIES XX:	*Analyzing a Film*
Macky Auditorium	**INTERRUPTUS I: LA DOLCE VITA**
Speaker:	Roger Ebert

SERIES XXI:	*Peace Keeping or Peace Making in the United Nations*
Memorial West Ballroom	**HAS NATO OUTLIVED ITS USEFULNESS?**
Chairman:	Mike Routsala
Speakers:	Leslie C. Green
	Jean-Jacques de Mesterton Radinsky
	James P. Murphy - Valentin Peschanski

12

Program page from last conference chaired by Howard Higman

5.

THE CONFERENCE ON WORLD AFFAIRS

When I came to Boulder in 1946 I made friends with George Zinke, a labor person who had also just joined the University staff and who had been with the National Labor Relations Board. We read in the press that a friend of ours from the war, Michael Ross, was going to make a speech in Estes Park in the middle of the summer, so we drove to Estes Park to hear him. We got there, but he had dropped out. We were furious. We would not have come, but we were there, so we decided to stay and listen to what was going on.

We heard a man named Louis Dolivet speak, a tall handsome Frenchman. A French communist more or less, he was editor of the *United Nations World* magazine. He made this fantastic speech about the new world which would appear after World War II, predicting the demise of old-style wars, Churchill, the Russian empire, and saying how the World Organization would take over. We were just transported with excitement. We asked him if he would come down to Boulder the next day and speak on the campus. He said he would if we would come and get him. We dashed home, got on the phone, and were very proud of ourselves to round up, by telephone overnight, a huge audience. I think we had over two hundred people who filled the Old Main Chapel. Dolivet stood there and mesmerized that audience, and then we went out and talked for about two hours. A professor of economics, James Dugan, said, "Howard, we ought to have him come back here when school is in session in the winter.

That fall, Bob Stearns, President of CU, installed a new Professor of Political Science in the Social Science Department, to the horror and anger of the faculty, who had not had a search committee, not made the nomination, not made the recommendation, not voted. He was installed from the top down. His name was Henry Ehrman. He had been thought, by the Hitler government, to be a German communist. He was incarcerated in a concentration camp, but bribed his way out, I believe, through the corrupt SS, using money from his family. He was allowed to escape to France. There he proceeded to screen the tourists who were coming to France from Germany, weeding out the ones who were actually Nazi Gestapo agents, sent as refugees to infiltrate and weaken the country for the coming push of the Germans into France. Others were honest refugees like Ehrman himself.

When the Germans captured France, he was on the list of the 10 most wanted ex-Germans , but he escaped to Free France. He was prominent enough to get special treatment and be shipped out of France and saved, hoping probably to go to Australia, New Zealand, South Africa, anywhere. He ended up in New York City and thought he was very lucky. The only job he could get at first was to translate for an encyclopedia, but he finally found himself as an instructor of prisoners of war in a camp in Virginia.

Someone called Stearns and said, "Ehrman is a brilliant man. You should hire him." So Ehrmann was installed as a professor of Political Science on the Boulder campus. The department members shunned him because of the way he got there. His office was next to mine and I saw him sitting in there alone. I marched in, sat down, chatted with him. He had a roll-top desk. I found him quite interesting and invited him over to my house for dinner. He had two sons, Michael and Paul, the age of my daughters, Anne and Alice. He lived in Chautauqua in one of those wooden houses. He could ski down to school. We became friends.

He wanted to have a model UN Assembly, with people representing the fifty countries of the United Nations and acting the roles of the countries in discussions of various issues. I thought that was an interesting idea and said that I would help him. So that became the idea of the United Nations Conference. I also wanted to get Louis Dolivet to speak on campus, so I wrote him and he wrote back saying that his contract required that he be paid $500. That was a lot of money in 1948. Ehrman and I made an alliance, and since Bob Stearns had brought him here, he had an "in" with the president. We went over to Stearns and proposed that we have a United Nations Conference on World Affairs and told him it would cost $500. There was a vote, we won and the University gave us the money. So, with great joy, we dreamed up this conference with one speaker from out-of-town, Louis Dolivet. The others were CU professors and people in Denver. We invited Dolivet, he agreed, and we organized a model assembly with CU students which Henry ran.

The Conference was to be in April, a week after spring vacation. On the first day of spring vacation we got a telegram from Louis Dolivet: "Must cancel plans to come to Boulder. Have been ordered to Italy to cover the March elections of the Italian government, which we in the press expect to produce a democratically-elected communist government in Italy." We were furious, upset, desperate. We could not tell the truth about why we had wanted to have the Conference in the first place; that we wanted Louis Dolivet. If I could have given the money back, I would have. We had to have the conference. All we wanted was Louis Dolivet. I decided to call Alger Hiss.

Hiss had been on the campus one month before, propagandizing for passage of a program to allow the Secretary of State to give money to European countries. The Secretary of State's name was George Marshall, and the program was to be called The Marshall Plan. Hiss had given a speech about it at Harvard, saying we had to rebuild the nations destroyed by World War II. We were the only country that came out of the war richer than when we went in. Everybody else was devastated - England, France, Germany, Japan, Italy, Russia. I had had lunch with Hiss, so I called him to see if he could come. He said no, he could not, but he gave me five names. I don't remember them, except the fifth was James P. Warburg of whom I had never heard. I called him on the phone and he said he could not come. I cried. He said, well, he could come for three days and he had a friend who could fill out the other two. So with heavy heart I accepted.

I went to Denver to get Warburg and bring him back to Boulder Sunday night for a reception in the basement of George Zinke's home, which was put on by junior and senior Social Science majors. They served Kool-Aid and cookies. I tried to take him out to dinner because he said he was hungry. At that time there were no restaurants in Boulder except on Pearl Street, where the steaks were about half an inch thick with a huge bone in the middle, and they were almost cooked in water. He slept in a room with my daughter Alice, who was two or three years old.

Warburg spoke at Macky Auditorium, and it was jammed. The reason it was jammed was that we had a tradition in those days of having students assemble in Macky once a month on a Monday at eleven for convocation; a practice that grew out of the ancient tradition of having chapel. American universities were originally Christian seminaries. So Macky was filled automatically.

Warburg walked in and gave a speech titled, "Halt, About Face," which absolutely electrified the campus. He suddenly became everybody's favorite candidate for president. Truman was running and Dewey was running on the Republican ticket. Henry Wallace was running, and was perceived by his enemies to be a communist. A Dixiecrat was running, someone from the South who was anti-Black. But the young socialists on campus preferred Warburg. The young communists were for Warburg. The Democrats were for Warburg. All week he marched around, like a guru, speaking to crowds of students. It was a sensational week, and, naively we thought that was the end of the Conference. We had gotten through it, and I was madly in love with Warburg.

The next fall, President Stearns called a meeting of the freshman, as they did in those days in Macky. In outlining the year on campus, he said that in the spring there was the annual United Nations Conference on World Affairs. I dashed on stage and said, "Bob, what are you talking about?" He said that we would not have a good thing like that not be repeated. So the second Conference on World Affairs occurred that spring. Warburg returned.

After the Conference, Warburg flew me and my wife Marion back to his house in New York. He owned half of Queens. His father was cum laude of the international Wall Street bankers. Later we were at his place in Connecticut, which was adjoined on one side by the house of Marshall Field. When Jimmy went into the house for a martini, Marshall Field turned to me and said, "You know, of course, you saved his life." I said, "What!" He said, "You did not know that? When he went to Boulder last spring he was contemplating suicide. He came back an absolutely rejuvenated man."

Warburg devoted the rest of his life to the elimination of war. That was during the breakdown of the American-Russian alliance. All kinds of big shots jumped out of windows and killed themselves, including our ambassador to England, because they believed the coalition between Russia and the U.S. was the reason Hitler had been defeated. When the alliance fell apart, the world just collapsed. Churchill was thrown out of office by the British; Truman started the all-out, anti-Russian attitude; the Russians rejected international control of atomic energy as an American plot. A wide degree of dissolution and disillusionment followed, and Warburg was among those who felt that everything had become hopeless.

So he came here that second year and stood in Macky and said: "One year ago there was a voice crying from the West over the telephone. Wistfully, I responded, and came to Boulder." We thought of the conference as Warburg week, because he came back the third and fourth years.

What we started in the first conference is still there. Nothing has been dropped. The things that have been added have to do with life style, culture, art, music. For example, one year we had a series called *Dyads* - relationships between two people, marriage, living together, non-sex. The Conference started with an emphasis on politics and economy, the United Nations, atomic energy. Now, the last three years have featured arms control and the threat of nuclear war, themes which had disappeared for about fifteen years. There was a period in the 1960s when the Conference featured Blacks, Chicanos and Indians, then their themes disappeared. You would see very few women on the list of speakers in the first fifteen years. I remember we used to have a panel called, *Wives,* and it was all right to have a wife speak on the program.

The big fight over content occurred during the Eisenhower years when the Conference took on the task of attacking Joseph McCarthy. One year we scheduled a series of panels on McCarthyism. The dean called me in after having seen the draft of the program and said, "I think you should avoid the word, 'McCarthyism.' After all, he is a United States Senator, and you can't attack a United States Senator." I said, "Of course you can. McCarthyism is evil, wicked and undesirable; our purpose is to attack it."

We had five days of panels attacking McCarthy. We had a McCarthy idolizer on campus, a student by the name of David Dwight Murphy, who was head of the McCarthy supporters. He attacked the panel on the grounds that it was unfair because there was no one in favor of McCarthy. One of the panelists, Sidney Harris of Chicago, agreed with him and said, "You may have my place tomorrow to defend McCarthy." The word came to me on Friday and I denounced Harris vigorously. I said, "We are not having anyone defend McCarthy. There is no such position. There is no such side as that."

I went to the meeting and it was jammed. Everyone had heard about it. Murphy demanded half the time. There were five speakers and he wanted half the time. I had to concede because one of the five speakers had given him his time. But I said he could have Sidney Harris' time and nobody else's, one-fifth of the time. He said he would not speak under the circumstances. I said, "Wonderful," loudly into the microphone, and the audience just roared with amusement. He backed off and took his one-fifth of the time.

I had a raging argument the rest of the semester with many of the faculty over my position that there were not two sides to the question, and there was no side that should be allowed to speak in favor of McCarthyism. I felt that Americans have this silly fairness doctrine that there are two sides to every question and both sides should get equal time. I was furious with them because, you see, in Los Angeles, thirty-five idiot Veterans of Foreign Wars claimed that UNESCO in the schools was communistic; the press and everybody said there were two sides to every question. So they gave half the time to the idiots and half to 3,000 scholarly school teachers and college graduates. People in Los Angeles were confronted with a lie for half the time and the truth for half the time. They voted for the lie and removed UNESCO from the Los Angeles schools.

This scheme of making any statement you want and getting half the time is perfectly ridiculous. I suppose that if some student decided to come forward and say that Howard Higman is a female, there would be two sides to the question. However, I was furious. McCarthyism was growing more powerful because there were two sides to every question.

The next year we got a new president, Ward Darley, who came up from the Medical School in Denver to replace Stearns. I later learned that the family of the pro-McCarthy student, Murphy, knew the Darley family in Denver. Around January I got a call from the President's office saying, "Professor Higman, Doctor Darley would like to talk to you a few minutes. Would you be free?" I said, "Certainly. What is it about?" "World Affairs Conference." So I went over and it soon became clear that Murphy had gone to Darley to complain about the unfairness of the conference on the McCarthy issue the previous spring. Dr. Darley said, "I do like controversy, and it is perfectly fair of you to put on all the controversy you want to in your World Affairs Conference, but you have to have both sides of the question." I said, "What do you mean, both sides?" "I have been told by Mr. Murphy that you excluded pro- McCarthy speakers from your Conference last year." I said, "Of course. There is no such side as that." "Well, I don't know about that," Darley replied. I said, "There is not a single person sponsoring this Conference who does not know that McCarthy is a fraud." He was not a bit persuaded. I said I didn't care, I was not trying to stamp out McCarthyism, but let people who feel that there is something to it organize their own conference, have a huge rally in Macky, if they want, but not us. We won't give our stage and our energy to perpetuating that which we know to be false. "Sir, our subject was not whether McCarthyism was good or bad, but how best to get rid of it, whether by ridicule, by law, by education or some alternative strategy. We only had differences of opinion about how to get rid of it, not about whether it was good or bad. If you were having a panel on tuberculosis cure and you had persons who believed in psycho-therapy, some who believed in sunshine and rest, some in exercise, some in diet, some in surgery, do you also have to have a Christian Scientist who believes in doing nothing?"

He said, "Oh, I see exactly what you mean. You can't have a rational discussion without an agreed-to-agenda from which to proceed. You put that down in writing, and I'll take it to the Regents."

So I wrote that out, stating that the purpose of the Conference was not to arrive at conclusions or engage in social actions but to present issues of the day within a dialectical frame of reference by persons who show mutual respect for the scholarly method of argument and evidence; to enable students to sharpen their awareness so they could better follow the news as it unfolded following the conference and arrive at their own opinions.

I don't think it would be possible to start a World Affairs Conference now. A scholar from Berkeley tried and failed. Washington University in St. Louis tried and failed. The German government had me give lectures to ten universities - Berlin, Frankfurt, Heidelberg - to help them start world affairs conferences. None of them did, and there is no way they could do it. We have had many universities visit our conference, send delegates to observe it to see if they can start one. But they never could.

The reason no one can create a conference on world affairs like this is because it created itself, and that's because it's reversed. Its organization is the reverse of everything else we humans do. Which is to say, normally, we decide to teach a course called philosophy, and normally such a course results in a collection of people who hold each other in fairly high regard. In other words they have some degree of integrity to their discipline, even though some breeches do occur between branches of the discipline. Generally speaking a discipline is organized around persons that admire each other somewhat.

This is not the case with the Conference on World Affairs, at all. The whole axiom of its success is based on the fact that it has no integrity, and therefore persons come who hold not only other persons who come in low regard, but even contempt. But because it's so big and so diffuse, they don't play in each other's playpens, even though sometimes they're on panels where they do express less than admiration for the other panelists. Some years ago the CIA created riots on the campus when they came to recruit. One of the older members of the Conference Committee who had been associated with the *Atlantic Monthly* said we shouldn't have another member of the committee who happened to have been in the CIA. We were able to diffuse that conflict. Not only did we have CIA people here, but we had no problem with students rioting when the CIA put on a five day panel on the role of intelligence in world affairs.

The Conference is a melange of people who are not like each other nor do they use the same language, and so they come back. Normally they go to meetings where they're social psychologists or child psychologists or geologists or oil diggers. Their conventions are all over America. I remember walking into the Palmer House seeing them and saying, "I bet they're social psychologists." Sure enough it was the American Social Psychological Association meeting. That's kind of scary but true.

This is not the case with the World Affairs Conference. The participants are overwhelmingly recruited by previous participants. The person who will take a week off, buy an airline ticket, come to Boulder for a week, work morning, noon, and night for five days, for no money and no particular prestige, will only come because people who have been here before say, "Gee, if you get invited to that, go." However, if I call up some stranger and say, "Buy yourself a ticket, come to Boulder, spend the week, we pay you nothing," that person will not come. Last year's Conference created this year's conference; so it goes back to James Warburg.

Its uniqueness is known around the world in Europe, Asia, Africa. You run into people everywhere who have been to the Conference. I ran into somebody in Cairo who said that he had been at the

Conference in Boulder. People from sixty or seventy countries have been here, and they remember it as a unique week. In 1967 I got a call from a professor of English named Robert Lee, and he asked, "Whom do you know in Poland?" I had just come back from Moscow and had stopped in Warsaw, but I realized that I didn't know anyone in Poland. "Why?" "I am an applicant for a Fulbright there. I want to go to Krakow." Then I remembered that we had the Ambassador from Poland to the United Nations come to the conference ten years earlier. His name was Borevsky.

I called Warsaw, not knowing if he was still in the government. I called the Foreign Office and asked for Borevsky. They said he could return my call on Monday. On Monday the phone rang and it was Borevsky. "Borevsky here." I said, "You probably don't remember me," and told him who I was. "Ah, that wonderful university in the center of the United States. I do remember. Highlight of my whole experience in America." He asked what he could do. I told him that I just wanted information. Could he help find out where Professor Robert Lee stood on the application for the Fulbright. He asked how the name was spelled, and so forth, and then said, "Yes, he has the Fulbright." I asked how he knew. "I am in charge."

There are thousands of things that have happened like that during the years of the conference. About the second year that Darley was president we had the first two communists who had come to America on a tour at the Conference. Darley called up and offered to have them stay in the President's house on campus. "It might save some trouble," he said.

Eleanor Roosevelt came the next year. About nine, on Monday morning, Darley called up and said, "Howard, I don't want to interfere, but I wanted to know if you'd object if we got a sound truck?" What? "Well, you probably don't know that Macky Auditorium is already full and it's two-and-a-half hours before Mrs. Roosevelt is going to speak. I thought it's a nice sunny day; we could put a sound truck outside so the students who can't get in can sit on the grass and listen to her."

I remember that when she spoke she was most excited about a brand new country that had been formed. She was radiantly eulogizing this wonderful new country that had been created out of Palestine. The main thrust was her tremendous shock at the introduction of the 20th century in the Middle East - television sets in the middle of tents, blankets and camels. It was the start of maybe four or five years when Israel was the conference main topic. I was actually crushed by the audience attending the Israel and Arab conflict talk. The two sides turned into a verbal war on our campus. Very polarized. One Israeli ambassador to the United Nations, who was on his way to the UN for the first time, was instructed to go to the World Affairs Conference first. He made his maiden speech in America at Macky; then went on to present his credentials to the Secretary General of the United Nations. We had enormous police security. Many from the Jewish community of Denver showed up for that one speech.

Henry Kissinger was here before he went into government. I had a fun thing with him. I called him in February 1960, at Harvard, and because it was a person-to-person call, I overheard the secretary tell the operator, "Professor Kissinger is unavailable." I said to the operator that he must be somewhere. Couldn't I get a number where I can reach him? The secretary heard the operator's annoyance and said, "Tell him I said he is unavailable for two weeks." I said, "I don't see why people would be unavailable for two weeks. I just talked to Bucky Fuller on the coast of Maine yesterday." She said, "I said he is unavailable for two weeks." So I lost. I don't like to lose. I was furious and I dialed the White House. A voice said, "White House." Kennedy had been President for about one month. I put four and four together; Harvard, Kennedy, Kissinger. I said, 'Henry Kissinger, please." A voice answered, "Allo." "Hi, Henry, this is Howard Higman." "Oh, how ever did you find me?" It was obvious to me that if his whereabouts were such a secret, the only place he could be was the White House. If his secretary wanted to conceal him she should have said that he was on a camel in the Sahara. Then I would have quit. But the secretary announced that he was somewhere. Because he was on a secret mission, no one at the White House switchboard knew he was there, so my call was put through.

Arthur Miller attended. At that time he had the top play on Broadway, *Death of a Salesman.* Fortunately, he was on the cover of *Atlantic Monthly* when we announced that he was going to be the keynote speaker. The students cared more about the keynote speech in those days. They don't care that much now. People asked, "Who the hell is Arthur Miller?" They had heard of *Death of a Salesman,* but didn't know who wrote it. No one knew playwrights except people who majored in English.

He was going with a woman named Norma Jean Baker. Later I learned it was her real name and Marilyn Monroe was her stage name.

Logistics

There are several hundred persons in Boulder, Colorado, who house, feed and entertain the participants. They can take it off their income tax if they want to, and many do. But if the participants had been paid by the University, as is usually done, and housed there at regular rates, and if they had their airfare paid, the cost would have been enormous - over a million dollars for a hundred participants a year. The people who house the participants and the participants become friends. They develop relationships. They begin to perceive of themselves as part of *our* annual conference on world affairs.

We have diffused the rules and regulations in such a manner that they're so badly organized that each person who is involved thinks that she or he is the center of the show. It's not controlled by any central creature.

The conference can easily be dissolved by anything causing it to revert to a system where it's financed by someone who's in charge, who has control over who become members of the Committee. The Committee has never turned down a person who wanted to serve on the Committee. Our whole aim is to play it like you do with oysters-with impediments. When an impediment comes into an oyster, instead of dying, the oyster surrounds it, and something insulates it from the rest of the oyster. In fact, we gather these up and call them pearls. That's been our technique. The *our* is a group; it's not a person. It's a very strong group that knows what it is doing.

The Conference is a fragile thing, almost organic. It takes lots of hard work to pull it off. It is self-propagating. People who come are excited about it. People who have been here want to return. It's always new and exciting.

First Skid Row Poverty Training Program, October 1964

6.

AN ACCIDENTAL SOLDIER IN THE WAR ON POVERTY

After Lyndon Johnson took over the presidency following John Kennedy's assassination in 1963, he authorized the establishment of the Youth Opportunity Center program to retrain old-line U.S. Labor Department bureaucrats to head up community centers for delinquent youth. Well, I was recruited to direct this War on Poverty Program by sheer accident.

It's possible, sometimes, when you receive a telephone call to know that it's going to take a very long time. You get a signal right off the bat. I was in a terrible rush one Saturday morning when the phone rang. It was Lois Badger, whom I knew as part of the Democratic party. She worked for the University of Colorado Extention Center in Denver. She said, "Howard, this is Lois."

I said, "Yes, Lois."

She said, "I've got to talk to you."

"Lois, I'm dashing out the door."

"Well it's very important, Howard, and I really do have to talk to you."

Editor's Note:

For this chapter, we have included three pieces that represent Higman's intense involvement in poverty issues.

"Lois, dear, I'll do anything you want, but I cannot talk to you now."

"Well, I'll pick you up Tuesday morning at eight o'clock."

I said, "I'll be ready."

On Tuesday morning I went out to her car. We were on the road to Denver when I asked, "Where are we going?"

She said, "We're going to Denver."

"Why?"

"We're going to the Federal building to meet Carl Haberl at the Office of the Department of Labor in Denver."

We reached the Federal Building and went up the elevator into his office. He took a long time starting out by saying that Lyndon Johnson wanted to develop Youth Opportunity Centers and to convert part of the Employment Service to work with dropouts, delinquents and the guys in pool halls.

Haberl said that staff from four Western states had volunteered to come to Denver for a three-week training program. Well, I knew nothing about any of that and told them so.

Lois responded, "Oh, you can do anything; you head the World Affairs Conference." I said I'd give it a try.

On the way back to my campus office, I remembered that I had two former students who might bail me out. Tom Adams had run the school for delinquent boys in Golden, Colorado, and Bob Hunter was working for the Mental Health Council of the Western Interstate Commission on Higher Education. I called and they came to my house. As we sat down, I told them about my plight. Tom said, "If we do it, we will not bring them to the campus and give them classes in minority group relations and counseling. Dropouts should be a part of our facility. They will freeze the minute they walk into a building that resembles a school." He further suggested that we go into the slums of Denver on Skid Row and rent a storefront for the class room. "When they walk in there, they'd be right at home," he continued. "We'll hire them at ten dollars an hour to discuss their life. They will be called *Basic Instructors* ."

I asked Adams to prepare a proposal to take to Washington.

Later we met and agreed upon a plan. Adams further suggested that when the trainees come to Denver, they are to bring only clothes they would wear to clean out a garage; blue jeans and shirts, no ties or suits.

We put the program together, moved into Denver's Oxford Hotel on Skid Row, located by the railroad tracks, rented a storefront to serve as a classroom, and brought the trainees into a world essentially foreign to them. We learned together. Here's the proposal that launched us.

1.
Proposal

I. Presenting the Problem

The most wasted resource of our nation today is the several million out of school, out of work youth who stand poorly prepared to enter adulthood as productive citizens but who will enter it nonetheless. Their horizons are meager. Their hopes have frequently turned into quiet retreat or noisy opposition. Our urban centers have little to celebrate and much to fear when they assess the future for many of their young citizens.

Disadvantaged youth today stand out in greater clarity than ever before in our nation's history. Their revolt is disorderly, frustrated, unclear and complex. We know a good deal about them. The major challenge today is to translate this knowledge into effective solutions to their individual plights and that of the community they inhabit. One solution is to assist these youth to prepare themselves for and to find employment and other meaningful roles which may give them a stake in an otherwise illusive society. This employment may be a first step toward other entries into useful social interactions.

This is a proposal to train personnel in state agencies of the Employment Security Program for managerial and staff positions in the Youth Opportunity Program. It is designed to break with traditional approaches for intensive education to specialized groups. It will break with tradition in the following ways:

The Setting : The trainees will learn in a natural setting of poverty and disadvantage. They will study in a rented building on Larimer Street in Denver (the main artery of Denver's Skid Row). This natural laboratory will provide them with a constant look at despair, conflict, disadvantage and poverty.

Involvement with the Setting: They will be housed in a respectable hotel, The Oxford Hotel, near Larimer Street and adjacent to Union Railway Station at the end of Seventeenth Street. They will have meals in the area and be encouraged to interact with those who live there. A surprisingly large number are youth who drift toward this section of Denver.

Getting in Touch with the Disadvantaged:: The trainees will be encouraged to seek out part-time employment in the area. The experience of searching for employment will give them new insights into the resistances, the barriers and plight of the disadvantaged.

Innovations in Teaching:: Perhaps one of the most creative plans in this program is to have part of the teaching done by the families and individuals who will be recruited from minority groups and poverty stricken Anglo families. Some will be youth of the area and circumstances. Through interviews, group interaction and sensitivity experiences of a new nature, the trainees will interact on a first-hand basis with those who know and feel most about being poor, why they are poor and why their prospects are dim. Avenues are open to this staff for the recruitment of these basic instructors. Skilled interviewers are available to direct these sessions.

II. *Suggested Curriculum for the Three week Intensive Course*

In keeping with the requests of Employment Security, the curriculum will devote two-thirds of its content to understanding the socially deprived young people from the economically disadvantaged sections of the city. The remaining one-third will be devoted to administrative principles of management for the Youth Opportunity Program.

1. *The Behavioral Science Sequence::* Content will be derived from the social and psychological sciences, principally: sociology, anthropology and social psychology. These lecture-seminars will present this content with a radical departure from the traditional pedagogical form. It will provide the conceptual and theoretical content on poverty and social and personal deviance. For instance; seminar sessions may be entitled:

A. Sociology of the Culture of Poverty

Dimensions of poverty and disadvantage

Deprivation - being alone and unable

The time continuum: unfulfilled futures

Image decay - mirrors in the back rooms

Opposition ideals (the quest for affluence)

Replacements for boredom

Masculinity - man as no-man

Urban living - people on people

Coming from a long line of dependent people

Joblessness

People on the move - rootlessness

B. Social and Personal Deviance - Causation

Individuals at odds

Social and cultural dimensions

Alternatives - social and psychological cloture to some
forms of deviance

C. Being Different

How it feels?

Stigmas

Near-groups in opposition (breaking the law)

Being different and deviant - the double trap

D. Foci—Ways Out

Breaking out of the system

Potentials for life - how to find them

Restoration of decent self image

Motivations for the disenchanted

Using the skills of inclusion

Expanding opportunities - within and without

E. The Administrative Principles for the management of the
Youth Opportunity Program.

The content will focus on human management techniques specifically designed for staff members who will be
dealing with disadvantaged youth. It will emphasize sensitivity experiences, group dynamics and role playing. The content

will not be presented in lecture sessions but rather through trainee-instructor interaction.

Formation of a social system - then running it

Administration and Policy

Decision-making

Leadership and charisma

The University of Colorado will grant graduate and undergraduate academic credit in the Department of Sociology to those students who desire to complete certain requirements in the pursuit of graduate work.

It is important to emphasize that the content of the training institute will be appropriate to several occupational positions in the Youth Opportunity Program, namely: program managers, assistant managers and supervisors.

Planning Symposium: We will hold a Planning-Evaluation Symposium at the Brown Place Hotel on Friday, 15 September, 1964, with at least twenty community activists representing various sections of the community.

This group will be given an opportunity to assess the proposed curriculum for the Institute.

< >

Our proposal was accepted. Tom Adams took it personally to Daniel Patrick Moynahan, the director of the U.S. Employment Security Office. I had called my friend, Adam Yarmolinsky, who worked in the White House, to ask him to arrange for Tom to deliver it. When Moynahan saw this three page proposal, he said, "We have over 280 of these and this one is the only one that's different. Most are fifty pages or more. I have no evidence that this one won't work, so I'll sign it." He did at once. His aide said to Tom, "You didn't include sensitivity training. That's required." Tom replied, "We don't accept the value of that process. How about adding a line, "We will sensitize the trainees to the conditions of poverty and delinquency rather then to themselves." This compromise was accepted on the spot.

In October, 1964 we began our experiment. Later we learned the serendipity of this event. In the summer of 1963, the Labor Department funded a program entitled CAUSE (Counselor Aides, University Summer Experience). One such program was conducted at the University of Denver. When a director in the Office of Economic Opportunity was asked to contact "that University out in Denver", the secretary inadvertently placed the call to the University of Colorado in Denver and reached Lois Badger. Therein lies the root of the accident.

I learned an awful lot in those four weeks in a program that cost less than $12,000. We wrote a book, *The Colorado Story*, to describe our adventure. It became the Bible of the War on Poverty and was reprinted time and again.

I don't know if it was Macaulay or Carlisle, but one was categorically wrong; there aren't great men, there are great groups, by accident or otherwise. From that Skid Row beginning, we trained over two thousand five hundred VISTA, WIN Program staff, lawyers, physicians, criminal justice workers, migrant Labor Council staff, counselors in Black Colleges and a host of other poverty warriors.

In the preface to the *Colorado Story*, I outlined our approach and thanked the University of Colorado.

Preface

When the President declared his war on poverty, there was less than an enthusiastic response from the universities and institutions of opinion in the United States.

Some persons have taken the view that the poor are always with us. Older persons remember in the height of the Depression when various programs attacking the problem of poverty were begun. Whether or not these programs might have resulted in the development of a professionalized body of technology, knowledge and a trained staff able to work in this field will not be known. Almost at the time of their inception, these programs were interrupted by the appearance of World War II,

Among other things, the war produced an apparent economic prosperity which gave rise to the slogan, *the economy of abundance*, and an unprecedented preoccupation with world affairs. Perhaps the most obvious change in the role of the university in postwar America has been in education and research concerning the problems of international relations, disarmament, foreign aid, war and peace.

In the 1930's, among the very few courses in Sociology at the University of Colorado, there were Criminology, Penology, Dependency and the Sociology of Poverty. An examination of the University curricula in the 1950's and 1960's reveals a disappearance of the subject of poverty as a social problem.

During the period of national hysteria in the early 1950's, sometimes referred to as the McCarthy era, educational institutions were under heavy attack. Many scholars took protection from public criticism by describing their efforts in neutral terms and writing politically sterile studies defended invariably by numbers replicable in computing machines.

The problem of poverty in the world threatened by international disorder and thermo-nuclear devastation was almost invisible. Magnificent new buildings were erected in areas of urban deterioration as evidence of America's material progress, but one block away from New York's Lincoln Center, Americans are still living in conditions at the subsistence level. Progress has been made. In the 1930's one third of the nation was ill-housed, ill-clothed and ill-fed. We know now that one-fifth of the nation remains in this condition.

The meagerness of the designs for urban renewal to date have taught us that merely tearing down the slums where these people live and replacing them with high rise apartment houses and insurance buildings may affect the landscape but not the problem, for the inhabitants merely must move elsewhere. Studies on the potential impact of automation on industries and the rapidly rising awareness of the disappearance of the need for the unskilled worker project for us the fact that left alone these problems will, far from solving themselves, become increasingly intolerable.

Although the university has characterized itself as primarily devoted to pure research and abstract thought, inspection will reveal that throughout history the university has been at the cutting edge of society itself.

It is in this spirit that the University of Colorado responded to the request of the United States Department of Labor to provide a training course for the use by counselors that would enable them to deal more effectively with the young men and women who seem to be outside the main current of American life. We chose to begin to tackle this problem by taking ourselves and our students to the problem itself.

The thought of returning the university to the scene of the human drama at the level of primary group relations suggests the possibility of the re-moralization of the students and the faculty relationship to the community.

2.
The Hampering Services Or The Hindering Professions
An Institute Summary

I have rediscovered Durkheim at this Institute. I discovered that people said one thing when they stood at this podium, something else when they were in work groups of twenty and still other things when they were in elevators. I am making this summary mostly from the elevator opinions, and I am going to call my remarks "The Hampering Services or the Hindering Professions."

Editor's Note:

Professor Higman delivered this summary at the Regional Institute on Undergraduate Social Service Education, May 3-5, 1965. in Salt Lake City, Utah

Our Classless Society

First I want to put what I have to say in the context of the Poverty Program. One of the reasons why we have the problems which the Property Program was set up to solve is the myth that we have a classless society. It may be easier for us to see our own roles in the Hampering Services if we look at some other group, such as the public schools, which offer a pretty good parallel. The fact that we have the so-called dropouts, with 28 percent of our youth not served by our schools, is partly due to our idea of the classless society. We strongly affirm the idea that we are all members of the middle class. If people aren't middle class, we'd like them just to vanish. That's called dropping out.

In England they wouldn't have this problem at all. They'd say, "He's the son of a workingman, isn't he? We'll put him in school for clock repair at age eleven and a half," This boy doesn't drop out of the British school system because he doesn't really get in.

In the 1930's we did recognize that a third of the nation was ill-housed, ill-clothed, ill-fed, in spite of Horatio Alger. We started serious work on this problem during the New Deal, but it was terminated to a large degree by the coming of World War II and the problems of world affairs. World affairs have occupied us ever since 1940, right up to the present time. We saw the magnificence of the Marshall Plan and Point IV. Americans began to learn to tithe for the underprivileged in Europe and Asia and Africa. Only now are we getting over the notion that ours is a completely affluent society and coming to realize that, if we can take care of people who live in mud huts in the Middle East, we might consider doing the same thing for people who live in adobe huts in Southern Colorado.

We have the problem now of trying to find out whether our established institutions—the schools, social welfare, and so on—will be able to adjust to this new urgency. I don't think we can answer that question for certain. We have in the discipline of sociology the idea of systemic inertia, which is that organizations come to have a stable equilibrium. You might phrase it this way: the social worker needs the caseload as much as the caseload needs the social worker.

A concrete example would be the way we have come to deal with unwed mothers. In Denmark, as you know, if an unmarried girl has a child, she is put into a dormitory where she lives with her child. While it is cared for in the nursery, she is encouraged to take courses in filing or typing or the practice of law—whatever is appropriate for her—and to earn as much as she can. If she can find the father of her child and get him to come live with her, that's fine. Three times out of four, there is established a home with a male, a female and a child. In any case, as soon as the girl's earnings are high enough, she voluntarily moves from dependence to independence. For the last 30 years we have, of course, done the opposite. If we find a man with a girl at two o'clock in the morning, that's a crime. We build systems that preserve themselves, so we could hardly condone the crime by providing help for the lawbreaker.

Professions and Professionals

To return to the central concern of this Institute, I have been hearing a good deal about the behavioral sciences. So I should like to say a word about how they are dealing with today's world. Consider sociology, which is my own field, so that I should attack it first. You could take all the articles published in the *American Journal* of *Sociology* for the last 20 years and dump them into an incinerator and it wouldn't make a great deal of difference. We have evolved finer and finer ways of doing more and more research about less and less with greater and greater mathematical skill and beauty, while we have dealt with nothing in Asia, Africa, India or Skid Row. In fact, to concern ourselves with anything as elementary as reality is unprofessional, and it's not the source of advancement. Not only is it important not to do research that is relevant to the world in which we live, but it's getting to be important to be sure that you do not teach the students about reality. First you give up the undergraduate students; and then you give up the graduate students; and I suppose the next stage is that you give up the administration.

I have been disturbed in the last few days at hearing about social work as a profession. I think the time has come for social workers to realize that people who *are* professionals don't talk about it.

You don't go to a medical meeting and hear someone getting up and talking about "medicine as a profession." You don't even hear the oldest profession talking about it as a profession; what you hear them talking about is what they do.

Also, I don't like the phrase, "social work as an institution," because I am afraid it is one. As I sometimes tell students about social climbers; everyone social climbs, but the only ones about whom we use this phrase are those whose social climbing shows.

At the Institute you have been talking about whether you should allow some material to go into the undergraduate school. Much of this, it seems to me, should be in high school. I think that you should also not worry about the Liberal Arts. What the students are complaining about is that we are old and they are young and we don't know that things have changed. The transmission of information has changed since we went to school, so that they know things as juniors in high school that we didn't find out until after we were married.

Education for Work

This Institute appears to recognize that there is in the field of social services and social welfare a need for persons *to work*. I think a majority of those present are willing for the students to be equipped with the skills—I don't mean having a peek at people who have the skills, but really acquiring skills— to do these jobs when they graduate with a BA degree.

I think there are two sets of persons who oppose this idea for opposite reasons. One of them is the behavioral scientist to whom I alluded before, who feels that the transmission of useful information to students is not professional. He uses the phrase the liberal arts, or he uses the phrase interesting research. So he would not want to participate in his department in anything as practical as equipping a student with the skill to recognize a case record, or to interview, or to add and subtract numbers in an agency. I think these persons are obsolete, but they are still with us.

Secondly, we have opposition from graduate social work professionals, and I think their problem is that they are the newest profession. Here the theory is that we mustn't allow the undergraduate to learn this sort of thing because that's what we teach in the graduate schools. I would give a warning here. If you insist on refusing to tell undergraduates what it is you have in the graduate school that they can't learn until they get there, you generate the suspicion that maybe the reason you won't tell them is that there isn't anything. The idea that a graduate physics department for example, would resent the thought of an undergraduate knowing physics is, of course, ridiculous. The more the student knows when he gets to you, the freer you are to send him further along his way. That means you have to stop having a standardized course for every student to learn 16 things, and stop being traumatic if he already knows some of them when he lands on your doorstep. The thing to do is to test him when he arrives. What he knows, skip, and get him on further.

The idea of democracy is one of our major values, but we are not going to be able to live in the world of the future with a homogenized population. There are going to be things other than graduate students, and you might as well evolve a name for them. There are going to be technicians, and they are going to have BA degrees. There are going to be technicians in physics, in chemistry. In medicine, doctors aren't going to insist that everyone have an MD degree. They've already invented a huge staff to serve them, medical technologists and a whole range of nurses who are doing things in public health and visiting nursing that doctors would have reserved to themselves 30 years ago. So in your profession a large base of the pyramid will not threaten the top if the top is willing to go up and make room for something below to help.

Support for Creative Programs

I sense a concern as to whether permission will be given for the programs which you would pursue. But I have found that the greatest support and tolerance for creative work in the struggle against poverty, illiteracy, dependency and deviance is to be obtained from the conservatives, from business. It is important not to institutionalize the ghosts of past conflicts and not to take a stance of caution and tentativeness and fear, and then wonder why you are not applauded uproariously by the world community.

When I was called on to present a rather novel program to a fairly conservative board of business men, I was told that I should expect rejection, because I was going to propose doing something on Skid Row in Denver. When I was through, I was astounded and I had a real learning experience because of the applause. These men came up and said, "Thank God, your university's finally getting its hands dirty!"

Cracks in the Opportunity Structure

There's a widespread notion that there are problems of motivation underlying poverty. There aren't. These people have the same motives you and I do—not that theirs are so high but that ours aren't either—education, medicine, a roof, food, clothes, children and so on. You will be told by some people that a kid will say: "I don't want a regular job. It'll interfere with my huntin' and fishin'."

The fact is that the problem is in the opportunity and not in psychological motivation. I have been able to convey this to Rotary Clubs with three statements, and I'm going to do the same for you. I want you to consider for a moment what you think my chances are of becoming the President of the United States. (I know what you're thinking.) I have a second thing to tell you. I'm willing. Now here's the point. Figure out what will happen to me in Boulder if I go around asking, "How do I get to be President?" "Will you help me get to be President?" I know better than to say things like that.

Well, in one part of the Poverty Program we interviewed boys whose fathers had never had a job since they came on the scene. Nor did they have an uncle who had a job, nor a male cousin who had a job. They didn't know personally a single man who had a job except for three hours unloading a box car. Usually one's life is somewhat like his father's, though a little bit different. These kids, who live in the world with us, do not live in the world of Louisa May Alcott at all. The question is a matter of urgency, and sometimes I think that we don't know that we're not here.

Today's Students: The Moral Generation

You're talking about education; you're talking about youth. What I would say is that we have a new generation of college students, and I would characterize this group by their shift in interest from politics to morals. The riot at Berkeley is conspicuous, but the underlying dynamic is universal. Not only in the United States but in South America and everywhere else, this behavior is moral. In politics, when we were New Dealers, we learned to expect to make a compromise, in which you got the biggest piece of pie you could get because you knew you couldn't get the whole pie. We had words like the New Deal and the Fair Deal. These were different ways to deal the cards from the same deck. The reason the Poverty Program is so significant is that we have a new deck, a totally new one, and it is the deck of economic abundance through technological advance. The world has enough food right now to feed a population of 30 billion people. The problems are not technological. They are social—who owns the land and who'll let who do what with what. The problems are human problems. The Malthusians couldn't have been more wrong. We have demonstrated it dramatically in the fact that the food—not the population—has increased geometrically in the United States. We have a surplus.

A Presbyterian minister told the Secretary of State in 1953 that he thought it would be a good thing if young Americans were in blue jeans and pup tents abroad instead of marching in Georgia in khaki. The Secretary of State said, "You don't understand the moral character of American youth. They do not have the stuff to do that sort of thing."

Later a candidate for the presidency made an off-hand remark about a Peace Corps. He had absolutely nothing in mind when he made the remark, and so he was embarrassed by the deluge of mail that came in to Washington. A great emergency arose, called we-have-to-create-something-to-deal-with-this. The subsequent outpouring of American youth into the Peace Corps is manifestation of a gigantic revolution. I call it moral. This generation is not going to look up to us if we don't, as someone said earlier, "get swinging."

The things that the Berkeley students would not do was to settle for anything else than all. My generation might have said, "Well, we got twenty-eight off, even though four might be expelled." The group of college students that we have to deal with today will not be satisfied with anything else than immediate, real and meaningful experiences. They will not only be willing to have, but they will demand, the kind of field experiences in their education that connect them rapidly with the real world out there of which they are very much aware. The pace of modern communications has broken down the ivory tower.

3.
Role (Code) Of The Volunteer
No role is universally applicable.

Whether poverty is defined as a measurable absence of monetary income, or in more general terms, as powerlessness — which might even include the powerlessness of an abandoned juvenile whose parents are well heeled, or the abandonment of an older person by both the community and younger children — the ACTION volunteer generally is perceived of as a person who has decided to be helpful.

Some volunteers are recruited precisely because they bring to the task either certain skills or knowledge of certain social structures which can be immediately applied. Other volunteers because of their commitment and their energy primarily bring power to the powerless.

Editor's Note:

This code was developed by Professor Higman and his training staff during the first year of the volunteer's training. From observations and experiences, the code emerged and was taught to subsequent groups. It remains applicable to most training today, either for volunteers or professionals who plan to work in human service programs. Most of this training was conducted for ACTION, the federal agency responsible for the administration of voluntary programs.

Non Zero Sum Game

Violence and the threat of violence obviously have played a significant role in social change. Whether or not it is necessary, and whether or not it is desirable is a frequently debated, highly controversial issue. However one comes down on that question, it will nevertheless be agreed that ACTION, RSVP, Foster Grandparents, the Peace Corps and VISTA are not amenable to the search for social change through violence, or what we commonly call confrontation. Congress did not establish VISTA for its own deselection. The overall philosophy of ACTION is the Non Zero Sum Game in which the processes of change are not based upon a division of the world into the angels, on the one hand, and the devils, on the other — with the hope of destroying, converting or exterminating the devils — but rather it is based upon a definition of the problem as an inadequate organization of all, with the hope of change, where although they may not all be equal winners, losers are minimized and the number of winners is maximized. The philosophy of the Non-Zero-Sum-Game can be communicated to volunteers in the process of training, giving them perspective to search for ways to solve problems without having to identify devils to be exterminated. It can be shown that whether or not one agrees with the wisdom of this policy from an ethical point of view, it certainly can be shown to be efficient and efficacious, because the alternative of identifying devils is to create a situation in which social change is likely not to occur. The primary result of this action has been seen to be a substitution of self-righteousness and a desire on the part of the volunteer who fails to effect any benefit for a client to rationalize his act as merely an identification of the cause of evil. We, today, call it having a level playing field.

Synergy

In the words of R. Buckminster Fuller, "A special and knowledgeable combination of cripples can be invincible." This is the principle commonly called synergy, whereby it can be shown that the whole can be vastly greater than the sum of its parts.

The Altruist

The volunteer can be trained to see that the proper posture is that of the altruist. The alternative is the posture of the egotist, who is concerned with what is in it for *me*, which at its worst merely leads to an acting out of neuroses against real and imaginary enemies. The altruistic volunteer is able to see that the only measurement of success he can employ is that there has indeed been a benefit accrued not to the organization nor to himself but to those whom he claims to be helping.

Selflessness may or may not be more than the appearance of selflessness. The appearance of selflessness can be taught easily. By means of role models it is possible to show the volunteer how his posture and his language can be used in such a fashion as to avoid celebrating his own self-interest.

The Tolerable Volunteer

The volunteer is not an employee. An employee trades his freedom and services, more or less willingly, for monetary remuneration, the use of which is his own business. The volunteer, on the other hand, has agreed, because of his acceptance of certain shared values, to devote his time and energy to a common cause. Although he is not as subservient to the boss as is the employee, he is not, on the other hand, a free agent to do or not to do whatever he pleases. He sensitively must learn the constraints upon his freedoms and choices imposed upon him by his decision to participate in the ACTION organization. If he is unwilling to accept these constraints, he is not entitled to the spiritual and material benefits that accrue to the volunteer.

There are two sorts of volunteers which ACTION does not need and cannot afford to perpetuate.

Righteousness

The first of these is self-deselecting, but is nevertheless wasteful of the energy and resources of the agency, if only by virtue of lost time and the costs that come with bad publicity. He is the volunteer who finds it useful to himself to march about identifying and celebrating what he perceives to be the individual person he chose to hold responsible for the plight of others which he denounces in high dudgeon. We refer to him as the person who seeks to substitute righteousness for commitment, skill and effort.

The Parasite

The second undesirable volunteer is the parasite who has found that with a guitar and a sleeping bag he can hide behind a furnace somewhere for twelve months — probably from the members of his nuclear family. He primarily wastes a slot that someone else would have used to advantage. He also creates a vast body of hostility to the agency in the public and in the members of Congress, who begin to see the agency as simply a haven for cultural dropouts.

Three Useful Volunteers

Warm Bodies

We might classify three useful categories of volunteers under the headings of warm bodies, boat rockers and ship sinkers. The problems of poverty are so vulgar that it is very difficult for a person to be useless. The word *warm body* was coined to refer to the volunteer who is exceedingly low profile and not very impressive to either the other volunteers or to the supervisors or the public generally, who has very little remarkable to say but goes about in a dependable, methodical way providing some useful services to some actual persons. For example, an individual who is free to act as an instrument of communication for persons who are housebound amongst the older, rural population through a steady and repetitious visiting program carrying things back and forth. Or an older person may be happy telling fairy tales to forty abandoned children of seasonally unemployed workers of the state of Florida, without whom they would have a life totally devoid of fairy tales. These are children for whom there is no meaning to the phrases, "Once upon a time. . ." and "Let's pretend. . ." Childhood fantasy is a prerequisite to successful adult accommodation.

Boat Rockers

Volunteers who rock the boat are sometimes visible and in some senses may even be thought to be irritating or nuisances, but on the overview are regarded retrospectively as having been creative and useful in their volunteer settings, with some measurable change to which they can point. They might be most persons' ideal volunteer.

Ship Sinkers

Finally, we have those who sink the ship. Even those volunteers must be loved. It may be that those who sink the ship are simply boat rockers with bad luck. Somehow their strategy went amiss and their project was closed down. We must avoid defining them as devils.

< >

Power

Poverty may be defined as powerlessness. Powerlessness may be observed in the individual who is in a situation in which there is nothing that he or she can do that will make any difference whatsoever as to what will happen to him or her tomorrow. Power derives from many sources: power derives from rectitude, beauty, enlightenment, physical strength, access to resources both material and non-material, energy and information. Although training can increase the access of the volunteers to each of these sources of power, probably no one source to power is greater than that of increasing information.

Teaching the volunteer how to increase information through listening, through attending meetings, and through arriving early at meetings and staying late, and cultivating conversational acquaintanceships with a large number of persons in the community, is exceedingly efficient. It can be seen that most of the specifics that have arisen in our learning how to train the effective volunteer could be subsumed in the acquisition of useful power, or the sensible avoidance of its loss.

Opportunity Structure

A fundamental concept in the agency of ACTION is the preference for the concept of opportunity structure over the alternative construct, lack of motivation. Inspection will reveal that the idea of motivation which is a psychologistic concept tends to lead to inaction and acceptance of the status quo. Usually the word, motivation, occurs negatively, as in lack of motivation..., "you can't motivate her," "he wasn't motivated." Our perception is that it is overwhelmingly more useful to use the sociologistic concept of opportunity structure which asserts that individuals are essentially equal — equally human, generous and selfish — and that their differences in behavior to a large degree are due to differences in perceptions of their real or imaginary opportunities. This enables us to analyze the situation in which we find persons in terms of how persons perceive their opportunity and to make modifications in their perceptions of their opportunities. This, of course, very fruitfully involves creating situations in which opportunities exist that had not existed before.

In this sense it can be shown that there is not any characterlogical difference between the so-called successful business executive and the grade-school dropout other than that which each is making a maximum use of his perceived opportunities — the difference being not in the person but in the situation in which they found themselves.

The Need for Feedback

Americans even more than other people are possessed of a cultural characteristic called, *The How Am I Doing Syndrome* . Karen Horney refers to it as the neurotic need for affection. Margaret Mead refers to this phenomenon as the success ethic with the response of others as the measure. David Reisman refers to the same phenomena as other direction. The ordinary volunteer comes to ACTION with these needs. The very unstructured nature to which ACTION seeks to address itself precludes the easy satisfaction of these needs on the part of the volunteer.

The Tolerance for Ambiguity

It can be shown that it is possible through training to enable the volunteer to suspend these needs for the duration of his service in ACTION and to acquire what has come to be called, tolerance for ambiguity. For the first time in his experience he finds that not only is it tolerable but that it can also be somewhat exciting and enjoyable to live in an existential situation in which tomorrow consists largely of surprises.

He can be taught survival skills showing that it is not necessary to fall all apart when supposed or expected plans fail to materialize.

Crisis

The Chinese do not have in the Mandarin language a character for the word crisis. They express this idea with two characters: danger — opportunity. The volunteer can be taught that those events which occur which an ordinary person defines as bad news can by careful examination normally turn into the volunteer's advantage. He can learn to analyze events which have been termed disadvantageous or unfortunate to determine what within them reveals to him a lever or a handle to pursue his goal.

Accidents

Less dramatic, but similar, is the need to train the volunteer to see that he can normally make use of accidents. He should give serious thought in his own life to the frequency of the occurrence of a crucial or important beneficial event which has in fact been the result, not of planning, but of efficient use of accidents.

Morale

He can be taught that high morale is something that can be asserted in place of good luck, good fortune and success experiences, which if you have there is no need for high morale. When you have resources, cooperation, a plan that works, the support of others, praise and recognition and the certain knowledge that you are doing what is right, you do not need morale. It is normal for the volunteer to be lacking any or all of these things. If he can persist under such circumstances, he has high morale. The morale of a group is directly related to the impenetrability of its barriers. For this reason it is necessary that ACTION training equip the volunteer with the awareness of his specialness.

Presentation of Self

Probably no single concept is more important for the preservation of the power of the agency itself and of the individual volunteer and, thus, the program, than what has come to be called, *POS*, or Presentation of Self. Through role playing the volunteer can be shown how his dress, speech, body language, reference to extraneous and irrelevant controversial opinions and display of self-serving needs limit his access to information, creditability, authority and informal influence.

The volunteer can be trained to see that it is actually a flattering fact that those who are seeking to work with hard-core problems create some degree of anxiety on the part of the community at large, and how it is that the community will therefore perceive the most negative possible construction in any interpretation of the meaning of the volunteers' acts. This is the reason that matters of speech and personal behavior become very much more important in the acquisition of power for the volunteer than they would be for other persons. Dress should invariably be chosen so as not to detract from the information that the volunteer is likely to get, since access to persons and information will turn out to be a principal tool or resource that the volunteer has to solve his problems. If a person can be referred to by dress, the volunteer is dressed wrongly: "The girl in the army jacket…" "The boy with the light bulb in his belt buckle…"

Wallpaper

Acquisition of information normally accrues to the volunteer who appears to be *wallpaper* and whose physical presence does not cause the community to freeze up.

Strangers

Some volunteers are not strangers to their community. They have certain advantages, but they also have certain disadvantages. It is well known that the stranger, as opposed to the familiar, has access to the ideas and persons and freedom for the making of suggestions and intrusion into the system that a non-stranger is denied. However, the stranger is also exceedingly visible, and it does not matter whether we are speaking of a neighborhood in the lower east side of Manhattan or a small town in rural Missouri, the neighborhood is still a face-to-face neighborhood of familiar faces, and the stranger is dangerous and suspected. He must learn quickly that he is exceedingly visible, that there is for him no place in which to hide.

The Invisible Medallion

Under the heading, The Invisible Medallion, the volunteer can be taught that it is vastly more exciting and demonstrably more efficient not to wear his heart on his sleeve. In the late Sixties volunteers who were willing to shave their beards and cut their hair found that they increased their authority and their power ten-fold with numbers of persons for whom at that time beards and long hair were certain signs of rejection. In any community there will be some symbolic piece of speech or garb which in that community can be identified as a signal to exclude the volunteer from full inclusion in the communications network.

Oh!

Without lying the volunteer who hears a startling or unacceptable bigoted expression of opinion from persons with whom he chooses to deal will not accelerate a quarrel or argument, but respond with the simple statement, "Oh!"

Van Ek's Law

Van Ek's Law was discovered as the proposition that the normal statement that one is innocent until proved guilty is essentially reversed in working in the ACTION program because of apprehension and the frequently unorthodox or unusual habitats of the ACTION volunteer — and here we are referring to working with ex-criminals, dropouts and perceived failures of various sorts, so the volunteer starts off as suspect. A brawl in a local tavern amongst a group of United States Marines, off-duty, is simply perceived by the community as "the high spirits of our fighting young men." On the contrary, the VISTA volunteer with a GSA car picked up in a "bust" is perceived exactly the reverse — as simply documentation for selfish decadence.

There is no one resource that the volunteer has to bring to maximize his power that is more significant to him than the preservation of his good name. Learning how to preserve his reputation points out that he cannot excuse himself by having reasons for having been defamed. We have ample proof that the volunteer who is seen emerging from the volunteer's house of the opposite sex early in the morning where the volunteer has taken shelter will get the credit for having violated the ten commandments whether or not this is indeed true. The statement has been made that in a rural setting if a male volunteer is going to tutor the town whore he should do so on the Civil War monument at high noon.

Van Ek's Law simply states that the proposition in response to a charge against a volunteer that it is false and not true will be of no help whatsoever. Volunteers who are reputed to be involved with drugs on an Indian reservation have lost their usefulness on the Indian reservation. The fact that the charge was false is unfortunate, but it is the charge and not the use of the drugs that has ruined the usefulness of the volunteer. When a thing private becomes public, it can never be private again.

Cooperation

Particularly with the young idealistic American it is both possible and necessary through training to show him that cooperation does indeed involve corruption. The person possessed of one hundred percent integrity can never cooperate, for the right person is never nominated, the right program is never decided upon, nor the right strategy the one that is going to be followed. Cooperation involves compromise. It is characterized by the contemporary American middle class. *Doing Your Own Thing* is not an adequate solution for the people who are living in poverty today. They are, indeed, doing their own thing, and it is not desirable.

Resistance by Partial Incorporation

Thus, the volunteer must understand that certain things are to be resisted by means of partial incorporation, or "There are many ways to skin a cat."

Plan B

There should always be a Plan B so that if Plan A is inoperative the result is not failure and stagnation but simply wiring around for an alternative.

IYDKDBIYDYACBIYDYCNH

If you don't know, don't, because if you don't you always can, but if you do you cannot not have. A vast body of volunteer failures in the first years of VISTA can be attributed to the fact that the volunteers were not trained to withhold action until they were relatively certain to whom it was they were speaking, or with whom they were dealing. Repeatedly came the phrase, "But, I didn't realize that they were..." "But I didn't know that..." The statement, "He who hesitates is lost," in ACTION should be replaced by the phrase, "He who hesitates survives."

Facts and Problems

He must learn the difference between a fact and a problem. The basic difference is that problems have solutions and facts do not.

Facts and Cues

You must not confuse facts with cues. The concept of a cue is a bit of information that while it may lead to a discovery of a fact, it should not be acted upon until further research and corroboration takes place. Half of those things which are cues today disappear and would have been misleading, and had they been acted upon, all would have been lost.

Lies

A volunteer must never lie. As soon as his credibility is gone, he is completely useless. Lying may be defined in the training as rendering another person's future unpredictable. When the lie is discovered, the price is extracted. The volunteer is emasculated. The program is damaged.

The matter of complete and full disclosure, however, is not consonant with an effective volunteer either. The line is difficult. It is not only unnecessary, but also unwise, to engage in over-communication, creating fear or hostility on the part of others or giving information that leads to the destruction of your program.

Fuzzing It

We have a concept that is difficult to define called *fuzzing it.* In the case of *fuzzing it,* although the volunteer does not make any statements that can be shown to be false, he does acquire the skill to cause the adversary person somehow to fail to comprehend or to lose interest in what it is that he would otherwise oppose. While we cannot get nearly everybody aboard to help us in the pursuit of ACTION goals, the next best thing is at least to neutralize the opposition, and give us the freedom to proceed. Fuzzing it is a code word and is a skill of those who do indeed survive.

Freezing It

There is the concept of *freezing it,* which means that positive benefits will accrue to a project whose staff acquires the discipline to refrain from participating in the survival of non-advantageous information, gossip and destructive speculation.

Freezing it is simply learning how to avoid in any way corroborating, supporting, enlarging or megaphoning on adverse information. This is a skill that can be acquired and again can contribute to the sum of the power and authority of any project.

Words Speak Louder Than Action

Training should equip the volunteer with the ability to realize that the statement, "Actions speak louder than words" is false. He will learn that words speak louder than actions, and essentially all of the hang-ups that arise will revolve around what somebody said. Therefore, what is said becomes exceedingly important to the volunteer. From the works of Wendell Johnson he can learn that he can acquire the skill of changing the levels of abstraction, wherein at higher levels of abstraction there may be cooperation and agreement, avoiding lower levels of abstraction where there would be dissonance, opposition and stalemate. This particularly can be a skill he can acquire in attempting to band slightly different groups of persons in a community to work together for a common purpose, before the town council, for example.

Translation

The concept of translation is a skill that can be taught which enables persons to phrase propositions in ways which at best meet with approval and at least minimize or lessen degrees of disapproval or anxiety. Concrete role playing games in these areas are excellent training exercises.

Secret Staff

The volunteer can be trained to acquire a secret staff. This will not only magnify his power and his project, but also enormously decrease his sense of loneliness and alienation. A secret staff is a phrase that applies merely to the fact that the volunteer has a consciously developed list written in a phone book of persons that he has found to call upon who will respond in a specific way for a specific purpose or use. The mere idea of doing this consciously, rather than in a haphazard sort of way as we all do in our daily lives, makes a significant difference both to the volunteer's morale and to his effectiveness in the scene.

God

The volunteer can be trained to know that every individual human being has a God or a value which to him needs no defense and is not something which is debatable. He can further learn that if he is to gain the cooperation of, or work with, an individual, it will be essential absolutely to honor and respect that individual's highest value and that he couch what it is he is doing at best in terms consonant with that person's definition of *good* but certainly couch it in terms that are not violative of that person's terms of *good*. It is particularly true when dealing with non-middle-class Americans whose vocabulary about their religious beliefs may be somewhat traditional when compared to that of the volunteer. He must understand with humility that all human beings, including himself, necessarily are possessed of vast bodies of superstitions without which action is unlikely.

The Second Law of the Volunteer

The volunteer can learn that the second most valuable Law of the Volunteer is to preserve his health and energy, for if he is not in a position to deliver even the minimal support of his own body, there is no possibility of his adding to the wealth of the powerless. To that end, he must learn to avoid exhaustion and realize that boredom is essentially a result of fear; that there are many things that he must not take personally.

The First Law of the Volunteer

The volunteer can learn that the first law of the volunteer is that he must preserve his good reputation, the loss of which makes him useless to everybody.

"Yanacuna," in the Quichua language of the old Inca's, means "a man who has his mind obscured with respect to the future." That was the word used—with exactly that meaning—to identify a savage. No other language in the world, whether modern or old, has managed to create such a perfect and eternally fitting definition of what truly savage is.

Our world today—and we all know it— is full of "Yanacuna's." We find some with degrees, and others full of honors. We find them giving advice and often, enjoying the highest positions as self-appointed saviours of humanity. We find them infiltrating everywhere and alienating whatever they come in contact with. They have no race, no color and no specified position within any ideological spectrum. They are everywhere. They are simply a disease; a frightening disease.

One of the few individuals I have known to deserve being called a MAN is Howard Higman. What could be more terrorizing to the modern "Yanacunas" than a man like Howard, being what he is, and doing the kinds of things he does?

Howard Higman is a combination of many virtues and many sins, which all put together, give us the true dimension of a friend and of a badly needed type of modern man. As a friend he has taught us how to enrich ourselves through challenging dialogue, and as a man, has shown us a method and a way of fighting the increasing menace of the modern "Yanacunas," by simply helping us discover how much of a "Yanacuna" still remains within each one of us.

—Manfred A Max-Neef
Pan American Union
Peru

7.

THE INFORMATION SOCIETY

Information may best be defined by what it is not. Information is in contrast to noise. Noise is meaningless perturbation in the sense environment. Information, on the other hand, is any perturbation in the sense environment which can be seen to have predictable recurring consequences.

The odor emanating from an empty can of sardines tossed into the trash is information. If there is a cat in the neighborhood, we can predict that the cat will overturn the trash can. The odor from the sardine can is a perturbation in the environment with a fairly predictable consequence. A streak of lightning in the air frequently will result in an individual's avoidance of standing free in an open field or close to a tall object. The sound of the rattler of a rattlesnake to some individuals is not noise but rather information, and will result in that individual's freezing in motion.

Dissemination of Information

The Post Office

The literature, both fact and fiction, of modern times, that is to say the last 400 years, was dominated by the post office. While the remnants of feudal aristocracy still received their messages in special

Editor's Note:

This piece is reprinted with the permission of the original publisher: Leonard Lewin, editor, Telecommunications: An Interdisciplinary Survey (Dedham:Artech House, 1979).

scrolls produced by ambassadors with couriers and attendants, the mass of humanity in the Western world was dominated by messages contained in *letters*. Not only did the arrival of letters and messages contained in the letters play a crucial role in fiction and non-fiction in modern times, but it is also significant that the Postmaster was the dominant figure in every small town or large city, who presided over the flow of the delivery of information from citizen to citizen or government to citizen or citizen to government and vied with the clergy, whose information was presumed to be associated with a supernatural network.

Electronic Communication

Electronic communication, which we know as the telegraph, the telephone, the radio, the television and the computer, has introduced a discontinuity in the course of human history of equal magnitude to the three previous revolutions: symbolic language a million years ago, writing ten thousand years ago, and printing 400 years ago.

The telegram, which was, of course, electronic communication transformed into a sort of letter, had the aura of special urgency because of the speed with which the message was transmitted, particularly over long distances. Thus, it was associated with serious matters such as death, induction into the army, casualties from warfare and birthdays. A serious exchange of thoughts in longhand by letter constituted a written record between two human beings bought at auction and reproduced in book form. There obviously is no counterpart in a collection of the exchange in telegrams; telegrams might be collected as a display of congratulations.

The distribution of information on a mass scale was primarily conducted by means of the printed word in newspaper, magazines and journals. Journals got their name from the thought that there was news each day, and thus the word *journal* derives from *day* as does journey, referring to how far one could travel on a horse in one day.

Small town editors complained that they did not indeed circulate the news; everyone in town knew it. Their problem was more that of archivist or recorder. When the editors *got the news wrong*, the townspeople descended upon them to correct them. It was not the information in the newspaper that was disseminated but rather the opinions and editorials espoused by the muckraker or the crusader that dominated the role of the newspaper. Information in the newspaper that was relevant was, or course, the advertisements, which were not dominated by persuasion but were announcements of what it was that was available, when, where and for how much. The fact is attested to by the relative energy spent in accuracy in newspaper advertisements in contrast with the energy spent for the accuracy in nonadvertising content.

Social Impact

Propaganda

We normally credit John Milton in his essay *Areopagitica* with the first clear expression of the ideas underlying the first amendment to the United States Constitution. This amendment, guaranteeing freedom of speech, is based on the notion that error should be free to be promulgated for the sophisticated reason that only with the promulgation of error, subsequently defeated in competition with truth, was truth itself to be defined. The idea of the difference between propaganda and facts became a major preoccupation with Western man during and after World War I. It was at this time that we began to get scholarly studies of the conscious management of the dissemination of information, or propaganda, as a major instrument of the struggle for the maintenance of power over the people. This occurred at the same time that telecommunication in the form of radio made its major debut.

While it could be argued that the promulgation of printed opinions in no way interfered with the opportunity of others to state their printed opinions, the use of limited and scarce airwaves presented a different problem. For this reason it was initially agreed that the society itself would control, by setting up rules, who would get to say what to whom on the airwaves.

Studies in the United States during the 1930s and 1940s showed repeatedly that persons believed that the news in the newspaper was highly likely to be incorrect, whereas the advertisements in the newspapers were highly likely to be correct. The reverse was true with radio broadcasts where it was believed that the news was highly likely to be correct, whereas the advertisements were highly likely to be incorrect. The reasons for this are fairly obvious in that the advertisements in the newspaper tended to refer to what was for sale, when, where and for how much, whereas radio advertisements contained persuasion and argument. The news on the radio, on the other hand, was restricted largely under the control of government to objectively verifiable shorthand assertions of events as they occurred.

With the frightening rise of totalitarian societies in Italy, Spain, Japan and Germany came the overtly conscious management of the dissemination of *information,* along with an enormous surge of interest in what we called *propaganda.* Some persons sought to define propaganda as a conscious distortion of information through the use of less than all the facts. Others defined propaganda as the use of information with an intention to influence the receiver of the information. Still others used the term propaganda to refer to the attempt to use information to create opinion.

Up to now telecommunications in the area of mass information has tended to be controlled almost entirely by the mass response. With the exception of the small effort of public broadcasting, television and radio are overwhelmingly restricted by the popularity of the offering as measured by scientific sampling.

Public Opinion

Prior to 1936, public opinion was a word invoked by persons with the hope of persuading other persons to join them. The truth of the claim was anybody's guess. The *Literary Digest* magazine claimed to know that public opinion insured an overwhelming defeat of Franklin Delano Roosevelt for his second term and the election of Alfred Landon to be President of the United States. We know in retrospect this disastrous prediction was based upon a simple error of what we would now call a stratified sample. The invention of the scientific public opinion poll, which we associate with Gallup, Roper and Harris, was probably as radical an invention, in terms of its social and political consequences, as the atomic bomb. The survival of political positions as well as their promulgators has become dependent upon how they are doing at the polls.

Electronic communications, in the form of a *face-to-face* fireside chat between President Franklin Delano Roosevelt and the masses of the American people, is given credit for his ability to father a major social revolution in the American lifestyle. However, the public relation firm of Whittaker and Baxter, in the managing the first election of Governor Earl Warren, and later of General Eisenhower and Richard Nixon in 1952, may be recorded by historians as conducting the first telecommunication presidential election. This marriage of scientific sampling, market research, telecommunications and computer projections has replaced the strong-willed, fortunate or brilliant business tycoons in the management of giant national and multi-national western corporations in the modern era. Names like Harriman, John Pew, J.P. Morgan, McCormick, John Deere and Henry Ford no longer explain the decisions of the corporate structure of the western economies.

The Telephone

Sixty years ago the cost of an individual personal telephone was approximately one third of a working man's monthly income. This, of course, accounts for the fact that he did not have a telephone, and also for the fiasco of the *Literary Digest's* selection of samples of voters from telephone books fifteen years later. Today the telephone company is the largest single corporate employer in the United States.

Let us notice the contrast between life with the telephone and life with the letter. One does not visit by letter, if letters are deep thoughts and feelings and can be published, read and reveal to us the inner person. The telephone *visit* is superficial, transitory and is characterized by such phrases as *touching base.* The telephone may be used as a thermometer to run a check or to determine the state of tension and well-being or the continuity of a previous relationship. The telephone is used by Americans as a thermometer, and conversely, as a device for sending out an alarm as well.

Secondly, the telephone compared with the letter is coercive. The voice seems to demand an immediate, clear-cut response. There is frequently a loss of reflection time on the part of the respondent on the telephone call. Whereas one may lay a letter down, read it over and over and reexamine it after his response to it; these options are not available to him in an exchange on the telephone. The bell of the telephone seems to act as a command. All of us have been infuriated by having service we were receiving in a department store interrupted by the ringing of a telephone as the person waiting on us stops to respond to the command, presumably coming from the other end of the telephone.

The telephone is active and, by comparison, the letter is passive. That the telephone as an instrument of invasion is attested to by the unlikely anomaly of the words, *the number is withheld at the request of the subscriber*, as well as the universal language of describing the desire for rest and rehabilitation as *getting away from the telephone.*

A unique advantage of the telephone call, contrasted to the letter, is the enormous potential for permitting the creative use of ambiguity. It would be exceedingly difficult to find letters in which the intent of the author is unclear. The message of the letter is clear, and the ambiguity can be preserved in face-to-face conversation. The telephone provides us with a superior mask for ambiguous exchange. This makes the telephone call a primary device for negotiation and adjudication for human differences. The phrase *May I say who is calling?* is primarily intended to facilitate the formation of strategies and the choice of tactics for what is expected to follow. The telephone call may be generative; that is, there is built into the telephone call rapid and extensive feedback which is slow or missing in the exchange of written letters, and as a result, the call itself may end up in conclusions that cannot be said to have been in the mind of either the initiator or the recipient of the telephone call.

The telephone call is a *dissolving message*. This characteristic of the telephone call is attested to be the alarm with which persons greeted the advent of the tape-recorded telephone call and the instance that the parties of the telephone call be informed that something was recording the call other than the human brain. We might well study the significant role of the dissolving message. The dissolving message is also attested to by the common practice of a subsequent letter saying, *this will confirm my telephone call,* or conversely the statement, *would you kindly put that in writing and slip it in the mail to me.* The phrase *I'll get back to you,* being an affirmation by denial, also attests to the general awareness of the ephemeral nature of the telephone communication. The phase, *I won't keep you,* means either *I got what I wanted* or *I guess I'm not going to get what I want.*

By the end of the nineteenth century, a change in society occurred from one largely constituted around nouns by which individuals were defined primarily by their Aristotelian essences, that is, individuals were perceived as subjects of sentences or as nouns. They had a clear-cut sense of identity, a high degree of continuity in space and time, and were characterized by such personalities as Abraham Lincoln, Henry Ford and J.P. Morgan. In the Aristotelian scheme, identities are defined as what the individuals *are*. However, with the appearance of the assembly line, the automobile and the telephone, the contemporary mobile society defines individuals as predicates, rather that subjects of sentences. They are what they are *doing*. In *The Lonely Crowd,* David Reisman discusses this shift as being analogous to a shift from *gyroscopes to radar.* We might add that the shift from the printed *passive* communications represented by the letter to the electronically transmitted spoken communication *active* represented by the telephone is a shift of the same order.

In a recent interview, Mr. William Baker, president of the Bell Laboratories, made these remarks which point up the magnitude of the role played by modern telephone networks:

> *It appears that the telephone is the principal organizing element in the ordering of an informational society. It appears that the switch telephone systems is as big an element as anything in reducing the entropy and bringing order in the broad philosophical sense... Since about 1945 the amount of information in the records doubles every seven years. It has been determined that a weekday copy of The New York Times has as much to read as the educated individual in the 16th century Europe absorbed in his lifetime. Now that imposes on society a huge burden because people can't absorb information any faster than about 40 bits (binary digits, the smallest measure of information) per second. Our evidence is that people today can't absorb information any faster than stone age people, so you can see that getting information fed to you faster over the phone becomes critical.*

James Flannegan, Director of the Acoustics Research Department of Bell Labs, has described a voice recognition system which will let a person in a checkless society call up his bank and have it send money from his account to a store to pay for a purchase. The computer succeeded in recognizing individual voices with 95 percent accuracy.

Saul Bucksbaum, Bell Labs' Vice-President for Network Planning states:

> *There won't be such a thing as a telephone in 50 years. We'll have an instrument, and at the press of a button you'll either turn it into a telephone or it will connect you with someone else or something else like a computer. You will be able to get a video display as well as a voice. You will have a communication terminal. When you get a busy signal your phone can monitor the*

line and complete the call as soon as the line is free. You will also have a display on the phone that will show what number is calling you. If you recognize it as that of someone you don't care to speak with you can ignore the ringing.

In 1900 a pair of copper wires carried one message. By 1918 a twisted pair could carry 12 channels. By 1950 a microwave link could carry 1,800 voice channels. By 1970 a coaxial cable carried 32,000 voice channels. Now a helical waveguide will carry 100,000 voice channels or the equivalent. The cost of delivering messages is falling at an exponential rate. We increasingly live in a *shrinking world*; in every sense, man around the world is again similar to primitive man in a single tribe since *accessibility* of information is almost universal.

Computation

A look at the effect of the new information technology on the speed and the cost of arithmetic computation illustrates the benefits derived from printed circuit and semiconductor technology. Carl Hegel calculates that one man takes one minute to do one multiplication at a cost of $12,500,000 for 125,000,000 multiplications. A desk calculator completes the multiplications in 10 seconds at one-sixth the cost of a man. A Harvard Mark I completes the calculation in one second at the cost of $850,000. Today a CDC 6600 does the job at 0.3 microseconds or at a cost of $4 in contrast to $12,500,000 for one man's effort.

In 1945 the labor for a million operations on a keyboard would take a month at a cost of $1,000, at the rate of a dollar an hour. In 1972 a computer could do a million operations for less than 6 cents, according to the futurist John McHale.

In the Organization for Economic Cooperation and Development Information Studies #3, 1973, *Computers in Telecommunications*, there is a list of possible services from a broad band switched network: advertising, pictorial consumer information, alarm (burglar, power failure, fire and so on), banking, facsimiles of documents, newspapers, emergency communications, communications between subscribers and computers, meter reading for utilities, the distribution of radio programs, shopping from homes, television originating and distribution, television-stored movies available on demand, educational television, telephone, computer-aided instruction, picture phone, video phone and voting. Buckminister Fuller has suggested the replacement of the representative system of government (Congress) with a national plebiscite on each specific issue after a public discussion of the issues conducted via telecommunications systems.

The Two Brains

Recent work in sociobiology is uncovering a distinct dualism in the human brain. The left brain is assigned the task of unilinear, sequential, logical thought proceeding from bit to bit to the whole, while the right hemisphere of the brain is assigned the process of a gestalt, a holistic leap. The traditional transmission of information through books and sentences associated with newspapers, journals and printing is characteristically that of the left brain. On the other hand, information transmitted by television, which is increasingly the source of news, would be right brained, starting with a holistic comprehension which then may be broken down into bits and pieces by analysis by the left brain.

The recent outcry that *Johnny can't read* may in fact reflect the replacement of the unilinear process of the left brain reading by a right brain gestalt awareness. In the pre-telecommunications era of the newspaper, a political campaign was waged, as in the example of the Lincoln-Douglas debates, by left-brained dialetical, unilinear, sequential argument characterized by logic. On the other hand, in the telecommunication world, the political campaign is waged by a 47-second television aphorism associating the candidate with either aversion or attraction. The most famous, *or infamous*, of these political advertisements for television was that of the Democratic Party in the 1964 presidential campaign which showed a little girl plucking off daisy petals followed in sequence by an explosion of a mushroom cloud and a picture of the Republican candidate, Barry Goldwater.

This shift from a unilinear, sequential arrangement of argument associated with books and the leftbrain by holistic, right-brained leap to conclusions first and reasons afterward, may be associated with the widespread disappearance of departments of debate from the college scenes of Western Europe and America in which debating teams stated logical propositions and carried on according to unilinear arguments for or against a proposition. It has been noted that the current so-called presidential debates in American campaigns do not have the character of debate but rather of a projection of images of two persons dividing the time equally. Departments of debate at universities have been largely replaced by departments of communication in which persuasion and advertising take on a holistic or right-brained character. Advertising in American newspapers during the 1920s and 1930s reflects the presentation of claims about the physical characteristics of the product being sold, whereas advertising since the advent of telecommunication seeks to create in the purchaser a feeling with reference to the product with little or no reference to the qualities or characteristics of the product itself. An advertisement for an automobile in 1928 gave its dimensions, its length, its width, its height, the amount of material used to manufacture the automobile and the horsepower of its engine. Advertisements for automobiles in the 1970s refer to what feeling the possession of such an automobile might induce in its owner.

Books are characterized by titles, chapters, paragraphs and sentences. They have a beginning, they proceed to the end, and then they stop, Television communication has no boundary lines, no margins, no paragraphs, no sentences, no beginning and no ending. A parallel can be found in the evolution of musical forms. This may be symbolized by the difference in music. In the classical music of Corelli, Vivaldi and Mozart one must learn, when growing up, when one should not applaud. Classical music, like chapters, paragraphs, and sentences in the written word, has a rigid and conventional form. Rock concerts, on the other hand, are lacking in the highly stylized form of classical music, and instead are free-flowing *happenings* characterized by the romantic form of the amoeba with no particular beginning or end.

The Noticers

In a quick examination of the three component parts of a university, we determined that in 1938 the university was possessed of x number of students, y number of professors and teachers, and z number of persons who were neither teachers nor students but facilitated the work of both. Forty years later, in 1978, the same institution had multiplied the number of faculty by 5, thus decreasing the teacher-student ratio. The striking fact, however, was that the number of persons associated with the university who were neither teaching nor studying was multiplied by 17. We might call these persons *noticers*, for they were neither teaching nor studying. They were noticing who was teaching, who was studying, what was being taught, what was being learned and represented an interface with a large community that funded and tolerated the academic activity. The gigantic rise in the number of *noticers* is directly correlated with the growth of relevance of information as opposed to the growth of activity in modern society as it is emerging.

The same observation could be made with reference to the growth of *noticers* if we can apply that title to the persons on the staffs of the elected officials in the House of Representatives and in the Senate of the United States, or the *noticers* currently employed in the White House as opposed to the line officers in the administration of the government. The same development would be characteristic in the Ford Motor Company in 1978 and that at the time of Henry Ford's personal dominion.

It is significant that in an interview in Paris between a manager of a Soviet corporation and a manager of a multinational Netherlands-based corporation, each revealed that with the advent of computer inventory their two jobs were converging and becoming surprisingly similar. With the ascendancy of telecommunications in management and decision-making, ideologies such as those of Adam Smith, on the one hand, and those of Karl Marx or Engels on the other, may become increasingly difficult to recognize as having a bearing on the conduct of an industry. Cybernetics in a rug factory in a socialist society and in that of a so-called free-enterprise system may be, in fact, identical.

Much is said about *information overload.* We predict that with a strong instinct for survival the individual human animal will maintain his/her sanity by a simple refusal to engage with the available information in the environment and consequently will carve out small, but habitable communities. These communities in the future will lack spatial definitions. A person's community may not be a block in a small town, but rather a list of frequently phoned individuals regardless of their physical location.

Telecommunications and the Future

Perhaps the most optimistic and hopeful projection one can make about the impact of telecommunications in the information society of the future is the appearance, only now, of the technical ability to monitor through satellites activities of groups and subgroups organizing for the expression of hostility by a use of arms. Although disarmament has been a goal spasmodically asserted from time to time by various groups in the world, only now is the mechanical means available to make universal world disarmament feasible because the primary logical reason for avoiding disarmament is the gnawing fear that the potential opponent has not done so. Man has, for the first time, the technical ability, if he chooses to use it, to agree to disarm and to be able, by satellite surveillance, to know that his potential enemies are keeping the bargain.

It has been argued that the new information society will destroy privacy and individuality. This may be incorrect for it may be argued that privacy was never a reality in the history of man. The fact that data banks know everything there is to know about an individual puts them in probably the same category as the brain of one's spinster aunt at the turn of the century. In the pre-telecommunications world of 50 years ago, most persons lived in small towns and rural communities, and in a town of 4,000 the two local bankers knew all that there was to know about everybody in town that could be stored in a telecommunications data bank today or tomorrow.

Not only may the widespread universal availability of knowledge make possible a rational allocation of the increasingly scarce resources of the earth's crust and eliminate disease and poverty, but it may also eliminate the need for irrational ideological pursuits based upon a zero-sum game. The technology of the Industrial Revolution produced a stingy material world described by David Ricardo's *Iron Law of Wages* which holds that most persons would have to live at a bare subsistence level as indeed is the case in the Third World today. That is a zero-sum game. The technology of the information society, on the other hand, is producing an exponential growth of food, goods and services making possible an ever-enlarging size of the pie, providing, in the words of R. Buckminister Fuller, *more and more* for *less and less.* For all to win it is no longer necessary for some to lose. That is a non-zero-sum game. The information society holds out the possibility that the non-zero-sum game can accommodate all persons around the world.

He asks you. He tells you. He beseeches you. He dismisses you. He plays the devil. He cleans the noses of cliches in the geyser of his paradoxes. You want to get at him, but he has moved away with the speed of a verbal Napoleon. His faith is hidden behind his sarcasms, his warmth behind the scorn. But sometimes his innocence and his convictions break through and overpower you. He is always a prizefighter, whether he knocks you down with a straight punch or with an oblique jab; and he is always his own show. You love him for the spectacle, and you love him for what he usually hides so well, and you are angry with him because he can't stand still and dim the lights of the playhouse, and you ask yourself: where is the real Howard? and then you realize that they are all real; in his fiction is his truth.

—Stanley Hoffman
Harvard University

8.

A LOOK AT TWO DECADES

As we opened a new decade, I was asked as a sociologist to write a piece about the seventies. It was sort of a New Year's prediction about the rest of the century, beginning with the '80s. I'm not sure, since I don't believe that prediction occurs, if it is really a guess, and I'm not sure how much of a guess it is or how much of a hope it is. I was startled by some people who read it, liked it and called up to say so, but who had friends who didn't realize that it was tongue-in-cheek.

I didn't realize it was tongue-in-cheek either.

Now, four years later, we can see some of the changes happening. Just after the article appeared, Southern California started to slip into the ocean. Someone called me and asked how I knew it would happen.

1.
Last Words on the Last Decade: The Seventies

Words speak louder than actions. It is interesting to notice the words that the Seventies generated. Language creates the reality in which we live. Just as the Ten Commandments were a reflection of what was of concern at the time, the rise of certain words in the Seventies testified

---

Editor's Note:

This piece first appeared as an article in the January/February 1980 edition of **Rocky Mountain Magazine** and is reprinted with the permission of representatives of the now defunct magazine.

221

to the sense of isolation felt by people during the decade. Two top words of the Seventies, right off the tips of our tongues, were *whatever* and *relate*. The word *whatever* is wonderfully versatile, expressing, as it does, the speaker's willingness to withdraw from any form of judgment, to avoid any expression of disapproval, whether strategic, ethical or moral. *Relate* implies similar removal; the suggestion that aloneness is the norm and a special word is needed to describe getting together.

Probably the dominant word of the times, courtesy of EST and Werner Erhard, was *experience*. The popularity of the word *experience* meant the demise of the word *had*. Where once we might have said that Albuquerque had its worst winter in years, we now say that Albuquerque experienced its worst winter. Were we used to say, *My wife had a cold last week*, we now say she experienced a cold. We used to say we had a Depression; now we say we may experience another one.

There is a profound significance in this change; the replacement of an active attitude with a passive attitude. In the sentence, *I had a cold*, there is at least the implication that one somehow had something to do with the cold. If one experiences a cold, he or she is only on the receiving end of the sniffles. A sentence recently appeared in the *Chicago Tribune* stating that the highways in Illinois had experienced larger cracks that usual this winter.

While the self-conscious Seventies may have been dubbed *the me decade*, those years have also been characterized by a strange twist on the use of the word *I*. *I* asserts an acceptance of personal responsibility, not only for one's own conduct, but also for its impact on others. The Seventies phrase *I think I can get behind that* was a cautious suggestion of the possibility of associating oneself with something that is going on, but certainly not as a leader, as is made clear by the word *behind*. More passivity and isolation.

As the word *I* came to be used differently, a suffix, *ist*, sprang to popularity as a way to make words help in the Seventies' task of categorizing people. As individuality became less important, group identity became more important. Thus, the word *racist* replaced the word *bigoted,* and the word *sexist* was leveled at people and practices that reflected the tradition of male dominance. The word *chauvinism,* traceable to a Frenchman, Nicholas Chauvin, who was excessively devoted to Napoleon, and classically applied to those affecting undue devotion to any flag, suddenly came to refer to anyone showing a lack of respect for women. The Seventies will be remembered as a time when public speakers, both male and female, tended to gasp after they used the word *he* or *him* (meaning all people) and hurriedly amended the sentence with *or she* or, *or her.*

Where there used to be *girls* a decade ago, there are now *women,* and where there used to be *colored people,* there came to be *Negroes* and now *Blacks.* There used to be *Oriental* people in America; during the Seventies they became *Asian. American Indians* turned into *Native Americans.* There used to be nationalities and then there were hyphenated Americans who are now *ethnic.*

If the word *ethnic* assumed new moral value, the word *nutrition,* along with everything else concerning one's health, experienced a religious conversion. What ever the medical virtues of vitamin tablets and organic edibles, they gained moral and religious overtones. Vegetarian food was perceived as morally superior to meat. Even certain vegetables, alfalfa and bean sprouts, for example, were considered morally superior to others, such as artichokes and potatoes. And, what ever jogging may do to the liver, the pancreas or the kidneys, joggers, too, claimed a moral superiority, fairly radiating it at intersections as they refused to alter their pace for automobiles.

Our national assumptions tended to change in the Seventies; we had a *crisis of confidence.* The imperial presidency, which reached its climax in the drama begun by the resounding reelection of President Richard Nixon, was terminated. And the President was done in by words. Even though his colleagues chastised him for it, television newsman Dan Rather, who covered the Nixon administration till the very end, acknowledged that fateful afternoon that President Nixon's final speech was accurate. Richard Nixon *had* undoubtedly been done in by words, the words on the tapes, and not by deeds. The words, *I am not a crook,* were labeled *affirmation by denial* by the press. Nixon used the phrase casually as one might say *I do not mean to interrupt you* or *Do not take this personally.*

And in the aftermath, presidents of the United States found it necessary to claim no rights to special transportation or to introductory music signaling eminence. It is not without significance that a Seventies American president chose to use the diminutive of the name *James* for his official signature.

Another nickname emerged with another rude awakening. The word *nuke* popped into the nation's vocabulary as Americans learned that their brilliant scientists and engineers, in designing new methods to extract energy from the heart of the atom, were fallible, and that the certainties of science could be undone by the conduct of those who managed science's creation. No one now mistakes Three Mile Island for a tropical resort.

In the Seventies the quantitative became the qualitative. Thus, in Colorado in the morning, one could hear on the radio that the air was *acceptable* air.

Americans learned some new words to go along with their changing assumptions. They learned that the sources of their new plastic clothing and plastic furniture, replacing wood and wool and cotton and silk and flax, were *hydrocarbons* dependent on the continuous supply of fossil fuel from somewhere in the Mid-East, which could be withheld, and the price of which could be determined by a *cartel* outside the control of the American decision-making system. So Americans combined a couple of words not heretofore used in tandem : *energy* and *crisis.*

Words like *significant* and *other* got tossed together too, as the historic codes governing the professed propriety of sexual conduct gave way to liberation, celebrated by the phrase *sexual preference.* Toward the end of the Seventies, it became evident that something had happened to male dominance, as the contemporary American male began to suffer from insecurity through the refusal of his live-in partner either to marry him or to agree to bear his children, and through the threat of female competition.

The American female claimed liberation, but suffered from the need to develop a prejudicial class structure to separate female superiors from the subordinates in the office scene. The words *affirmative* and *action* joined hands.

As the Seventies became more liberated, Clark Gable lost once and for all his preeminence for having shocked a nation from coast to coast when, in *Gone With the Wind,* he made his famous utterance, *Frankly, Scarlett, I don't give a damn.* It's hard to imagine what words would have to be put in Gable's mouth to shock audiences: *Frankly, Miss Lovelace...*

Another word, *process,* flourished in the Seventies. Peace was not called *peace,* it was called the *peace process;* the Constitution became the *Constitutional process.* Couples, odd and otherwise, were embroiled in the *relationship process.* We were certain the *process* would work out correct and proper solutions, and despite our disillusionment, we trusted the process. The words *In God We Trust* on our coins could have been replaced with the phrase, *In Process We Trust.*

The word *computerized* gained momentum in the Seventies. A major fact of the decade was the ultimate triumph of electronic communication and electronic computation. No greater change in the history of the world ever occurred than the decrease in the cost of computing a square root by using an $11 pocket calculator. Computers also led the way to a growing sense of isolation, of the absurdities of action: *After all, there is nothing we can do about it, it's in the computer,* as though computers themselves devised the rules and regulations.

No one has yet noticed the unrecognized *isolation generation.* They came in with the wave of a future that disappeared during the Seventies. These people first appeared in the Sixties and early Seventies as the counterculture. They professed their intention to destroy the establishment. They refused to shave; they wore blue denim that they disfigured with holes and patches; they refused to marry the men or women with whom they slept. It was their intention to abolish the corporate structure, which they said was funding the destruction of the earth through industrial, economic and military complexes. They penetrated the universities as teaching assistants and assistant professors.

Then their younger brothers and sisters came of age, and, observing their elders' failures, in no way regarded them as role models. Arriving on the college campuses at the end of the Seventies, this new crop began to resurrect sororities and fraternities and the mickey mouse activities of years gone by. This was quickly labeled *nostalgia*. Instead of absenting themselves from libraries, they crowded them. They stopped taking courses in sociology and began the search for courses that led to instantaneous and immediate employment. Business schools flourished. Courses in economics began to be jammed. This generation still wore blue denim. But it was *designer* blue denim.

The *isolated generation* was that group of befuddled, still-hip Americans between the ages of 25 and 40. The late Sixties and early Seventies went by and left them in the wake.

One of the major soft-voiced ideas of the Seventies was the *media event*. Increasingly, we began to realize that television talk shows were actually commercials promoting, for instance, the authors of books published by presses owned by corporate structures that not only controlled the television network, but also films, radio stations, newspapers. Toward the end of the decade the term *media event* began to be heard less and less as media events became indistinguishable from reported news.

As for the reported news, journalism in the Seventies was dominated by the post-Watergate discovery of *investigative reporters* and the consequent deterioration of the news to the levels of trivia. A number of *investigative reporters* (as if there were a legitimate category of reporters who didn't investigate stories) exhibited a strange hunger for the profoundly irrelevant. Magazines because excessively and superficially *peopled*.

Two great television programs emerged, diametrically opposed to one another, each with the same audience. On the one hand, *60 Minutes*, while skirting slander and libel, managed to leave the audience with what is perhaps the lesson of the decade, the certain knowledge that nearly everybody is a scoundrel. And on the other hand, a charming young man named Donahue, who facing an audience of benign middle-class women with station wagons and children in the primary grades, was nevertheless able to present a range and a variety of conduct convincing everyone that while there may not be heroes, there were certainly no devils, but instead a fascinating array of alternatives. Donahue's earnest moral relativism perfectly reflected the decade.

The Seventies will be remembered as a period when all sorts of things experienced a very verbose end, some grand oral malaise, just prior to the beginning of the new world and a new vocabulary that appeared after January 1st, 1980.

2.
The Challenge of the Eighties

I am addressing *The Challenge of the Eighties* to the teachers of the world, and by the word *teachers* I include school administrators, principals, superintendents and the support staff of the entire educational system. To do that, I am going to discuss the world fifty years ago. Second, I will discuss how it is that world disappeared, which it has. And last, I will list ten specific challenges which persons are facing right now in the world.

Recall, if possible, the world as it was when I was a child fifty years ago. Some remember that world as it was; others do not remember but may observe that there are those of us who exist who do not even realize it has gone away, and some cannot imagine that such a world ever did exist.

When I was sixteen, there were horses. Horses are, of course, a form of solar power which pulled most of the plows and most of the wagons and moved most of the food; horses even delivered milk in New York City as late as when I was sixteen, fifty years ago. That is why we still refer to the measurements of electric motors in terms of horsepower.

Fifty years ago, most of the bread eaten by Americans was made in kitchens in individual homes. My mother had fifty-pound sacks of flour in what was called a flour bin; one whole day a week was devoted to the process of the manufacture of the bread for the coming week.

Fifty years ago, most of the clothes worn by people were made in each home. The sewing room in the home was a major room and the sewing machine was a standard piece of equipment. Even quilts and bedding were manufactured in the home. Fifty years ago, laundry was done in the home by hand in a rudimentary way with laundry tubs and scrub boards, but if you were fancier, you would have a washing machine run by gasoline or electricity that rotated around with two big rubber ringers, and that was followed by a full day of ironing, first by flatirons on stoves and then by fancy electric irons; and my mother had a mangle of which she was very proud, a great big roller heated by gas through which sheets could be run.

Fifty years ago, clothes were made of cotton or linen or wool or silk, and clothes were repaired in the evenings. Women had baskets with little wooden objects they shoved into stockings and then they wove threads back and forth and crosswise, removing holes from the stockings. These objects were called darning eggs. It seemed endless, the need to darn stockings. Today, those of you who know, know that most clothes are made of petroleum and are discarded rather than repaired.

A large part of the summer was devoted to the preservation of food that was harvested during the summer and fall in such a fashion that it could supply food throughout the winter. There were no Bird's Eye frozen foods in those days.

This difference is very important to remember. When I went to school fifty years ago, eighty percent of Americans did not go as far as high school. Until that time an eighth grade certificate was thought to be the terminal formal educational degree. The people who went on to high school were a small elite handful who were going to be used in the mercantile world, keeping books and writing bills, carrying on correspondence in offices, or in a few cases, preparing for the few occupations that were required in the universities. But the main body of persons did not go to college or the Harvard Business School; they learned to be a Rockerfeller or a Vanderbilt or a John Pew or a Harriman in the field of industry and business, not on college campuses. Persons who got their adult roles learned them by apprenticeship in eighty percent of the cases, and most women had *women's roles*, most men had *men's*, but some reversed them.

This started out with household chores when children were four years old or else a child could crawl under the granary and gather eggs; later, when little Jimmy was six years old, he would slop the pigs; when a little older he could shock the wheat; when still a little older, he could herd cows. Still older, he might mow hay on a stack-a-horse. The girls would learn from an aunt or a mother or another woman how to make bread, how to do laundry, how to sew, how to make clothes and mend them, how to keep house, how to tend children. Boys would learn agriculture or plumbing or plastering. Roads were built by men on the end of shovels and picks, slowly unfolding a road. There was no way you could imagine their coming home at night and then changing into jogging clothes to go to jog.

The primary means of the socialization of the young was apprenticeship and jobs. These jobs ran on a linear scale with meager rewards for small jobs steadily increasing to a top level of the highest paid reward. Child labor laws, which correctly prevented the abuse of children, had an unfortunate secondary effect which has been disadvantageous: the elimination of that later socialization into work and meaningful lives.

Fifty years ago, most of the lawyers who were members of Congress had never been to law school. Lawyers tended to become lawyers as apprentices in law offices and then passed the bar.

Fifty years ago, there was no way that my mother could have left my father and gone to Washington for a month and a half. Without her, he could not have eaten, he could not have had clean clothes. Today, with laundromats and frozen foods, it is very easy for any member of the family to sustain life, materially at least, in the absence of the other members.

In the twenty-year period from 1950 to 1970, the number of farm families in America dropped from twelve million to two million, and those ten million farm families did not just disappear from the Earth, but rather they moved into empty cores of cities.

An interesting fact known by some of us who know is that, in spite of much publicity, there is not actually any shortage of food. A few years ago, Idaho coughed up a record number of potatoes. If they had hit the market freely, potatoes would have been free, but they did not hit the market because of farm support prices. We have sustained an artificial scarcity in milk, butter, cheese and farm products ever since the days of Franklin Roosevelt in order to maintain a price to enable the farmer to sustain his standard of living. So, we have enough milk and enough butter in storage in the government to feed the hungry world now. We call the non-growing of food the Farm Bank and the Soil Bank.

In the world of apprenticeship, the whole burden of the socialization of the child was not thrust upon the school system. The primary education occurred in the real world of chores, tasks, apprenticeship and work. Remember delivery boys? They used to deliver groceries to your kitchen door. There are no more delivery boys in the present world.

What I am going to say is this: I am a teacher. I was not going to be a teacher until after World War II. I was going to be in advertising and business and commerce, but somehow during the war I changed my perspective about the values in life. When I was offered a teaching position in 1946 at a beginning salary of one-third of the income of the starting salary of another job, with the U.S. Steel Corporation, I took the instructorship and the academic vows of poverty. A teacher obviously derives a sense of satisfaction from working with the young and observing the growth and maturation of persons. It is an alternative to the delight one can get from succeeding in competition for higher and higher salaries and material rewards which are associated with business executives, successful professional attorneys and persons in real estate. The teacher today can no longer transmit to the young, as they did when I was alive, a solid set of fixed values so that one could plan a life to unfold according to a pre-plan. I recall that I had a total plan for my life, including marriage, family, occupation, residence. That I did or didn't do any of these things is immaterial. The point is, one tended to have such a plan. The contemporary young have no such sense of certainty about the future and have changed from a rigid plan to another one of *readiness*. This is illustrated by the fact that we have trunks in attics and in basements and *they* have backpacks and are prepared to pick up and move on a moment's notice. It is difficult for them to answer the question of where they would like to be twenty-four months hence. Likewise, it is necessary to be two-fisted; that is, to have more than one plan, so they can be idealistic and realistic at the same time, pessimistic and optimistic at the same time, prepared to relate to changing circumstances.

I am going to list now the ten issues that I think our students will confront in the coming decade, one way or another.

First, resolving the ethical problems and reaching moral consensus on issues presented by the new technologies in biology. I am speaking, for example, of genetic engineering, and the intrusion into the birth process and the heredity process. Fifty years ago, the idea of establishing a family was based on a total and complete ignorance of the genetic possibilities of a specific union between a father and mother, and certainly no knowledge about the probable physical characteristics of the offspring before it was born. That has changed.

Second, preserving individual personality in a world of decreasing individual independence and of increasing inter-dependence, with increasing awareness of the vast numbers of others with whom we share the world.

Third, finding a replacement for the vanishing roles of dependence of women on males which characterized the dominant lifestyle of America until almost now, which accounted to some degree for the stability of the family. Today there is an alarming increase in the number of children who are reared in a one-parent household, although they may switch on weekends.

Fourth, replacing the salubrious rewards of the work ethic in a nation of increasing material glut.

Fifth, reconciling the demands for equality and human rights with the demands for civil liberty. We have demands for equality characterizing human rights as evidenced by the Civil Rights Movement, the Women's Lib Movement, the Union Movement, on the one hand; and on the other hand, we have demands for liberty which give rise to civil rights as characterized by the repression of dissidents around the world, the elimination of pluralism in behavior in many societies, and the excessive regulation of and infringement upon individual liberty. Our nation has been more interested in liberty than in equality. It is no coincidence that we have a Statue of Liberty but we do not have a Statue of Equality.

Sixth, preserving quality, which is to say, elitism and meritocracy in a world of increasing demands for equality and populism. Sometimes the charge of elitism is hurled like some kind of sin. We do not have any objection to elitism in professional athletics, in acting, in the arts, in writing and music; we do not demand that all pianists be dead-level equals or that we cannot celebrate our finest pianist, our finest flutist, our fines violinist. Our schools must simultaneously do two contradictory things. In celebrating and honoring the few, the exceptional, the superior we all benefit from, we must provide value and worth and dignity to those who occupy the very useful roles further down the line. We will always have some sort of pyramid, creating the higher as the fewer. But we need not depress, punish and deprive those of us who are ordinary people.

Seventh, finding a replacement for the vanishing role of the free competitive market in the setting of prices and product priorities. The free competitive market has disappeared as a result of the technological integration of production. Even though the Reagan Administration would seek to turn the economy over to a free competitive market, it cannot be done, for the simple reason that there is not one. Deregulation is not deregulation; it is the shifting of prices administered by the corporate structure instead of the government structure. It is certainly not the marketplace. In other words, we need to find out how to deal with the corporation as *Mother*.

Eighth, finding a replacement for the vanishing role of apprenticeship as the main source of socialization of the young. Can the school system actually replace the role of the older man or woman who was primarily responsible for the daytime life of eighty percent of the young during their maturation fifty years ago?

Ninth, preserving our physical safety from the threat of the new demands arising in an awakening of the Third World around the globe. This awakened awareness is, of course, a result of the information revolution. My grandmother used to say, "*What you do not know will not make you angry.*" But, increasingly, everyone knows that there is no innate right that one-third of the world should have a very high standard of living by exploiting the resources coming from another third which is forced into poverty. The toppling of the Shah of Iran was a direct result of the invention of the cassette tape recorder whereby the word could spread even among a group of pre-literate persons.

Finally, the tenth challenge, and by far the most serious, is living with the bomb. The United States/Soviet Union arms race, the proliferation of thermonuclear weapons throughout the rest of the world, accidental detonations and finally, obviously, terrorist use of atomic weapons, are factors which must be considered in facing this challenge. While it is true that a unilateral disarmament on the part of either of the great powers would certainly lead to instability and atomic war, it is equally true that steady proliferation and growth of nuclear weapons will likewise result in world destruction.

The increasing diversion of more and more labor and materials to non-consumer goods in the form of weapons which, if used, will end human life on Earth, is not only dangerous folly but is also uneconomic. When workers are paid to make tanks which they cannot ever buy, the supply of spendable money increases without any symmetrical increase in purchasable goods, thus destroying the level of living and creating a steady increase in prices for the shrinking store of consumer goods.

In the long run, this arms race, if not reversed, will destroy the civilian economy and private property, individual freedom, human rights and civil liberties; the very things which political leaders claim they are organized to defend.

These are the challenges that face you and me as teachers of the young in the decade to come.

Firstly, the word no is not in Higman's vocabulary. When he calls and asks that you make a speech or appear at a meeting, there is only deadly silence from him when you answer, "No", citing a thousand reasons, all good ones, too, why you cannot come to Boulder, Denver or some Godforsaken spot where the only way to get there is by a little bitty airplane that flies through little bitty holes in a mountain.

Secondly, the rat never asks for anything for himself, thus making you feel like a miserable heel for not complying with his request. It's always for the damned students or the poverty program or some other jazz that he wants things.

That Higman, he's a miracle. No one else could pull off such operations. Plenty of people are just as smart as he is, but not many are as with it as he is; without him life would be very much duller.

—*Paul Jacobs*
Ramparts Magazine

9.

SNIPPETS

Howard Higman was able to capture the essence of a topic with a one liner or a short analysis. We call them Snippets. They are his observations about persons, events, theories, creeds and social issues. Howard was never speechless; he held an opinion on most every topic.

PERSONS

Jean Stafford

A friend of mine throughout my life, Jean Stafford had a great influence on me. She was the only hippie in Boulder during the Depression. Her father wrote Westerns under an assumed name for money. He wrote in the back of their house with no shirt, and smoked. Her mother had big red cheeks, was optimistic and happy. Jean hated her guts. Jean had two older sisters and a brother. The brother was interested in nature and farming near Fort Collins. The older sister, Margie, was a painter.

Jean and I were secret intellectuals in the eighth grade. We read Eugene O'Neill's *Strange Interlude* out loud to each other. She had a sword, a real sword of her father's, and she wore it to school, dragging it all the way.

Editor's Note:

Some of these observations have appeared in earlier chapters but are repeated because including them is essential to certain discussions.

Jean put herself through college by posing as a model. I have a whole slew of charcoal pictures of her as a model. Jean would have nothing to do with the fraternity-sorority world. Her heroes were people like George Fulmer Reynolds, who taught English language. She got her BA and MA summa cum laude in three-and-a-half years and won a scholarship to attend Heidelberg University, which she claimed she never would have gotten if they had known that Jean was a woman's name. She went to Heidelburg for one year, 1938, just before the war. She wrote letters saying that when she went to class, she had to say "Heil Hitler". She was there during the purging of the Jews from the schools. She wrote a dissertation on divine and profane love in English poetry.

Jean came back here after one year in Germany. She took a job at Stevens College, a sort of anti-intellectual girls school. She held a huge ceremonial burning of *Readers Digest,* which was being used as a text. She was fired.

She went to New York and was hit by a car which smashed her face. Once I had made a death mask of her and she remembered it. I sent her this mask for her surgeon to use to put her face back together. She sued the guy who hit her, and, in the course of things, they were married. They moved to Boston. His name was Robert Lowell, Amy Lowell's nephew. He was a poet laureate. Jean and he had a hell of a time. He was also an insane, converted Catholic; went to mass several times a day; became very weird. Jean then wrote a book and won a prize which established her as one of America's top writers.

She left Lowell and married an anti-Semitic publisher; left him and married A.J. Liebling. The world noticed that after she married Liebling she stopped writing. He was a very famous labor writer who wrote for the *New Yorker.* They lived in the Village. When he died I tried to call her. When I finally got her number, Harry Bridges answered the phone. Strange. Harry Bridges was the boss of the Longshoremen; a communist labor leader. He once spoke on the CU campus. Jean and I had a long relationship. She civilized me in English literature.

< >

Eleanor Roosevelt

Eleanor Roosevelt entered my life before I knew her personally. My mother and father regarded the Roosevelts as evil and a traitor to their class. I cried all night as a high school student when I found out Roosevelt had trounced Herbert Hoover, who was my family's total hero.

Then, in college, I became deeply concerned about politics and the coming threat of Adolf Hitler. I was influenced by a Marxist professor of philosophy named Joseph Cohen, who took the *Moscow Daily News,* and thought then that Hitler was vastly worse than the Communists. I became an avid devotee of Roosevelt. For the bombing of Pearl Harbor, I am eternally grateful. It is my belief that if the Japanese had not bombed Pearl Harbor, Hitler might have destroyed Western civilization. I know my hero Roosevelt was unpopular; he was going to get involved in putting down the aggressor dictators: Mussolini, Franco and Adolf Hitler. But four out of five Americans were not a bit appalled by Adolf Hitler. As a matter of fact some even perceived of him as having saved Western civilization from the ravages of Bolshevism, after the collapse of the Weimar Republic.

In 1955 Mrs. Roosevelt's son, Elliot moved to the mountains in Colorado and sent a son to college in Fort Collins and a daughter to college in Boulder. Her name was Chandler, and although it was true that she was betrothed to a man she would later marry, a Texas oil person, she was squired around town by a friend of mine, Lyle Taylor. This is how it was that we were able to get Mrs. Roosevelt to agree to come to open the Conference on World Affairs in 1955. Her granddaughter Chandler persuaded her grandmother to open the eighth World Affairs Conference.

When she came to town she of course was housed in the home of the President of the University, Ward Darley. He had a very fancy lunch after her opening speech at 11 a.m. She was seated on his right and, since I was the chairman of the conference that had invited her, I was seated on her right. Next to me was the president of the student body. Well, understandably Mrs. Roosevelt didn't look at me for one minute. She instead carried on her conversation with her host, the President. I was talking to the student body president and I used the word *McCarthy*. I used it in a generic sense, I wasn't talking about the Senator himself, but I did utter the word McCarthy, and Mrs. Roosevelt rose, almost levitated off her chair, turned and looked at me and said, "McCarthy! I had an occasion to speak to that young man the other day, and I said, 'Young man, I don't approve of anything you are doing. He said, 'Mrs. Roosevelt don't get excited...' And I said I'm not excited, I'm indignant!" She slapped the table and her water glass fell over.

She added, "I am a delegate, as you know, to the United Nations, and we have to fill out a list of organizations to which we belong for the Attorney General. I belong to an organization called *Aid to Yugoslav Mothers*. I don't care whether Mr. Tito is a communist or not. I'm in favor of the aid to Yugoslav mothers. I also know that the organization is going to fold. I have not resigned. I filled out my sheet. Subsequently a person called me in and said, 'Mrs. Roosevelt, you filled out your sheet of the organizations to which you belong, but you forgot to sign it.'" Mrs. Roosevelt smiled seraphically, and said, "I know Senator McCarthy has looked into this list and labeled a half of them communist."

From that modest beginning she continued to come back to Boulder to make speeches on behalf of the things of which she was in favor. The first year I got a message from her, stating that she would arrive at my house Tuesday evening. I had over a hundred persons coming for dinner in my three-story house. Everyone in town of course knew that Mrs. Roosevelt would be here for dinner. Friends who barely knew my wife would call and offer to bring a salad. She had to explain that all had been taken care of. As I was watching through the window on that Tuesday night, a car drove up, and she got out. I dashed out. She got out of the car, looked at me, and said, "Young man, I know that you and I have the same objectives. Don't waste your time trying to be polite or flattering. Make the most use of the time I am here." Believe it or not, I was bright enough to obey her. I took her round the side of my house to the garden in the back, put her in a chair and came inside. I went up to the room on the top floor, and said, "Mrs. Roosevelt is in the garden."

"What did he say?" one asked loudly.

"Mrs. Roosevelt is in the garden."

It got louder and louder, and the house evacuated. The person who came out first was the wife of an anthropology professor. When she saw Mrs. Roosevelt she started running and crying; she leaped in the air; Mrs. Roosevelt grabbed her and held her like a child in her lap.

Later, we came in for dinner. I had been remodeling the house. That was my aerobics in those days, and I had torn out a window by the dining room table. The window that was torn out was hideous, and I realized I'd done nothing to conceal the half-torn window. When she walked by, she looked at it and said, "Oh! A pre-Raphaelite garden! How beautiful!" I thought, that will never, ever be finished. And that's true to this day.

Of course, at the appropriate time, her driver came and she left. And that was my first encounter with Mrs. Roosevelt.

She came back, occasionally, to make speeches, supporting Adlai Stevenson. I remember one particularly. One question asked in the discussion period was should we go on testing the atomic bomb in Utah. Those of you who remember will recall that Adlai Stevinson said no and Dwight Eisenhower said yes. They asked Mrs. Roosevelt where she stood. I remember thinking that I'd have to change my own position as she began her speech. She said it would be a wonderful thing if the human race had preached the understanding that it was not necessary for people to murder each other in conflict. But unfortunately it is not the case. There is war; there are weapons; there are dangers. I could hear her beginning to defend the testing of the bomb. I remember my soul left my body and went across the stage of Macky auditorium to the other side to join her in her position of being in favor of testing. But at the end of her lengthy careful speech she said, "In spite of all this, I am against it." Her rhetoric was flawless.

My soul went back into my body. That was when I learned one of her secrets, which was that she always spelled out all the reasons that people had for the things of which she didn't approve. That told the audience when she told them her position, they couldn't say she didn't understand.

Later, Quigg Newton, the President of the University and former Mayor of Denver, called me and said, "Mrs. Roosevelt wants me to ask you, Howard, to be the regional director for the American Association of the United Nations." I said, "What?" "It's an organization that's her main life now. It covers the states of Colorado, New Mexico, Montana, Wyoming and Washington. You will have a supply of money—not a salary; it's a volunteer job for you but you will have money to hire a secretary, as well as cover travel costs and hotel bills."

So the next four or five years I spent travelling around, seeing Mrs. Roosevelt often, in Seattle, San Francisco, Oregon, Washington, Wyoming and Colorado. What I know is that everything Mrs. Roosevelt had to say was *how* to get something done. We came to call that instrumental speech. She never spoke about how she felt about something, it was always about why we should do what we should do and *get it done.*

There was a congressman from the state of Michigan who was a violent anti-Russian. He had been at the University of Colorado at Macky auditorium speaking the night before at a Denver meeting where Mrs. Roosevelt was the main speaker. It was sponsored by a Denver minister who was a great friend of this congressman. I blurted out how much I despised this congressman who was promoting the cold war. I was tipped off by a Denver group that I had hurt this minister's feelings and that it was a shame that I had done so since he was a sponsor of the United Nations himself. The following day I went to the luncheon at which Mrs. Roosevelt was sitting behind me. I couldn't see her but it was reported that she was smiling seraphically when she heard me say again how much I disliked this congressman.

I then realized that I made a mistake. Once I had told my daughter Alice that I disliked a woman who put out a cigarette in the uneaten yolk of an egg at breakfast in the movie *Rebecca*. Alice said, "No, you didn't mean to say that you disliked that woman; you disliked her putting out her cigarette in the yolk of an egg." So I said at the luncheon, I did make a mistake and I am sorry for that, I don't mean I don't like the congressman—I mean to say I don't like what the congressman said. Mrs. Roosevelt is reputed to have smiled in a big way. And that's the way it was.

One time she spoke to me in the St. Francis Hotel in San Francisco. We had got on the same elevator going to a meeting on the United Nations and she said, "Oh, Professor Higman I think you've got a cold!" That's the closest she ever got to anything other than what to do, when to do it and how to do it.

When Franklin Roosevelt died, I learned that the effective Vice President was Jimmy Burns, not Harry Truman. The Roosevelts had no interest in or knowledge of Harry Truman. Mr. Truman was not even informed of the Manhattan Project, the secret development of the atomic bomb. He was, of course, summoned to the White House. I think it's wonderful that he was more conscious of the fact that we had no President than of himself. He turned to say to Mrs. Roosevelt, "Mrs. Roosevelt, what can I do for you?" She looked back at him, according to Jimmy Burns, who told Paul Porter, my boss, and said, "Mr. Truman, you have asked the wrong question. The question is not what you can do for me, but what can we do for you, Mr. President."

You may or may not recall that when Truman ascended to that office, it was generally predicted that there was no way he would be able to perform or function at all. It was a foregone conclusion that Thomas Dewey, the Mayor of New York, would become the real President. Truman was not perceived to be "with it." And, as you know, he turned out to be one of the greatest presidents in American history.

Truman appointed Eleanor Roosevelt to the delegation to go to London to create the United Nations. Establishment figures said, "Mr. Truman, you've made a mistake; you can't appoint Mrs. Roosevelt to the United Nations; she knows nothing at all about politics, world affairs or State Department matters." Presumably Truman pushed a button, called a secretary and started to dictate letters putting down everybody who opposed her appointment. When the ship left New York for London, Eleanor Roosevelt was part of the delegation.

The establishment men said, "What the hell are we going to do with her.?" They finally came up with a clever scheme; to create a meaningless subdivision of the meetings. They named it *Human Rights*. Human Rights was not a subject the governments felt they had any authority over whatsoever. Human rights was kind of like what is going on now—with people who don't want you to kill lobsters—animal rights. If women in Saudi Arabia have a different status, that's their business, not ours. If people have harems and a hundred and ten wives, that's none of our business. Human rights was not a thing with which government was involved. It's not like Civil Rights at all.

Then they created this thing called the Human Rights Council and put Mrs. Roosevelt in it to get rid of her. She ended up Chairman of the Council, and of course other people put their stellar gang in it as well. They ended up writing a charter on human rights to the horror of the United States government. There was no way in the world the U.S. government would sign such a thing.

However, to start with, we claimed it had nothing to do with international affairs; it was local affairs. And of course we later signed it. Some said the Soviet Union would have us before the World Court ten times a day for the disparate way we treated Blacks in America. Not until the decision of the Supreme Court did we feel that Negroes had an equal right to eduation. In fact, I've discovered that the average American has no knowledge that human rights has not been a long tenant of our government's position. It is, in fact, brand new. I ask people who they think was the first president to approve of it. They say, "Wilson?"-No. "Roosevelt?"-No. "Hoover?"-No. "Kennedy?"-No. "Johnson?"-No. We did not sign the human rights charter until President Carter. And when he did sign it he made the State Department livid; they thought it totally irresponsible to bring human rights into this country. Right now in America, people think human rights is something we've had since 1776. No way. Mrs Roosevelt educated us and the world about the human condition. We owe her a great debt of gratitude.

TEACHING

Any time your name gets in the paper, you're a dead duck.

Although I'm a liberal, I'm also a conservative. Look at all the things I've saved. Physical things all over the place. I've been a Calvinist since childhood.

Democracy is rule by the people. This means that if people believe that fluorine in the drinking water produces pregnancy, you do not have fluorine in the drinking water. The best societies, Meocracies, ones ruled by one, are unlikely and can be neglected.

Freedom is policed primarily by its being used. The professor who speaks freely and honestly creates the environment for academic freedom. Academic freedom can be lost through self-induced restraint by a professor who fears the consequences for his style of life that might ensure him from becoming unpopular. Unfortunately, this sort of erosion of academic freedom can occur even in the absence of any pressure from society, the community or his colleagues.

Once a student asked, "How do you survive?" I said, "Well, it's very simple. Just learn to always put your worst foot forward, and the more they dig the more uninteresting you become. It's called 'scratch a Communist and find a Presbyterian.'" I survive because I've learned to run with my enemies. Others fail because they only run with their friends.

This may sound funny, but to my way of thinking the University is my church. A church is a meaningful thing in the pursuit of virtue and truth. No individual person possesses all of these, but the collective impact of the University (or the church) in the world is the long-run pursuit of truth and virtue.

I was greedy. I decided I wanted to know everything.

Teaching is like being a successful preacher. The best classes have a student who opposes what I say. Good teaching involves a quarrel between the professor and the students. I like teaching rebellious students. I say to them, "I'm your problem. If you're going to have a successful revolution, you've got to get guys like me defeated".

I've never corrected anything because I've discovered that when you correct things, you draw more attention to them than when you don't. Nothing worth anything doesn't have enemies.

The English language should not disappear one word at a time, even because of political correctness. I am anti-political correctness violently, steadfastly and proud of it.

CREEDS AND THINGS

The trouble with Harry is that he suffers from delusions of miniature. I noticed that I was getting more fame for things I didn't do, good or bad. Being a coward, I didn't defend it or say anything.

I can't bear to get rid of anything. I don't like change.

You don't invite someone to your house who wrote a letter saying you served bad food.

I fear this new technology because it will leave persons with no place to hide.

Amercians are anti-expert. They do not like experts. Any American who gets up in a group and speaks like an expert will be ignored. What he needs to say is, "I don't know anything about this, but it seems to me...... ." Then he'll get the group's attention.

We hide in groups. The reason we're so interested in self-help groups, which is simply the pooling of ignorance by people sitting in a circle, is that we have no "selves". We have only relationships with others.

Middle-class man is without place, time and identity. Unlike the classical Greek, with his understanding of order, proportion, balance and structure, middle-class man is like the Paleolithic Indian. His dinner is in the forest.

Computers are vastly overrated. They are showoffs with speed. They have no tolerance for ambiguity which is the most distinguishing aspect of human life.

< >

On God

I was born a secular Presbyterian and was rigidly and severely socialized in the First Presbyterian Church of Boulder. As a child I became aware of a personal God, who was not always kind. I believed my ancestors sat in Heaven and observed all my behavior while I was a little boy. I longed for privacy.

After my liberation from the unpleasant aspects of the possibility of other people's infinite mortality, existing on the other side, and the experience of a personal God who could monitor my private behavior, I didn't think much about religion until I became a college professor. In the early fifties, a graduate student asked me, "Why is God dead?" I answered, "It's simple, the personal God is dead because of the lessening of fear due to science and technology, especially the invention of the pill and the supermarket." My parents and grandparents were gravely afraid of unwanted pregnancies and scarcity.

I see today's life as the best of all possible worlds. I cite the steady progress of the longevity of life on earth around the world since the Industrial Revolution and the application of science and technology to man's covenant. I note the historical impact of the outbreak of scientific and rational civilization in Europe and the spread of the English language and the adoption of Western dress across the world.

Every civilization is born with a religion it never abandons, followed by answering a religious question; "What is Good or God"? After that answer is found, civilization concerns itself with politics, who gets what and how as well as the rules for getting it. Next follows the search for technical and scientific answers to how the biological and material world exists. Finally, a preoccupation with what is beautiful: art, soccer, rock music, the classics, follows.

I believe I am living in the declining phase of Western Christian civilization and in the emerging heroic phase of the new global civilization. I witness signs of its appearance and am optimistic about its arrival. So far, the human race is the greatest achievement of Good and it will be unified by answering the basic question: What is good for every person as opposed to non-humans or only some humans? I look for the new theology to develop a political system characterized by the spread of democracy, freedom and the right for every individual to determine the value of his or her personality. The dogmatic absolutism of science and technology is being replaced by relativism, defining truths within specific frames of reference. Robert Oppenheimer defined science as a self-destroying system. We are moving toward a pragmatic answer to the question: What is real?

My optimism springs from the successful elimination of the last major threat to world civilization which violated the covenant of liberalism, humanism, relativism and pragmatism, primarily in the person of Adolph Hitler.

I think of how seldom I hear any discussion of or heated debates over the issues raised by immortality or the efficacy of prayer. I wonder if my friends have accommodated their own personality with what it is they do and think. Some high level discussions by world leaders I have read about do reflect the converging syntheses on a higher dialectic of the liberal, humanistic and pragmatic values inherent in their religions which may help the survival of humankind.

In my current conception of God, which is of course quite different from the one to whom one prays or plans to sit beside, I firmly know there are no persons who make choices or make the effort to preserve their own lives, knowing that it is the one thing they cannot, in the long run, apparently do.

When Buckminster Fuller was asked if he believed in God, he snapped back and said, "Of course not. Look out the window. Do you see the cars, the trees, the street? Do you believe in them? You don't believe in *It*. It's out there. I don't believe in God. It's out there. It is the Universe."

< >

Puritanism, Capitalism and Communism

In classic Puritan Europe, persons were taught to avoid hell or perdition where you lived eternally upside down in lava if you failed to do the right thing. This view was promoted in Dante's *Inferno*. To avoid this terrible fate, you must engage in individualism, work, thrift and washing.

The puritan ethic led to the accumulation of wealth over and above that necessary to keep warm, to be fed, to love, to live, to laugh, to play, to revere. This accumulation of wealth was a necessary prerequisite to the Industrial Revolution, the life of the factory, plant and capitalism. Puritanism reached its extreme caricature in Massachusetts over and above that of Europe. It can be equated with Freud's concept of guilt. The greater the guilt, the greater the anxiety and propensity of the guilty to work instead of play. Those early Americans had the highest incidence of the need to work than any other people on earth. As a consequence, they accumulated the largest amount of material wealth.

The only reason persons will knock themselves out, get up before dawn to work until midnight to save it and wash it, is to receive rewards. In Puritanism, the rewards came after you died. We call it postponed rewards; salvation, being in heaven on clouds with harps. Puritans were ascetic and severe and Godly.

Today, this Puritan reward has little currency in developing nations. Their biggest problem is to move from a tribal society to a modern industrial state without Martin Luther. It is highly unlikely that the belief in eternal heaven and hell will dominate the people of developing countries. While Puritans were concerned with individualism, these nations are communal. Plantation society is not very productive. It's leisurely. The accumulation of wealth requires some form of coercion. The Communist leaders of the Twentieth Century were and are the new Puritans: Mao, Stalin, Castro, for example. However, there are two differences from our Puritans: First, they do not believe postponed rewards will be in heaven on clouds with harps, rather the good life for them and their children is here on earth, right now. They practice thrift and washing, ascetic and severe, communistic style. Secondly, their societies are communal rather than individualistic. They use a form of assembly line rather than the individual working at a lathe for his own reward as ours did.

Americans want a replica of our government in these new countries. A liberal government has free elections, a loyal opposition and civil rights including the right of minorities to drop out and continue to exist. Liberty, whether you verbalize it or not, is probably the value you hold most dear, more than democracy or material wealth. While Communism degrades liberty, Puritanism eschews Communism. The group decides in ours. A few decide in theirs.

We tend to judge other societies as bad, call them totalitarian because they abolish opposition, don't hold free elections or champion human rights for minorities. Probably a certain level of literacy, wealth and civil rights is a prerequisite for the kind of society we have in the United States and Western Europe. It is an idle hope to suppose that right-wing or left-wing totalitarian nations will tolerate a free society because the prerequisite conditions do not exist in many of them. Thus we have the current ideological conflict.

< >

Family Values: The Loss of Muscles.

I am concerned about the debate over family values. No one writes or talks about the root causes. Many under 40 years of age have no sympathy for children who get into or cause trouble. I will explain why later. They see these children as wicked who need to be punished because they have lost family values. Some say the government is to blame by forcing women to take jobs in order to keep the family going. They do not believe their problem can be solved by social programs, do-good actions or funding. They frame the problem as a matter of sin. Former Vice President Dan Quayle attacked the *Murphy Brown* television show for its promotion of unwed motherhood. He called it sinful. He and others do not understand that sin has nothing to do with the problem.

Actually, family values have changed because of the change in women's roles during and since World War II. Historically most women worked at home to nurture a family. We see demonstrably the disappearance of this way of life. Our culture has been changed by the great impact of materialism, in the true sense, not Marxism, but social reorganization. In the twenties, when I was young in Boulder, I could tell you who lived in every house on 11th Street. People stayed put. There was only one woman in Boulder who was divorced and persons gossiped about her. To be divorced is nothing now. When I taught 600 freshmen in an introductory sociology course during the sixties, I would ask them every Christmas to raise their hands if their mother and father were still married. Less than half did. The majority had four or more parents. This is not a breakdown in family values; rather, it is the result of a total change in the instruments of survival.

Before World War II, family members were interdependent and they used their muscles to survive. Every house on my block had a sewing room. Either the mother, the landlady or a hired seamstress sewed and sewed. They made all the clothes and linens. I wore only those homemade clothes until the third grade when I got store bought ones. Sewing machines had pedals and women ran them with the muscles in their legs. At night they took their little basket of worn socks and used a little darning bottle to reweave them into restored socks. They said, "A man works from sun to sun, but a woman's work is never done."

On Mondays, my mother turned our house into a laundry, as most other women who ran households did. They had zinc tubs and a washing board. They hung the laundry on a clothes line with clothes pins to let them dry in the sun and wind. They used their own muscles.

On Tuesdays, they ironed. The first iron I remember was a piece of metal placed on a hot stove. Much later, electric irons were introduced. But they still ironed with the muscles in their arms on ironing boards. Some got fancy and used wringers and a mangle located in the basement to do their sheets.

They worked in kitchens for hours. My mother had a California cooler with ice around it to keep the food cool and fresh. Most had 500 pound bins to hold flour from which they manufactured bread, pies, cookies, cakes and other pastries. I remember eating the first piece of store-bought bread. The house was a little factory. That has largely disappeared since World War II.

In August, the canning began. I never understood why it was called canning; they used glass mason jars and Kerr lids. They put up tomatoes, peaches, pears, peas, jelly, jams and everything from the garden. These were sealed with paraffin. Most houses had a fruit room in the basement where the jars were stored on shelves like books in a library. Women went downstairs to select the fixings for meals. They ran their own little restaurants.

Then World War II came. Technology appeared; muscles began to disappear. My father had built our house by boring bit holes with his arm muscles. He had no electric saw or drill. Highways were built by men using picks, sledge hammers and shovels. Today they sit on expensive machines, unfolding the highway as they go along.

The country's new labor force is largely a bunch of robots. The things that everyone once did have changed. Farming was largely a family enterprise with a job for even four year olds. Today, agribusiness provides the nation's food. When I was young, we slopped pigs with food piled near the kitchen door. Stuff left over from cooking or meals was given to the pigs.

Work was done by muscles until the 1920's. By the 1930's, electric tools arrived. Women's jobs began to disappear. Today you can get your whole dinner at Safeway in 30 minutes, ready to put on the table. Stores even sell watermelons already cut.

Before World War II, women coming out of college had to choose; on the one hand, they could become a Mrs. and operate a little factory at home for the family. Others could choose a career. Few did. The technology invented during World War II and after destroyed the family factory. Sewing rooms disappeared, bit by bit. Dishwashers became fashionable; canning was discontinued. Home-produced food has largely vanished. We now live in a society of technological dependency. The only way most young persons today can learn about this vanished way of life is through seeing million dollar movies that reconstruct life in the 1880's or at the turn of the century. Many think it's quaint. *The Waltons* on television gave us images of that pre-war family culture. Thus, many of these young people and the other critics of family values miss the point. With women at work and out of the home, many children have no binding role to the family. Many are left to fend for themselves after school. Some find their recreation in the gun. To blame the mother for this vast change in our society is foolish.

We, as a society, will never and cannot return to the pre-war American family. The issue is not a loss of family values, it is a change in the material basis of our culture. Our task is to find ways to accommodate these changes and no longer point the finger of blame at those who have not coped well with the loss of muscles. Once the glue that held a family together was the interdependency of work roles: today it is compassion and there's precious little of that.

< >

Telemarketers: Fair Game

First I need to tell you, if the caller is a person who have been calling for their organization for years, as with light bulbs made by veterans, I tell them to write to me about it. If they're raising money for left-handed blind people, I say send me a letter. They're not this new abhorrent thing at all.

I'm talking about something new, these telemarketers who get you to the phone. They might just as well have opened your front door while you were at dinner and walked in. These callers are fair game; I'll give you some examples of how to cope with them .

The phone rings and a guy says, "I'm calling you about storm windows."

"Storm windows?"

"Yes. We're having a special sale on storm windows."

"Oh! We don't have any. I think that's wonderful. I'll tell you what we need, then you can tell me how much it costs.

Then I set the phone down on a table. Later I come back to the phone and say, "Well I've done the third floor and there are three rooms and they have eight windows and they're five feet tall and twenty-eight inches wide, except for one and that's thirty-six."

Then I say that I'm going to do the next floor, set the phone down and come back later. I do this for each floor, then I say, "Okay, that's all the storm windows, and so I'll tell you what I want."

"What?"

"I want cloisonné."

"What?"

Cloisonné; the frames that are porcelain, with decorations."

He says, "No, no."

"What do you mean, 'no, no"?"

"Oh, no. They're aluminum."

"Aluminum? My wife has a tremendous aversion to that. Someone left an aluminum pan here and she called me to come take it out into the alley. She said, 'I can't be near aluminum.' I'm awfully sorry." Then I hang up.

< >

Here's another example. The phone rings. I answer it and someone says, "We're calling you about carpet."

"Carpet?"

"Yes. You probably know that there was a hotel to be built down near the train station in Denver. Well, they've canceled it and all the manufacturers have said that it would be cheaper to sell the carpet locally. We'll install it for the very low price of eight dollars per yard."

"Do you have green?"

"Yes, we've got green."

"And yellow?"

"Yeah."

"Patterned?"

"Patterned or plain."

"Oh by the way, I forgot to ask you about stains."

"Oh, that's the main reason they're used in a hotel. They're made of fibers that are resistant to any kind of stain. You can pour iodine or ink on them, mop it up with a sponge, and you can't see it anywhere."

"Well I can't use your carpeting after all."

"What?"

"We love stains in rugs. The main thing we do when we come in our house is look at the stains. Because each stain has a story. I wouldn't be at all interested in a carpet that wouldn't have stains." And I hang up.

< >

Here's another one. I bought a little house for Elizabeth, my daughter, and a roofing company called me, and they said, "We see you've bought a house over on fifteenth. Have you looked at the roof very carefully? It's in very bad repair, and we'd like to come around and give you a bid for a new roof."

"Well that's just an illusion."

"What?"

"It's only an illusion. It doesn't have a roof at all, because we like to sleep outdoors, in sleeping bags, in the open rain. It's fun when it drips on your nose."

I go on like that and finally he hangs up.

< >

But the one I love best I do all the time, though I'm getting fewer and fewer calls. A woman calls and says she's from a subsidiary of one of the long distance lines, like Sprint or MCI. She says, "I'm doing a survey."

"So am I. Who are you?"

"I'm ..."

"How long have you been working there?"

"About a month."

"Where?"

"We operate out of Lafayette."

"How much pay do they give you?"

"Uh, five seventy-five an hour."

"Well, I'm doing a survey on..."

At about that point a man's voice comes on and says, "What's going on here?"

The next one is about when you buy something from Penney's or some other store. About a month after you buy something they call you to see if you want to buy a maintenance contract (which I don't buy, ever). This is how it goes. A woman phones and says, "Mr. Higman?"

"Yes?"

"How are you today?"

"What?"

"How are you today?"

"Excuse me, but what do you plan to do with the information?"

Or this one. A man calls up from Sprint or AT&T long distance. I let him talk for a while. Then I say to him, "I've got only one thing of interest to say to you; I neither have nor use a telephone."

THE NEW YORK TIMES OBITUARIES
FRIDAY, DECEMBER 1, 1995

Howard Higman, Academic Impresario in Colorado, Is Dead at 80

By Robert McG. Thomas Jr.

Howard Higman, the agile-minded academic impresario whose annual World Affairs Conferences at the University of Colorado attracted a dazzling and diverse array of fun-loving intellectuals, died on Nov. 22 at Boulder Community Hospital. He was 80.

Officially, Mr. Higman was a sociology professor, but that was merely an academic cover for his role as the thinking person's Nathan Detroit, the founder and proprietor of the oldest established permanent free-wheeling gabfest in academia, a week-long extravaganza of discussion and debate that was once compared to a cross between a think tank and a fraternity party.

Whatever it was, it has lasted 49 years.

Lured by the chance to meet and debate articulate, quick-witted specialists from diverse backgrounds and disciplines, the conference's participants over the years included such diverse personalities as Eleanor Roosevelt, Henry Kissinger, Abba Eban, Henry Steele Commager, Buckminster Fuller, Marshall McLuhan, Brian Wilson of the Beach Boys, Arthur Miller, Ted Turner, Ralph Nader and Roger Ebert, a perennially popular panelist who proved he could hold his own with the reigning resident wits when he inverted Veblen to sum up the week-long conference as "the leisure of the theory class."

Mr. Higman, the son of a miner turned contractor, was born in a hospital on the Colorado campus and grew up, as he once acknowledged, wanting to know everything. A brilliant man known both for the breadth and depth of his knowledge, he apparently majored in art as a Colorado undergraduate and then switched to sociology in its graduate school only because everything-there-is-to-know was not a recognized discipline.

Although Mr. Higman served on various government committees over the years and spent four years directing a Vista training program, his abiding passion was the conference, which he started as a young instructor in part to offer students at Colorado, known at the time as a party school, an alternative to skiing - thinking.

The conference, which began with a single speaker in 1948, was originally designed as a one-shot tribute to the United Nations, but it proved so popular that the university ordered Mr. Higman to make it an annual event.

It attracted major attention in 1953, the height of Senator Joseph McCarthy's anti-communist crusade, when Mr. Higman stacked the panels with speakers who turned the conference into a continuous attack on the Senator's tactics.

A measure of the conference's popularity was that the 125 invited participants not only received no stipends for spending a week serving on one panel discussion after another, they had to pay their way to Boulder. There, at least, room, board and local transportation were provided. The panelists bunked with local families and were driven around town by Colorado students who also served as waiters, bartenders and awed acolytes.

Like an astute hostess who makes it a point to seat the Duchess next to the dustman, Mr. Higman, who once arranged a debate between Timothy Leary and G. Gordon Liddy, was a master at orchestrating creative tensions. Among other things, he required participants to take part in at least one discussion on a topic they knew nothing about. And to assure that his panelists would talk about what they knew and not what they had boned up on, he made it a point not to disclose the list of topics or panel assignments until after the participants had gathered in Boulder.

The subjects of the 200 overlapping panel discussions could be profound ("Third World Development - Women as a Force of Change") or otherwise ("The Resurgent Condom").

Such a rich smorgasbord attracted 30,000 townspeople and Colorado students each year. Even so, the university suspended the conference this year, saying it had gotten out of touch with its student interests.

For all the appealing atmosphere of the week-long conference, a chief attraction was Mr. Higman himself, a man of such enormous intellectual range that he taught himself architecture and gardening because he could not afford to hire skilled professionals, and, for the same reason, made himself into an accomplished French chef.

For all his brilliance, Mr. Higman could also be something of an absent-minded professor. During a stay with a friend in Washington, for example, he once cooked an elaborate meal for 30 guests, but forgot to invite anybody, leaving his host, John Midgley, to eat beef Wellington for three weeks.

Known as everything from dictatorial to lovable, Mr. Higman could sometimes be impatient with the world, especially when it failed to keep up with his own inventive mind. Unwilling to wait for the development of portable telephones, for example, he had 17 installed in his house so one would always be handy.

He is survived by his wife, Marion, and three daughters, Anne and Elizabeth of Boulder, and Alice Reich of Denver.